PENGUIN BOOKS

Mythos

Stephen Fry is an award-winning comedian, actor, presenter and director. He rose to fame alongside Hugh Laurie in *A Bit of Fry and Laurie* (which he co-wrote with Laurie) and *Jeeves and Wooster*, and was unforgettable as General Melchett in *Blackadder*. He hosted over 180 episodes of *QI*, and has narrated all seven of the Harry Potter novels for the audiobook recordings. He is the bestselling author of four novels – *The Stars' Tennis Balls*, *Making History*, *The Hippopotamus* and *The Liar* – as well as three volumes of autobiography – *Moab is My Washpot*, *The Fry Chronicles* and *More Fool Me*.

MYTHOS

STEPHEN FRY

PENGUIN BOOKS

PENGUIN BOOKS

UK | USA | Canada | Ireland | Australia
India | New Zealand | South Africa

Penguin Books is part of the Penguin Random House group of companies
whose addresses can be found at global.penguinrandomhouse.com.

First published by Michael Joseph 2017
Published in Penguin Books 2018

008

Copyright © Stephen Fry, 2018

The moral right of the author has been asserted

Set in 12.15/14.33 pt Garamond MT Std
Typeset by Jouve (UK), Milton Keynes

Printed and bound in Great Britain by Clays Ltd, Elcograf S.p.A.

A CIP catalogue record for this book is available from the British Library

ISBN: 978–1–405–93413–8

www.greenpenguin.co.uk

Penguin Random House is committed to a
sustainable future for our business, our readers
and our planet. This book is made from Forest
Stewardship Council® certified paper.

ΓΙΑ ΤΟΝ ΈΛΛΙΟΤΤ ΜΕ ΑΓΆΠΗ

FOREWORD

I was lucky enough to pick up a book called *Tales from Ancient Greece* when I was quite small. It was love at first meeting. Much as I went on to enjoy myths and legends from other cultures and peoples, there was something about these Greek stories that lit me up inside. The energy, humour, passion, particularity and believable detail of their world held me enthralled from the very first. I hope they will do the same for you. Perhaps you already know some of the myths told here, but I especially welcome those who may never have encountered the characters and stories of Greek myth before. You don't need to know anything to read this book; it starts with an empty universe. Certainly no 'classical education' is called for, no knowledge of the difference between nectar and nymphs, satyrs and centaurs or the Fates and the Furies is required. There is absolutely nothing academic or intellectual about Greek mythology; it is addictive, entertaining, approachable and astonishingly human.

But where did they come from, these myths of ancient Greece? In the tangle of human history we may be able to pull on a single Greek thread and follow it back, but by picking out only one civilization and its stories we might be thought of as taking liberties with the true source of universal myth. Early human beings the world over wondered at the sources of power that fuelled volcanoes, thunderstorms, tidal waves and earthquakes. They celebrated and venerated the rhythm of the seasons, the procession of heavenly bodies in the night sky and the daily miracle of the sunrise. They questioned how it might all have started. The collective unconscious of many civilizations has told stories of angry gods, dying and renewing gods, fertility goddesses, deities, demons and spirits of fire, earth and water.

Of course the Greeks were not the only people to weave a tapestry of legends and lore out of the puzzling fabric of existence. The gods of Greece, if we are archaeological and palaeoanthropological about it all, can be traced back to the sky fathers, moon goddesses and demons of the 'fertile crescent' of Mesopotamia – today's Iraq, Syria and Turkey. The Babylonians, Sumerians, Akkadians and other civilizations there, which first flourished far earlier than the Greeks, had their creation stories and folk myths which, like the languages that expressed them, could find ancestry in India and thence westwards back to prehistory, Africa and the birth of our species.

But whenever we tell any story we have to snip the narrative string somewhere in order to make a starting point. It is easy to do this with Greek mythology because it has survived with a detail, richness, life and colour that distinguish it from other mythologies. It was captured and preserved by the very first poets and has come down to us in an unbroken line from almost the beginning of writing to the present day. While Greek myths have much in common with Chinese, Iranian, Indian, Maya, African, Russian, Native American, Hebrew and Norse myths, they are uniquely – as the writer and mythographer Edith Hamilton put it – 'the creation of great poets'. The Greeks were the first people to make coherent narratives, a literature even, of their gods, monsters and heroes.

The arc of the Greek myths follows the rise of mankind, our battle to free ourselves from the interference of the gods – their abuse, their meddling, their tyranny over human life and civilization. Greeks did not grovel before their gods. They were aware of their vain need to be supplicated and venerated, but they believed men were their equal. Their myths understand that whoever created this baffling world, with its cruelties, wonders, caprices, beauties, madness and injustice, must themselves have been cruel, wonderful, capricious, beautiful, mad and unjust. The Greeks created gods that were in their image: warlike but creative, wise but ferocious, loving but jealous, tender but brutal, compassionate but vengeful.

Mythos begins at the beginning, but it does not end at the end. Had I included heroes like Oedipus, Perseus, Theseus, Jason and Herakles and the details of the Trojan War this book would have been too heavy even for a Titan to pick up. Moreover, I am only concerned with *telling* the stories, not with explaining them or investigating the human truths and psychological insights that may lie behind them. The myths are fascinating enough in all their disturbing, surprising, romantic, comic, tragic, violent and enchanting detail to stand on their own as stories. If, as you read, you cannot help wondering what inspired the Greeks to invent a world so rich and elaborate in character and incident, and you find yourself pondering the deep truths that the myths embody – well, that is certainly part of the pleasure.

And pleasure is what immersing yourself in the world of Greek myth is all about.

Stephen Fry

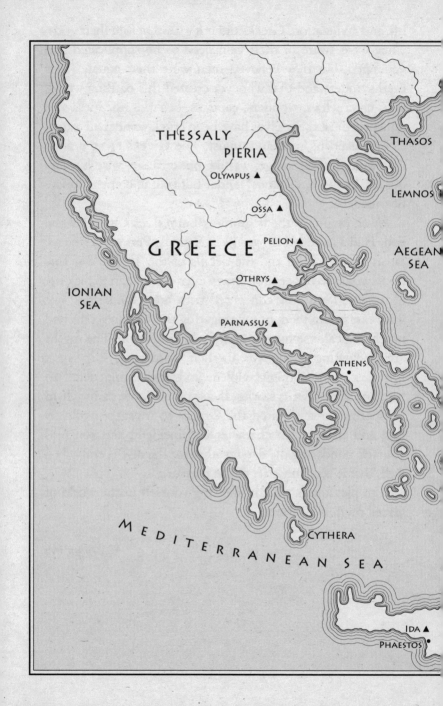

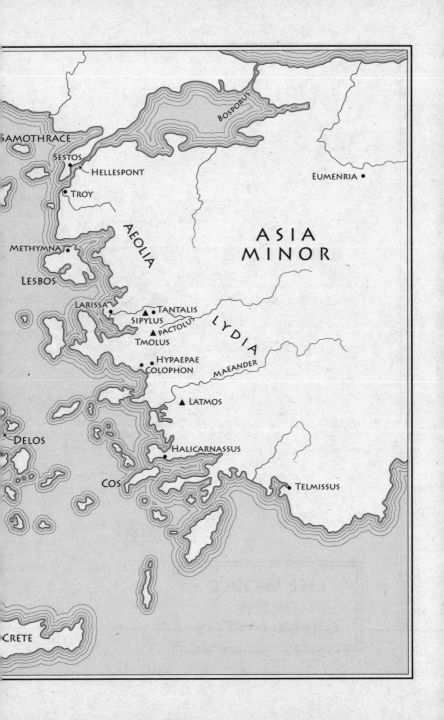

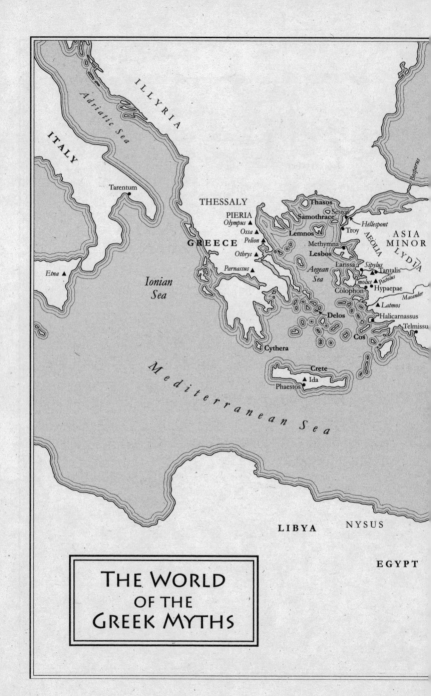

THE WORLD
OF THE
GREEK MYTHS

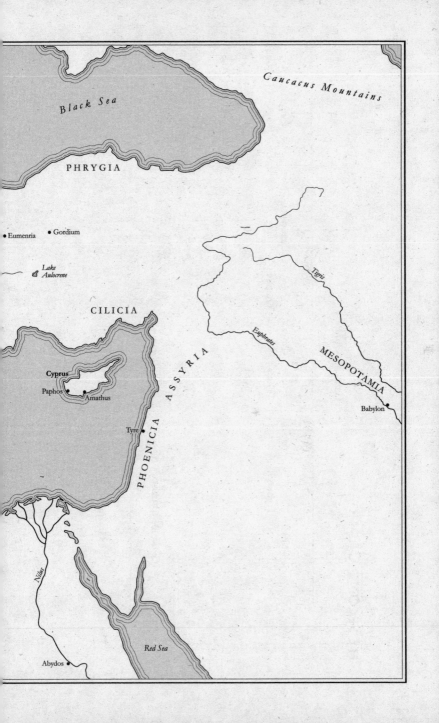

THE SECOND ORDER

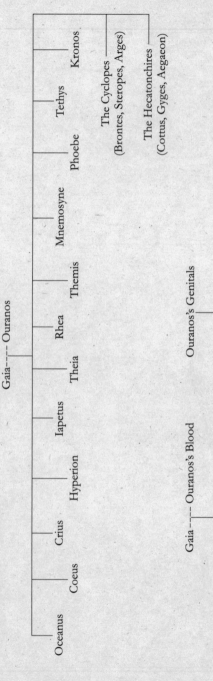

THE OLYMPIANS

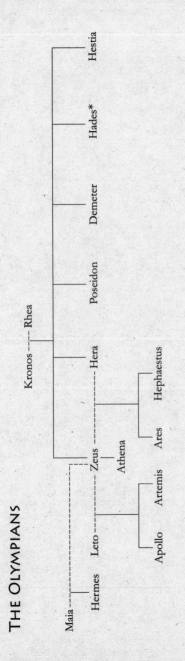

*Hades is not technically an Olympian, as he spent all of his time in the underworld.

The Beginning
PART ONE

OUT OF CHAOS

These days the origin of the universe is explained by proposing a Big Bang, a single event that instantly brought into being all the matter from which everything and everyone are made.

The ancient Greeks had a different idea. They said that it all started not with a bang, but with CHAOS.

Was Chaos a god – a divine being – or simply a state of nothingness? Or was Chaos, just as we would use the word today, a kind of terrible mess, like a teenager's bedroom only worse?

Think of Chaos perhaps as a kind of grand cosmic yawn. As in a yawning chasm or a yawning void.

Whether Chaos brought life and substance out of nothing or whether Chaos yawned life up or dreamed it up, or conjured it up in some other way I don't know. I wasn't there. Nor were you. And yet in a way we were, because all the bits that make us were there. It is enough to say that the Greeks thought it was Chaos who, with a massive heave, or a great shrug, or hiccup, vomit or cough, began the long chain of creation that has ended with pelicans and penicillin and toadstools and toads, sea-lions, seals, lions, human beings and daffodils and murder and art and love and confusion and death and madness and biscuits.

Whatever the truth, science today agrees that everything is destined to *return* to Chaos. It calls this inevitable fate *entropy*: part of the great cycle from Chaos to order and back again to Chaos. Your trousers began as chaotic atoms that somehow coalesced into matter that ordered itself over aeons into a living substance that slowly evolved into a cotton plant that was woven into the handsome stuff that sheathes your lovely legs. In time you will abandon your trousers – not now, I hope – and they will rot down in a landfill or be burned. In either case their matter will at length be set free to become part of the atmosphere of the planet. And when the sun explodes and takes every particle of this world with it, including the ingredients of your trousers, all the constituent atoms will return to cold Chaos. And what is true for your trousers is of course true for you.

So the Chaos that began everything is also the Chaos that will end everything.

Now, you might be the kind of person who asks, 'But who or what was there *before* Chaos?' or 'Who or what was there before the Big Bang? There must have been *something*.'

Well, there wasn't. We have to accept that there was no 'before', because there was no Time yet. No one had pressed the start button on Time. No one had shouted *Now*! And since Time had yet to be created, time words like 'before', 'during', 'when', 'then', 'after lunch' and 'last Wednesday' had no possible meaning. It screws with the head, but there it is.

The Greek word for 'everything that is the case', what we could call 'the universe', is COSMOS. And at the moment – although 'moment' is a time word and makes no sense just now (neither does the phrase 'just now') – at the moment, Cosmos is Chaos and only Chaos because Chaos is the only thing that is the case. A stretching, a tuning up of the orchestra . . .

But things are about to change very quickly.

THE FIRST ORDER

From formless Chaos sprang two creations: EREBUS and NYX. Erebus, he was darkness, and Nyx, she was night. They coupled at once and the flashing fruits of their union were HEMERA, day, and AETHER, light.

At the same time – because everything must happen simultaneously until Time is there to separate events – Chaos brought forth two more entities: GAIA, the earth, and TARTARUS, the depths and caves beneath the earth.

I can guess what you might be thinking. These creations sound charming enough – Day, Night, Light, Depths and Caves. But these were not gods and goddesses, they were not even personalities. And it may have struck you also that since there was no time there could be no dramatic narrative, no stories; for stories depend on Once Upon a Time and What Happened Next.

You would be right to think this. What first emerged from Chaos were primal, elemental principles that were devoid of any real colour, character or interest. These were the PRIMORDIAL DEITIES, the First Order of divine beings from whom all the gods, heroes and monsters of Greek myth spring. They brooded over and lay beneath everything . . . waiting.

The silent emptiness of this world was filled when Gaia bore two sons all on her own.* The first was PONTUS, the

---

* This trick of virgin birth, or *parthenogenesis*, can be found in nature still. In aphids, some lizards and even sharks it is a reasonably common way to have young. There won't be the variation that two sets of genes allow; this is the same in the genesis of the Greek gods. The interesting ones are all the fruit of two parents, not one.

sea, and the second was OURANOS, the sky – better known to us as Uranus, the sound of whose name has ever been the cause of great delight to children from nine to ninety. Hemera and Aether bred too, and from their union came THALASSA, the female counterpart of Pontus the sea.

Ouranos, who preferred to pronounce himself Ooranoss, *was* the sky and the heavens in the way that – at the very beginning – the primordial deities always *were* the things they represented and ruled over.* You could say that Gaia was the earth of hills, valleys, caves and mountains yet capable of gathering herself into a form that could walk and talk. The clouds of Ouranos the sky rolled and seethed above her but they too could coalesce into a shape we might recognize. It was so early on in the life of everything. Very little was settled.

---

* Indeed *ouranos* is the Greek word for 'sky' to this very day.

THE SECOND ORDER

Ouranos the sky covered his mother Gaia the earth every-where. He covered Gaia in both senses: he covered her as the sky still covers the earth to this day and he covered her as a stallion covers a mare. When he did so, something remarkable happened. *Time began.*

Something else began too – what shall we call it? Personality? Drama? Individuality? Character, with all its flaws and failings, fashions and passions, schemes and dreams. *Meaning* began, you might say. The seeding of Gaia gave us meaning, a germination of thought into shape. Seminal semantic semiology from the semen of the sky. I will leave such speculation to those better qualified, but it was nevertheless a great moment. In the creation of and conjoining with Ouranos, her son and now her husband, Gaia unwound the ribbon of life that runs all the way to human history and our own very selves, yours and mine.

Right from the start, the union of Ouranos and Gaia was gratifyingly productive. Twelve robust, healthy children came first – six male, six female. The males were OCEANUS, COEUS, CRIUS, HYPERION, IAPETUS and KRONOS. The females, THEIA, THEMIS, MNEMOSYNE, PHOEBE, TETHYS and RHEA. These twelve were destined to become the Second Order of divine beings, earning themselves a legendary name.

And somewhere, as Time crept into being the clock began, the clock of cosmic history that still ticks today. Perhaps one of these newborns was responsible, we can look into that later.

Not content with these twelve strong beautiful brothers and sisters, Ouranos and Gaia gave the world yet more progeny – two distinctive, but distinctly *not* beautiful, sets of triplets. The three CYCLOPES came first, one-eyed giants who gave their father sky a whole new range of expressions and modulations. The eldest cyclops was called BRONTES, thunder,* next came STEROPES, the lightning, and then ARGES, brightness. Ouranos could fill the heavens with flashes of lightning and crashing thunder. He gloried in the noise and spectacle. But the second set of triplets Gaia bore sent even greater shudders through him and all who saw them.

Perhaps it is kindest to say that they were a mutational experiment never to be repeated, a genetic dead end. For these newborns – the HECATONCHIRES† – each had fifty heads and a hundred hands and were as hideous, fierce, violent and powerful as anything that had yet been released into being. Their names were COTTUS the furious, GYGES the long-limbed and AEGAEON the sea goat, sometimes also called BRIAREOS the vigorous one. Gaia loved them. Ouranos was revolted by them. Maybe he was most horrified by the thought that he, Lord of the Sky, could have fathered such strange and ugly things, but I think that like most hatred his revulsion was rooted in fear.

Filled with disgust, he cursed them: 'For offending my eyes, you shall never see light again!' As he roared these furious words, he pushed them and the Cyclopes back into Gaia's womb.

---

* The brontosaurus or 'thunder lizard' got his name from Brontes. The novelist sisters from Yorkshire *may* have too. Their father was born 'Brunty' but changed it to Brontë, perhaps to lend a grand peal of classical thunder to his Irish name, perhaps in honour of Admiral Nelson who had been made Duke of Brontë – the dukedom was located on the slopes of Etna and is believed to have derived its name from the Cyclops slumbering beneath.

† Pronounced heck-a-ton *key*-rays – the *hecaton* means 'hundred' and the *chires* 'hands' (as in 'chiropractor').

Gaia's Revenge

We have good cause to wonder here what 'he pushed them into Gaia's womb' really means. Some people have taken it to indicate that he buried the Hecatonchires in the earth. Divine identity at this early time was fluid, how much a god was a person and how much an attribute is hard to determine. There were no capital letters then. Gaia the Earth Mother was the same as *gaia*, the earth itself, just as *ouranos*, the sky, and Ouranos the Sky Father were one and the same.

What is certain is that in reacting like this to the three Hecatonchires, his own children, and in treating his wife with such abominable cruelty, Ouranos was committing the first crime. An elemental crime that would not go unpunished.

Gaia's agony was unbearable and inside her, alongside the trio of writhing, flailing three-hundred-handed clawing and a hundred-and-fifty-headed butting Hecatonchires, there sprang up a hatred, a most terrible and implacable hatred against Ouranos, the son she had borne and the husband with whom she had given birth to a new generation. And, like ivy twisting round a tree, there grew a plan of revenge.

The piercing pain of the Hecatonchires still gnawing at her, Gaia visited Othrys, a great mountain that looks down over what we now call the central Greek region of Phthiotis. From its peak you can see the plain of Magnesia reaching down to the blue waters of the western Aegean as they curl round the Malian Gulf and embrace the sporadic scattering of islands called the Sporades. But Gaia was consumed with too much pain and too much fury to enjoy one of the world's most charming views. On the summit of Mount Othrys she set to work fashioning a most unusual and terrible artefact from its rock. For nine days and nights she laboured until she had produced an object which she then hid in the cleft of the mountain.

Next she took herself off to visit her twelve beautiful, strong children.

'Will you kill your father Ouranos and rule the cosmos with me?' she asked each in turn. 'You will inherit the sky from him and together all of creation will be our dominion.'

Perhaps we imagine that Gaia – Mother Earth – is soft, warm, bountiful and kind. Well, sometimes she is, but remember that she banks down fire inside. Sometimes she can be crueller, harsher and more terrifying than even the wildest sea.

And talking of the marine world, the first of the children that Gaia tried to win to her side were Oceanus and his sister Tethys.* But they were in the middle of negotiating a share of the oceans with Thalassa, the primordial goddess of the sea. All of this generation were stretching and flexing their muscles at this time, establishing their areas of expertise and control, nipping, growling and testing each other's strength and dominance like puppies in a basket. Oceanus had conceived the idea of creating tides and currents, which were to run like a great salt river around the world. Tethys was about to have his baby – no sin in those early days of course: propagation would not have been possible without incestuous couplings. She was pregnant with NILUS, the Nile, and would go on to give birth to other rivers and to at least three thousand Oceanids or sea nymphs, attractive deities who moved as easily on dry land as in the waters of the sea. They already had two fully grown daughters: CLYMENE, who was the lover of Iapetus, and the clever and wise METIS, who is due

---

* 'Tethys' is also the name palaeontologists give to the great ancient sea that was an ancestor of the Mediterranean.

to play a very important part in what is to come.* The pair were happy and looking forward to life on the ocean wave, so neither saw any reason to help kill their father Ouranos.

Next Gaia visited her daughter Mnemosyne, who was busy being unpronounceable. She seemed a very shallow, silly and ignorant being, who knew nothing and appeared to understand less. This was deceptive, for each day that passed she got smarter and smarter, more and more well informed and more and more capable. Her name means 'memory' (giving us the word 'mnemonic'). At the time of her mother's visit, the world and the cosmos were very young, so Mnemosyne had had no opportunity to prime herself with knowledge or experience. As the years passed, her endless capacity for the storage of information and sensory experience would make her wiser than almost anyone. One day she would mother nine daughters, the MUSES, whom we shall meet later.

'You want me to help you kill Ouranos? Surely the Sky Father cannot die?'

'Dethrone or disable him, then . . . it is no more than he deserves.'

'I will not help you.'

'Why not?'

'There is a reason and when I know it I will remember it and tell you.'

Exasperated, Gaia went next to Theia, who was also paired off in another sibling union, to her brother Hyperion.

---

* Since there were perhaps three thousand Oceanids it would be fruitless to list them, even if all their names were known. But it is worth introducing CALYPSO, AMPHITRITE and the dark and fearful STYX who – like her brother Nilus – was to become the deity of a very significant river. One more Oceanid merits a mention, but only because of her name – DORIS. Doris the Oceanid. She went on to marry the sea god NEREUS and by him mother many NEREIDS, friendly nymphs of the sea.

In due course she would give birth to HELIOS the sun, SELENE the moon and EOS the dawn, quite enough parenting to be getting on with, so they too showed no interest in Gaia's plans to depose Ouranos.

Despairing at her pallid and unadventurous brood's refusal to live up to what she imagined to be their divine destinies – not to mention repulsed by how loved up and domesticated they all appeared to be – Gaia next tried Phoebe, perhaps the most intelligent and insightful of the twelve. From the earliest age shining Phoebe had shown that she possessed the gift of prophecy.

'Oh no, Mother Earth,' she said, when she had heard Gaia's plan. 'I could take no part in such a plot. I see no good coming from it. Besides, I'm pregnant . . .'

'Damn you,' snapped Gaia. 'Who by? Coeus, I bet.'

She was right, Phoebe's brother Coeus was indeed her consort. Gaia stormed off with renewed fury to visit her remaining offspring. Surely one of them had the stomach for a fight?

She called on Themis, who would one day be regarded everywhere as the embodiment of justice and wise counsel,* and Themis wisely counselled her mother to forget the unjust idea of usurping Ouranos. Gaia listened carefully to this wise counsel and – as we all do, whether mortal or immortal – ignored it, choosing instead to try the mettle of her son Crius, who consorted with her daughter by Pontus, EURYBIA.

'Kill my father?' Crius stared at his mother in disbelief. 'B-but how . . . I mean . . . why? . . . I mean . . . oh.'

'What's in it for us, mother?' asked Eurybia, who was known as 'the flint-hearted'.

---

* Themis later became a personification of law, justice, custom – *mores*, the rules that govern how manners and things are or should be.

'Oh, just the world and all that's in it,' said Gaia.

'To share with you?'

'To share with me.'

'No!' said Crius. 'Leave, mother.'

'It's worth considering,' said Eurybia.

'It's too dangerous,' said Crius. 'I forbid it.'

Gaia turned with a snarl and sought out her son Iapetus.

'Iapetus, beloved boy. Destroy the monster Ouranos and rule with me!'

The Oceanid Clymene, who had borne Iapetus two sons and was pregnant with another, stepped forward. 'What mother could ask such a thing? For a son to kill his own father would be the most terrible crime. All Cosmos would cry out.'

'I must agree, mother,' said Iapetus.

'A curse on you and a curse on your children!' spat Gaia.

A mother's curse is a terrible thing. We shall see how the children of Iapetus and Clymene, ATLAS, EPIMETHEUS and PROMETHEUS, met their ends.

Rhea, the eleventh of Gaia's children to be asked, said that she would have no part in the plan, but – throwing up her hands to stop a savage torrent of abuse from her mother – suggested that her brother Kronos, the last of these strong beautiful children, might very well like the idea of deposing his father. She, Rhea, had heard him many times cursing Ouranos and his power.

'Really?' cried Gaia. 'You say so? Well, where is he?'

'He's probably mooching around down by the caves of Tartarus. He and Tartarus get on so well. They're both dark. Moody. Mean. Magnificent. Cruel.'

'Oh god, don't tell me you're in love with Kronos . . .'

'Put in a good word for me, mummy, please! He's just so dreamy. Those black flashing eyes. The thunderous brows. The long silences.'

Gaia had always thought that her youngest's long silences indicated nothing more than dullness of intellect, but she sensibly refrained from saying so. After assuring Rhea that she would of course recommend her warmly to Kronos, Gaia sped down, down, down to the caves of Tartarus to find him.

If you were to drop a bronze anvil from the heavens it would take nine days to reach the earth. If you were to drop that anvil from the earth it would take another nine days to reach Tartarus. In other words the earth is halfway between the sky and Tartarus. Or you might say Tartarus is as far from the ground as the ground is from the sky. A very deep, abysmal place then, but more than just a place. Remember Tartarus was a primordial being too, who was born out of Chaos at the same time as Gaia. So when she approached him, they greeted each other as family members will.

'Gaia, you've put on weight.'

'You look a mess, Tartarus.'

'What the hell do you want down here?'

'Shut up for once and I'll tell you . . .'

These testy exchanges won't stop them, at a future date, from mating and producing TYPHON – the worst and deadliest of all the monsters.* But just now Gaia is in no mood for love or for trading insults.

'Listen. My son Kronos – is he nearby?'

A resigned groan from her brother.

'Almost certainly. I wish you'd tell him to leave me alone. He does nothing all day but hang around looking at me with his eyes drooping and his mouth open. I think

---

* Typhon gave us typhus, typhoid and the deadly tropical storm, the typhoon. Later we will meet two of Typhon's repulsive offspring by a half woman, half water snake, called ECHIDNA.

he's got some kind of man-crush on me. He copies my hairstyle and leans limply against trees and boulders looking miserable, melancholy and misunderstood. As if he's waiting for someone to paint him or something. When he's not gazing at me he's staring down into that lava vent over there. In fact there he is now, look. Try and talk some sense into him.'

Gaia approached her son.

The Sickle

Now, Kronos (or Cronus as he sometimes styled himself) was not quite the pained and vulnerable emo-like youth that Rhea's and Tartarus's descriptions may have led us to picture, for he was the strongest of an unimaginably strong race. He was darkly handsome, certainly; and yes, he was moody. Had Kronos the examples to go by, he would perhaps have identified with Hamlet at his most introspective, or Jaques at his most self-indulgently morbid. Konstantin from *The Seagull* with a suggestion of Morrissey. Yet there was something of a Macbeth in him too and more than a little Hannibal Lecter – as we shall see.

Kronos had been the first to discover that brooding silence is often taken to indicate strength, wisdom and command. The youngest of the twelve, he had always hated his father. The deep and piercing venom of envy and resentment was beginning to unravel his sanity, but he had managed to hide the intensity of his hatred from all but his adoring sister Rhea, who was the only member of his family with whom he felt comfortable enough to reveal his true self.

As they made their way up from Tartarus, Gaia poured more poison into his receptive ear.

'Ouranos is cruel. He is insane. I fear for myself and for all of you, my beloved children. Come boy, come.'

She was leading him to Mount Othrys. You recall the strange and terrible artefact that I told you she had wrought and hidden in the cleft of the mountain before she went visiting each of her children? Gaia now took Kronos to that place and showed him what she had made.

'Pick it up. Go on.'

Kronos's black eyes glittered as they took in the shape and meaning of this most strange object.

It was a sickle. An enormous scythe whose great curved blade had been forged from adamantine, which means 'untameable'. A massive aggregate of grey flint, granite, diamond and ophiolite, its half-moon blade had been refined to the sharpest edge. An edge that could cut through anything.

Kronos plucked it from its hiding place just as easily as you or I would pick up a pencil. After feeling the balance and heft of it in his hand, he swung it once, twice. The powerful swish as it whipped through the air made Gaia smile.

'Kronos, my son,' she said, 'we must bide our time until Hemera and Aether dive into the waters of the west and Erebus and Nyx prepare to cast the dark –'

'You mean we must wait until evening.' Kronos was impatient and quite lacking in poetry or finer feeling.

'Yes. Eventide. That is when your father will come to me, as he always does. He likes to –'

Kronos nodded curtly. He did not wish to know the details of his parents' love-making.

'Hide there, in that very cleft where I hid the sickle. When you hear him covering me, and he grows loud in his roars of passion and groans of lust – strike.'

Night and Day, Light and Dark

As Gaia predicted, Hemera and Aether were tired after twelve hours of playing and slowly Day and Light slipped down westwards into the sea. At the same time, Nyx slipped off her dark veil and she and Erebus threw it over the world like a shimmering black tablecloth.

As Kronos waited in the cleft, sickle in hand, all creation held its breath. I say 'all creation', for Ouranos and Gaia and their offspring were not the only beings to have reproduced. Others had multiplied and propagated too, with Erebus and Nyx the most productive by far. They had many children, some terrible, some admirable and some lovely. We have already seen how they gave birth to Hemera and Aether. But then Nyx, without Erebus's help, gave birth to MOROS, or Doom, who was to become the most feared entity in creation. Doom comes to every creature, mortal or immortal, but is always hidden. Even the immortals feared Doom's all-powerful, all-knowing control over the cosmos.

After Moros came a great rush of offspring, one after the other, like a monstrous airborne invasion. First came APATE, Deceit, whom the Romans called FRAUS (from whom we derive the words 'fraud', 'fraudulent' and 'fraudster'). She scuttled off to Crete where she bided her time. GERAS, Old Age, was born next; not necessarily so fearful a demon as we might think today. While Geras might take away suppleness, youth and agility, for the Greeks he more than made up for it by conferring dignity, wisdom and authority. SENECTUS is his Roman name, a word that shares the same root as 'senior', 'senate' and 'senile'.

A pair of perfectly ghastly twins were next: OIZYS

(MISERIA in Latin) the spirit of Misery, Depression and Anxiety, and her cruel brother MOMOS, the spiteful personification of Mockery, Scorn and Blame.*

Nyx and Erebus were just getting into their stride. Their next child, ERIS (DISCORDIA), Strife, lay behind all disagreements, divorces, scraps, skirmishes, fights, battles and wars. It was her malicious wedding present, the legendary Apple of Discord, that brought about the Trojan War, though that epic clash of arms was a long, long way in the future. Strife's sister NEMESIS was the embodiment of Retribution, that remorseless strand of cosmic justice that punishes presumptuous, overreaching ambition – the vice that the Greeks called *hubris*. Nemesis has elements in common with the eastern idea of karma and we use her today to suggest the fateful retributive opposition the lofty and wicked will one day meet and which will bring them down. I suppose you could say Holmes was Moriarty's Nemesis, Bond was Blofeld's and Jerry was Tom's.†

Erebus and Nyx also gave birth to CHARON, whose infamy would grow once he took up his duties as ferryman for the dead. HYPNOS, the personification of Sleep, was born to them too. They were also the progenitor of the ONEROI – thousands of beings charged with the making and bringing of dreams to the sleeping. Amongst the Oneroi whose names are known to us were PHOBETOR, god of nightmares, and PHANTASOS, responsible for the fantastic manner in which one thing turns into another in dreams. They worked under the supervision of Hypnos's son MORPHEUS, whose name itself suggests the morphing, shifting shapes of the dream

---

* Momos (MOMUS to the Romans) would go on to be worshipped in a seriocomic literary way as the guiding spirit of Satire. Aesop incorporated him into some of his fables and he is the hero of a lost play by Sophocles.

† The Romans, perhaps confusingly, called Nemesis INVIDIA, which is also the Latin for 'envy'.

world.* 'Morphine', 'fantasy', 'hypnotic', 'oneiromancy' (the interpretation of dreams) and many other verbal descendants of Greek sleep have survived into our language. Sleep's brother THANATOS, Death himself, gives us the word 'euthanasia', 'good death'. The Roman's called him MORS, of mortals, mortuaries and mortification.

These new beings were frightening and loathsome in the extreme. They left on creation a terrible but necessary mark, for the world seems never to offer anything worthwhile without also providing a dreadful opposite.

There were, however, three lovely exceptions:† three beautiful sisters, the HESPERIDES – nymphs of the west and daughters of the evening. They heralded the daily arrival of their mother and father, but with the soft gold of the gloaming rather than the dread black of night. Their time is what movie cameramen today call 'magic hour', when the light is at its most beguiling and beautiful.

These then were the offspring of Nyx and Erebus, who even now were shrouding the earth in the darkness of night as Gaia lay waiting for her husband for what she hoped would be the last time and Kronos lurked in the shadows of that recess in Mount Othrys, keeping a firm grip on his great scythe.

Ouranos Gelded

At last, Gaia and Kronos heard from the west the sound of a great stamping and shaking. The leaves on the trees

---

* Neil Gaiman's *Sandman* character, Dream, is also known as Morpheus, and formed the inspiration for the character Morpheus played by Laurence Fishburne in the Wachowskis' *Matrix* films.

† *Four* exceptions perhaps. Hypnos is not so bad after all. The longer you live, the fonder you become of him. And talking of living long – perhaps Geras isn't too awful either. So five.

shivered. Kronos, standing silently in his hiding place, did not tremble. He was ready.

'Gaia!' roared Ouranos as he approached. 'Prepare yourself. Tonight we shall breed something better than hundred-handed mutants and one-eyed freaks . . .'

'Come to me, glorious son, divine husband!' called Gaia, with what Kronos thought a distastefully convincing show of eagerness.

The horrible sounds of a lustful deity slobbering, slapping and grunting suggested to him that his father was attempting some kind of foreplay.

In his alcove Kronos breathed in and out five times. Never for a second did he weigh the moral good of what he was about to do, his thoughts were only for tactics and timing. With a deep inhalation he raised the great sickle and stepped swiftly sideways from his hiding place.

Ouranos, who had been preparing to lie on top of Gaia, sprang to his feet with an angry snarl of surprise. Walking calmly forward, Kronos swung the scythe back and swept it down in a great arc. The blade, hissing through the air, sliced Ouranos's genitals clean from his body.

All Cosmos could hear Ouranos's maddened scream of pain, anguish and rage. Never in creation's short history had there been a sound so loud or so dreadful. All living things heard it and were afraid.

Kronos leapt forward with an obscene cry of triumph, catching the dripping trophy in his hands before it could reach the ground.

Ouranos fell writhing in immortal agony and howled out these words:

'Kronos, vilest of my brood and vilest in all creation. Worst of all beings, fouler than the ugly Cyclopes and the loathsome Hecatonchires, with these words I curse you. *May your children destroy you as you destroyed me.*'

Kronos looked down at Ouranos. His black eyes showed nothing, but his mouth curved into a dark smile.

'You have no power to curse, daddy. Your power is in my hands.'

He juggled before his father's eyes his grisly spoils of victory, burst and slimy with blood, oozing and slippery with seed. Laughing, he pulled back his arm and hurled the package of genitals far, far from sight. Across the plains of Greece they flew and out over the darkening sea. All three watched as Ouranos's organs of generation vanished from sight across the waters.

Kronos was surprised, when he turned to look at her, that his mother had covered her mouth in what appeared to be horror. Tears were leaking from Gaia's eyes.

He shrugged. As if she cared.

Erinyes, Gigantes and Meliae

Creation at this time, peopled as it was by primal deities whose whole energy and purpose seems to have been directed towards reproduction, was endowed with an astonishing fertility. The soil was blessed with such a fecund richness that one could almost believe that if you planted a pencil it would burst into flower. Where divine blood fell, life could not help but spring from the earth.

So no matter how murderous, cruel, rapacious and destructive the character of Ouranos, he had been the ruler of creation after all. For his son to have mutilated and emasculated him constituted a most terrible crime against Cosmos.

Perhaps what happened next is not so surprising.

Great pools of blood formed around the scene of Ouranos's castration. From that blood, the blood which fell from the ruined groin of Ouranos, living beings emerged.

The first to push themselves out of the sodden ground were the ERINYES, whom we call the Furies, ALECTO (remorseless), MEGAERA (jealous rage) and TISIPHONE (vengeance). Perhaps it was an unconscious instinct of Ouranos that caused such vengeful beings to rise up. Their eternal duty, from the moment of their chthonic – or out-of-the-ground – birth, would be to punish the worst and most violent of crimes: relentlessly to chase the perpetrators and to rest only when the guilty had paid the full and dreadful price. Armed with cruel metallic scourges, the Furies flayed the very flesh from the bones of the guilty. The Greeks with characteristic irony nicknamed these female avengers the EUMENIDES or 'kindly ones'.

Next to rise from the soil were the GIGANTES. We have inherited 'giant', 'giga' and 'gigantic' from them, but while they were certainly possessed of prodigious strength, they were no greater in stature than their half-brothers and sisters.*

Finally, in that instant of pain and destruction were created also the MELIAE, graceful nymphs who were to become guardians of an ash tree whose bark exuded a sweet and healthful manna.†

As all these unexpected new beings emerged alive from the blood-soaked ground, Kronos stared at them in disgust and scattered them with a sweep of his scythe. Next he turned to Gaia.

---

* Their names signify not their size but their chthonic origins – generated from the earth, 'Gaia-gen' if you will. Gaia's name, incidentally, became worn down to *Ge* in later Greek. She is still there in earth sciences like 'geology' and 'geography', not to mention the later environmental studies that have restored her full name – James Lovelock and his popular 'Gaia Hypothesis' being a prime example.

† The sugars of the 'manna ash', which still grows in southern Europe, give their name to today's sweetener Mannitol.

'I promised you, Earth Mother,' he said, 'that I would release you from your gnawing agony – hold still.'

With another sweep of the scythe he sliced open Gaia's side. Out tumbled the Cyclopes and Hecatonchires. Kronos looked down at his parents, both of them now bloody, panting and snarling like angry wounded animals.

'No more shall you cover Gaia,' he said to his father. 'I banish you to live out eternity beneath the ground, buried deeper even than Tartarus. May you sulk there in your fury, gelded and powerless.'

'You have overreached yourself,' hissed Ouranos. 'There will be revenge. I curse your life, that it be ground out in slow remorseless perpetuity, its immortal eternity an insufferable burden without end. Your own children will destroy you as –'

'As I destroyed you. Yes, I know. You said. We'll see about that.'

'You and your brothers and sisters, I curse you all, your straining ambition will destroy you.'

The 'striving, straining one', or TITAN, is the title we reserve for Kronos, his eleven siblings and (much of) their progeny. Ouranos meant it as an insult, but somehow the name has resounded through the ages with a ring of grandeur. No one, to this very day, would be insulted to be called a Titan.

Kronos met these curses with a sneer and, corralling his mutilated father and newly freed mutant brothers at the point of his sickle, he led them down to Tartarus. The Hecatonchires and Cyclopes he imprisoned in the caves, but his father he buried even deeper, as far from his natural domain of the heavens as he could contrive.*

---

* At least the deposed Sky Father has the consolation of the planet Uranus named in his honour – it being the convention that the planets take the *Roman* names of the gods they represent.

Brooding, simmering and raging in the ground, deep beneath the earth that once loved him, Ouranos compressed all his fury and divine energy into the very rock itself, hoping that one day some excavating creature somewhere would mine it and try to harness the immortal power that radiated from within. That could never happen, of course. It would be too dangerous. Surely the race has yet to be born that could be so foolish as to attempt to unleash the power of uranium?

From the Foam

We return now to the great arc in the heavens traced by Ouranos's severed gonads. Kronos had flung the Sky Father's junk, if you recall, far across the sea.

We can watch it now. Near the Ionian island of Cythera it drops, splashes, bounces, rises up again and finally falls and half sinks beneath the waves. Great ropes of semen trail in its wake like ribbons from a kite. Where they strike the surface of the sea a furious frothing is set up. Soon all the waters bubble and boil. Something arises. From the horrors of patricidal castration and unnatural ambition it must be – surely – something unimaginably ugly, something terrible, something violent, something appalling, that promises only war, blood and anguish?

The whirlpool of blood and seminal fluid foments, fizzes and foams. Out of the spindrift of surf and seed emerges the crown of a head, then a brow and then a face. But what kind of face?

A face far more beautiful than creation has yet seen or will ever see again. Not just someone beautiful but Beauty itself rises fully formed from the foam. In Greek 'from the foam' can be rendered as something like APHRODITE, and this is the name of the one who now lifts herself from the spume and spray. She stands on a large scallop shell, a demure and gentle smile playing on her lips. Slowly she alights onto a beach on Cyprus. Where she steps flowers bloom and clouds of butterflies arise. Around her head birds fly in circles, singing in ecstasies of joy. Perfect Love and Beauty has made her landfall and the world will never be the same.

The Romans called her VENUS, and her birth and arrival on the sands of Cyprus on the scallop shell were never better portrayed than in Botticelli's exquisite painting, which once seen is never forgotten.

We leave Aphrodite making her home on Cyprus and return to Kronos, who is on his way back from the dark caves of Tartarus.

Rhea

When he arrived on Mount Othrys, Kronos found his sister Rhea waiting for him. The sight of her darkly handsome brother, a huge sickle dripping blood in his hand, thrilled her to the point of internal explosion.

His authority was established: none of his brother or sister Titans dared question him.* His father was powerless and Gaia, who found she could take no joy in the violent overthrow she had set in motion, withdrew into her realm and into a more passive existence. She never lost her strength, authority or high status as Mother Earth and ancestress of all, but she no longer ventured forth to interact or conjoin. Kronos was the master now. After a great feast in which his

---

* The females of the race can be called 'Titanesses'.

achievement in unmanning and unseating Ouranos was roaringly and most unmusically sung, Kronos turned to the blushing, trembling Rhea and pulled her aside to make love to her.

Rhea's joy was complete. She had played her part in helping the brother she adored achieve mastery of all creation. And now they were united. More than that, in the fullness of time she began to feel a child moving inside her. A baby girl, she felt sure. Her happiness was unclouded.

Kronos, on the other hand . . . His already dour disposition was darkened by something else. The words of his father Ouranos began to echo in his head:

Your own children will overthrow you as you overthrew me.

Over the coming weeks and months Kronos watched with sullen foreboding as Rhea's belly filled and swelled.

Your own children . . . your own children . . .

When the day came for her confinement, Rhea laid herself down in an alcove in the mountain – the same recess in the rocks, in fact, where Gaia had concealed the scythe and Kronos had hidden. Here she gave birth to a beautiful baby girl whom she named HESTIA.

The name was hardly out of Rhea's mouth before Kronos stepped forward, snatched the child from her arms and swallowed it whole. He turned and departed without so much as a hiccup, leaving Rhea white with shock.

The Children of Rhea

Kronos was now lord of earth, sea and sky, with the scythe the symbol of his authority. His sceptre. The earth he took from Gaia, the sky from Ouranos. With threats of violence he wrested dominion over the sea from Pontus and Thalassa and from his siblings Oceanus and Tethys. He trusted no one and ruled alone.

Still Kronos continued to take his pleasure with Rhea and still she consented, loving him hopelessly and trusting that the monstrous eating of their firstborn had been some sort of aberration.

It was not. Their next child, a boy she called HADES, was devoured in just the same manner. And then another baby girl, DEMETER. Next was POSEIDON, a second boy, and finally a third girl, HERA. All of them swallowed whole with as much ease as you and I might gulp down an oyster or a spoonful of jelly.

By the time Kronos consumed Hera, Rhea's fifth pregnancy, her love for Kronos had turned to hate. That same night he seized her and made love to her again. She swore to herself that if she became pregnant he would never take her sixth child. But how could she prevent him? He was all powerful.

One morning she arose and felt the familiar nausea. She was pregnant. Her divine instincts told her that her sixth was to be a boy.

She left Othrys and took herself off in search of her mother and father. For all that she had contributed to their downfall she retained a daughter's trust in their wisdom and good will. She knew too that their fury at her part in their ruin was as nothing to their undying hatred of Kronos.

For three days her calls to Gaia and Ouranos rang round the hills and caves of the world.

'Earth Mother, Sky Father, hear your daughter and come to her aid! The son who cut you and cast you out has become the foulest of ogres, the most depraved and unnatural creature in all the world. Five of your grandchildren has he eaten. I have one more baby inside me, ready to come into the world. Teach me how to save him. Teach me, I beg, and I will raise him to revere you always.'

A deep and terrible rumbling was heard far below. The ground shook beneath Rhea's feet. The voice of Ouranos came roaring into her ears, but within it she heard too the calmer tones of her mother.

Together the three of them hatched a marvellous plan.

The Switch

In order to set this marvellous plan in motion Rhea went to Crete to confer with a she-goat named AMALTHEA. Also living on the island were the Meliae, nymphs of the manna-bearing ash tree. If you remember, they had sprung from the soil soaked by Ouranos's blood, along with the Furies and the Giants. After an encouraging conversation with Amalthea, Rhea conferred with these mild and sweet-natured nymphs. Satisfied that the things she needed to achieve on Crete could be achieved, she returned to Mount Othrys to prepare for her time.

Kronos had seen by now that his wife was expecting and he readied himself for the happy day when he could consume the sixth of his children. He was taking no chances. The prophecy of Ouranos still rang in his ears and the superstitious pangs of paranoia that ravage all despotic usurpers grew fiercer in this ur-Stalin each day.

Gaia had told Rhea about a certain stone – an object of perfect magnetite just the right size for their purposes, smooth and shaped like a bean – which could be found in the hills not far from Mount Othrys itself.*

---

* In fact the area of central Greece where Mount Othrys stands is called Magnesia to this day: it gave its name to magnesium, magnets and, of course, magnetite. Manganese too, through a spelling mistake.

In the mornings Kronos liked to stride from one end of Greece to the other visiting each of his Titan brothers and sisters, outwardly to consult with them, in truth to make sure that they were not plotting against him. At the time she knew he would be on the seashore, visiting Oceanus and Tethys, Rhea went to the place that Gaia had described, found the stone and took it home to Mount Othrys, where she swaddled it in linen. The plan was coming together.

One afternoon not long afterwards, with Kronos near enough to hear her but far enough away to take some time to arrive, Rhea began to scream the screams of childbirth. Louder and louder came her agonized howls, tearing the fabric of the air until, after a sudden silence, they were replaced by the best impression she could give of a baby's first gasping cries.

Sure enough, Kronos approached. His shadow fell over Rhea.

'Give me the child,' he said.

'Dread lord and husband –' Rhea cast him an imploring look. 'Will you not let me keep this one? Look at him, so sweet, so innocent. So harmless.'

With a rough laugh Kronos snatched the tightly wrapped baby from Rhea's cradling arms and bolted it down in one great gulp, swaddling linen and all. Down it went like the others, never touching the sides. Punching his breastbone once, then twice, Kronos gave a loud belch and left his tormented wife to her grief-stricken sobs.

The moment he had gone, the sobs turned to hysterical, barely suppressed chokes and screams. Chokes and screams of laughter.

Catching her breath and rising from her bed Rhea slipped down the mountainside and made her way to Crete, travelling as fast as anyone could in so heavily pregnant a state.

The Cretan Child

Rhea's accouchement on Crete was easy enough. Tenderly assisted by the she-goat and the Meliae she prepared to give birth in the safety and comfort of a cave on Mount Ida. Soon she was delivered of a quite transcendently beautiful baby boy. She named him ZEUS.

Just as Gaia had recruited her youngest child Kronos in order to take revenge on her son and husband Ouranos, so Rhea vowed she would rear this, her youngest child, to destroy her husband and brother Kronos. The dreadful cycle of blood-lust, greed and killing that marked the birth pangs of the primordial world would continue into the next generation.

Rhea knew she must return to Mount Othrys before Kronos noticed her absence and suspected that something was wrong. As had been arranged, the goat Amalthea would suckle the baby with her rich and nutritious milk while the Meliae would feed him on the sweet and wholesome manna that wept its gum from their ash trees. In this way young Zeus could grow up on Crete strong and well nourished. Rhea would visit him as often as was possible, to tutor him in the arts of revenge.

Although this is the best-known version, there are many different accounts as to how Zeus escaped the attention of the great Kronos, god of earth, sky and seas. One records that a nymph named ADAMANTHEA suspended the infant Zeus by rope from a tree. Strung up between earth, sea and sky he remained in this way invisible to his father. It is a pleasingly Daliesque image – the baby who would become the mightiest of all beings gurgling, babbling and chuckling in mid-air, hanging between the elements over which he was destined to rule.

The Oath of Allegiance

While, unknown to his father, Zeus grew strong on goat's milk and manna in Crete and learned to walk, talk and understand the world around him, Kronos summoned his Titan siblings to Mount Othrys to renew their pledges of loyalty and obedience.

'This is our world now,' he told them. 'Fate has decreed that I must be childless, the better to rule. But you must do your duty. Breed! Fill the world with our Titan race. Bring them up to obey me in all things and I will grant you lands and provinces of your own. Now, bow before me.'

The Titans bowed low and Kronos gave a grunt of satisfaction that was the closest he ever came to an expression of happiness. The vengeful prophecy of his father had been averted; the eternal Age of the Titans could begin.

The Cretan Boy

Kronos may have grunted with satisfaction, but Moros, the figuration of Destiny and Doom, smiled – as he always does when the powerful exhibit confidence. On this occasion Moros smiled because he could see that Zeus was flourishing on Crete. He was growing into the strongest and most striking male in all creation – indeed his radiance had become almost painful to look upon.* The goodness of goat's milk and the nurturing potency of manna had given him strong bones, a clear complexion, sparkling eyes and glossy hair. He

---

* As is often the case with extraordinarily attractive people. It is incumbent upon us to apologize or look away when our beauty causes discomfort.

made the journey, to use the Greek terms, from *pais* (boy) and *ephebos* (teenager) to *kouros* (youth) and thence into a fine example of what we might call today a young adult. Even now the first downy outlines of what was to become a legendary and mighty example of the art of the beard were showing themselves on his chin and cheeks.* He possessed the confidence, the unforced air of command, that marks out those destined to lead. He was quicker to laughter than anger, but when his ire was roused he could frighten every living creature within his orbit.

From the first he exhibited a blend of zest for life and strength of will that filled even his mother with awe, and some attested that Amalthea's milk conferred extraordinary capabilities on the youth as he grew. To this day Cretan guides entertain visitors with tales of the young Zeus's remarkable powers. They tell the story (as if it happened within their lifetimes) of how, as an infant playing with his beloved nanny-goat and unaware of his own strength, Zeus accidentally snapped off one of her horns.† By virtue of his already prodigious divine powers, this broken horn instantly filled itself with the most delicious food – fresh bread, vegetables, fruit, cured meats and smoked fish – a supply that never gave out no matter how much was taken from it. Thus originated the celebrated Horn of Plenty, the CORNUCOPIA.

Zeus's determined mother visited Crete whenever she felt able to slip away from the ever watchful Kronos.

---

* The question of how long it took for immortals to be weaned, to walk, talk and grow into adulthood is a vexed one. Some sources maintain that Zeus grew from a baby into young manhood in a single year. Divine time and mortal time seem to have run differently, just like those of dogs and humans do, or elephants and flies, for example. It is probably best for us not to concentrate in too literal a fashion on the temporal structure of myth.

† Zeus was often playful. The Romans called him JUPITER or JOVE, so he had quite literally a jovial disposition. 'The Bringer of Jollity', Gustav Holst calls him in his orchestral suite *The Planets*.

'Never forget what your father did. He ate your brothers and sisters. He tried to eat you. He is your enemy.'

Zeus would listen as Rhea described the unhappy condition of the world under Kronos.

'He rules by fear. He has no sense of loyalty or trust. This is not the way, my Zeus.'

'Doesn't that make him strong?'

'No! It makes him *weak*. The Titans are his family, his brothers and sisters, nephews and nieces. Already some are beginning to resent his monstrous tyranny. When your time comes you will exploit that resentment.'

'Yes, mother.'

'A true leader forges alliances. A true leader is admired and trusted.'

'Yes, mother.'

'A true leader is loved.'

'Yes, mother.'

'Ah, you laugh at me, but it is true.'

'Yes, m—'

Rhea slapped her son.

'Be serious. You are no fool, I can see that for myself. Adamanthea tells me that you are intelligent, but impetuous. That you spend too much time hunting wolves, teasing the sheep, climbing trees, seducing the ash-tree nymphs. It is time you were properly schooled. You are sixteen now and soon we must make our move.'

'Yes, mother.'

The Oceanid and the Potion

Rhea asked her friend Metis, wise and beautiful daughter of Tethys and Oceanus, to prepare her son for what was to come.

'He is clever, but wayward and rash. Teach him patience, craft and guile.'

Zeus was captivated by Metis from the start. He had never seen such beauty. The Titaness was a little smaller than most of her race, but endowed with a grace and gravity that made her shine. The step of a deer and the guile of a fox, the power of a lion, the softness of a dove, all allied to a presence and force of mind that sent the boy dizzy.

'Lie down with me.'

'No. We shall go for a walk. I have many things to say to you.'

'Here. On the grass.'

Metis smiled and took his hand. 'We have work to do, Zeus.'

'But I love you.'

'Then you will do as I say. When we love someone, we always want to please them do we not?'

'Don't you love me?'

Metis laughed, though in truth she was astounded by the halo of glamour and charisma that radiated from this bold and handsome youth. But her friend Rhea had asked her to undertake his education and Metis was never one to betray a trust.

For a year she taught him how to look into the hearts and judge the intentions of others. How to imagine and how to reason. How to find the strength to let passions cool before acting. How to make a plan and how to know when a plan needed to be changed or abandoned. How to let the head rule the heart and the heart win the affection of others.

Her refusal to allow their relationship to take on a physical dimension only made Zeus love her more. Although she never told him so, Metis returned the love. As a result there existed a kind of crackle in the air whenever the two were close.

One day Zeus saw Metis standing over a large boulder and bashing its flat surface with a small round-ended stone.

'What on earth are you doing?'

'Crushing mustard seeds and crystals of salt.'

'Of course you are.'

'Today,' said Metis, 'is your seventeenth birthday. You are ready to go to Othrys and fulfil your destiny. Rhea will be here soon, but first I must finish a little preparation of my own devising.'

'What's in that jar?'

'In here there is a mixture of poppy juice and copper sulphate, sweetened with a syrup of manna provided by the Meliae, our friends of the ash tree. I'll put all the ingredients together and shake them up. Like so.'

'I don't understand.'

'Look, here is your mother. She will explain.'

As Metis looked on, Rhea outlined the plan to Zeus. Mother and son gazed deep into each other's eyes, took a deep breath and swore an oath, son to mother, mother to son. They were ready.

Rebirth of the Five

Midnight. The thick cloth that Erebus and Nyx threw across earth, sea and sky to mark the end of Hemera's and Aether's diurnal round blanketed the world. In a valley high up on Mount Othrys, the Lord of All paced alone, banging his chest, restless and miserable. Kronos had grown into the most foul-tempered and discontented Titan of all. Power over everything gave him no satisfaction. Since Rhea had – without explanation – banned him from the conjugal bed, sleep had been a stranger to him too. Denied its healing balm his mood and digestion, neither good at the best of times, had worsened. The last of the babies he had swallowed seemed to have provoked a sharp acid reflux that the previous five had not. Where was the joy in omnipotence when his stomach griped and his thoughts stumbled blindly in the thick fog of insomnia?

His heart lifted to a state approaching something like happiness, however, when he heard, unexpectedly, the sound of Rhea's low sweet voice humming gently to herself as she came up the slope towards the mountaintop. Loveliest sister and dearest wife! It was quite natural that she had been a little upset by his consumption of their six children, but she surely understood that he had had no choice. She was a Titan, she knew about duty and destiny. He called out to her.

'Rhea?'

'Kronos! Awake at this hour?'

'I have been awake for more days and nights than I can count. Hypnos and Morpheus have made themselves strangers to me. Full of scorpions is my mind, dear wife.' Macbeth, another murderer deprived of sleep and plagued by dark prophesies, was to say the same thing, but not for many years yet.

'Oh tush, my love. Cannot the wit and craft of a Titaness surpass those silly sleep demons? There is nothing Hypnos and Morpheus can do to soothe your aching body, to calm your racing mind, to ease your wounded spirit, that I cannot match with something sweet and warm of my own.'

'Your sweet warm lips! Your sweet warm thighs! Your sweet warm —'

'Those in time, impatient lord! But first, I have brought you a present. A lovely boy to be your cupbearer.'

From the recess stepped Zeus, a radiant smile lighting up his handsome face. He bowed and proffered Kronos a jewelled goblet which the Titan snatched greedily.

'Pretty, very pretty. I might try him later,' he said casting an admiring eye over Zeus and drinking down the contents of the goblet in one greedy draft. 'But Rhea, it is you that I love.'

It was too dark for him to see that Rhea had hoisted one eyebrow into an arch of contemptuous incredulity.

'You love me?' she hissed. '*You? Love? Me?* You, who ate all but one of my darling children? You dare talk to me of *love*?'

Kronos gave an unhappy hiccup. He was undergoing the strangest sensations. He frowned and tried to focus. What was Rhea saying? It could not be that she no longer loved him. His mind was even more foggy and his stomach even more turbulent than usual. What was *wrong* with him? Oh, and there was something else she had said. Something that made no sense at all.

'What do you mean,' he asked in a voice thick with confusion and nausea, 'by saying that I ate "all but one" of your children? I ate *all* of them. I distinctly remember.'

A strong young voice cracked through the night air like a whip. 'Not quite all, father!'

Kronos, the nausea rising in an alarming surge, turned in shock to see the young cupbearer step from the shadows.

'Who ... who ... whoooooooooo!' Kronos's question turned into a sudden uprush of uncontrollable vomiting. From his gut, in one heaving spasm, erupted a large stone. The linen in which it was once wrapped had long since been dissolved by stomach acid. Kronos gazed at it stupidly, his eyes swimming and his face white. But before he could understand what he was seeing he was assailed by that horrible and unmistakable feeling that tells a vomiter there is more to come. Far more.

Zeus leapt fleetly forward, picked up the regurgitated boulder and hurled it far, far away, much as Kronos had once flung Ouranos's genitals far, far away from the exact same spot. We will find out later where it landed and what happened.

Inside Kronos the compound of salt, mustard and ipecacuanha continued to do its emetic work.* One by one he spewed up the five children he had swallowed. First out was Hera.† Then came Poseidon, Demeter, Hades and finally Hestia, before the tormented Titan collapsed in a paroxysm of exhausted panting.

If you recall, Metis's potion also included a quantity of poppy juice. This immediately began to take somniferous effect. Letting out one last great rumbling groan, Kronos rolled over and fell into a deep, deep sleep.

With a cry of exultation Zeus bent over his snoring father to grasp the great sickle and administer the *coup de grâce*. He would sever Kronos's head in one blow and raise it up in triumph before the world, creating a victorious tableau that would never be forgotten and that artists would depict until the end of time. But the scythe, forged by Gaia for Kronos, could not be used against him. Powerful as Zeus was, he was unable even to pick it up. He tried once, but it felt as if it was fixed to the ground.

'Gaia gave it to him and only Gaia can take it away from him,' said Rhea. 'Let it be.'

'But I must kill him,' said Zeus. 'We must be revenged.'

'His mother Earth protects him. Do not anger her. You will need her in the time to come. You will have your revenge.'

---

* The potion was prepared by Metis and it would be nice to think that is where our word 'emetic' comes from, but I don't think it does.

† Although in birth order Hera had been the last to be born before Zeus, she now counted as the second child. A kind of reverse seniority operated as they emerged from Kronos's gullet. Zeus became officially the eldest of the children while Hestia, having been the firstborn, was now considered the youngest. It makes sense if you are a god.

Zeus gave up his attempts to move the scythe. It was vexing that he could not behead his hated father as he lay there snoring like a pig, but his mother was right. It could wait. There was too much to celebrate.

In the starlight over Mount Othrys he and his five liberated siblings laughed and stamped and hooted and howled with delight. Their mother laughed too, clapping her hands with joy to see her radiant sons and daughters so well and so happy, out in the world at last and ready to claim their inheritance. Each of the five rescued ones took it in turn to embrace Zeus, their youngest but now eldest brother, their saviour and their leader. They swore allegiance to him for ever. Together they would overthrow Kronos and his whole ugly race and establish a new order . . .

They would not, despite their parentage, call themselves 'Titans'. They would be *gods*. And not just gods, but *the* gods.

The Beginning
PART TWO

CLASH OF THE TITANS

At the summit of Mount Othrys, Kronos lay stretched out on the ground. The other Titans had not yet learned of Zeus's rescue of his brothers and sisters, but it seemed likely that when they did they would react with furious violence. Under cover of the night Rhea and her six children slipped away, putting as great a distance between themselves and Titan country as they could.

War, Zeus understood clearly, was inevitable. Kronos would not rest as long as his children lived and Zeus was just as determined to dethrone his father. He heard louder than ever the sound he had heard within him since infancy: a softly insistent whisper from Moros telling him that it was his destiny to rule.

The bloody, violent and destructive conflict that followed is known to historians as the TITANOMACHY.* While most of the details of this ten-year war may be lost to us, we do know that the heat and fury, the explosive power and colossal energy released by the battling Titans, gods and monsters caused mountains to bellow fire and the ground itself to quake and crack. Many islands

---

* Hesiod, in the eighth century BC, offers us the fullest extant account, but other poets also sang of it; an epic called the *Titanomachia*, by the eighth-century Eumelus of Corinth (or possibly the legendary blind bard Thamyris of Thrace), is tantalizingly mentioned in other texts, but remains lost to us. Hesiod describes the pitched battle that shook the earth like this: 'The boundless sea rang terribly around, and the earth crashed loudly: wide Heaven was shaken and groaned, and . . . reeled from its foundation under the charge of the undying gods, and a heavy quaking reached dim Tartarus and the deep sound of their feet in the fearful onset and of their hard missiles. So, then, they launched their grievous shafts upon one another, and the cry of both armies as they shouted reached to starry heaven; and they met together with a great battle-cry.'

and landmasses were formed by these battles. Whole continents shifted and reshaped themselves and much of the world as we know it now owes its geography to these seismic disturbances, to this literally earth-shaking conflict.

In a straight fight it is almost certain that the combined strength of the Titans would have been too much for their young adversaries. They were stronger and more remorselessly savage. All but Clymene's sons Prometheus and Epimetheus sided with Kronos, far outnumbering the small group of self-styled gods ranged against them under Zeus's generalship. But just as Ouranos had paid dearly for his crime of imprisoning the Cyclopes and Hecatonchires inside Gaia, so Kronos was about to pay for the blunder of imprisoning them in the caverns of Tartarus.

It was the wise and clever Metis who advised Zeus to go down and release his three one-eyed and three hundred-handed brothers. He offered them freedom in perpetuity if they would help him defeat Kronos and the Titans. They needed no further encouragement. The Gigantes too chose to side with Zeus and proved themselves brave and tireless fighters.*

In the final decisive battle the pitiless ferocity of the Hecatonchires – not to mention their surplus of heads and hands – combined quite marvellously with the wild electric power of the Cyclopes whose names were, if you recall, Brightness, Lightning and Thunder: Arges, Steropes and Brontes. These gifted craftsmen hammered their mastery of storms into thunderbolts for Zeus to use as weapons, which he learned to fling with pinpoint accuracy at his enemies, blasting them to atoms. Under his direction the Hecatonchires picked up and hurled rocks at furious speed, while the Cyclopes harried and dazzled the enemy with lightning

---

* See Appendix on p. 399.

44

shows and terrifying peals of thunder. The hundred hands of the Hecatonchires scooped and launched, scooped and launched innumerable rocks at the enemy like so many demented windmilling catapults until, bludgeoned and battered, the Titans called for a ceasefire.

We will leave them, their great bloodied heads bowed in full and final surrender, and take a moment to look at what else had been going on in the world while battle raged for those ten terrible years.

The Proliferation

The fire and fury of war had scorched, enriched and fertilized the earth. New growth burst through to create a fresh, green world for the triumphant gods to inherit.

If you remember, Cosmos had once been nothing but Chaos. Then Chaos had spewed up the first forms of life, the primordial beings and the principles of lightness and darkness. As each generation developed and new entities were born and in turn reproduced, so *complexity* increased. Those old primordial and elemental principles were spun into lifeforms of ever greater diversity, variety and richness. The beings that were born became endowed with nuanced and unique personalities and individuality. In computer language, it was as if life went from 2 bit to 4 bit to 8 bit to 16 bit to 32 bit to 64 bit and beyond. Each iteration represented millions and then billions of new permutations of size, form and what you might call *resolution*. High definition character, such as we pride ourselves in having as modern humans, came into existence and there was an explosion of what biologists call *speciation* as new forms burst into being.

I like to picture the first stage of creation as an old-fashioned TV screen on which a monochrome game of *Pong* played. You remember *Pong*? It had two white rectangles for rackets and a square dot for a ball. Existence was a primitive, pixellated form of bouncing tennis. Some thirty-five to forty years later there had evolved ultra hi-res 3-D graphics with virtual and augmented reality. So it was for the Greek cosmos, a creation that began with clunky and elemental lo-res outlines now exploded into rich, varied life.

Creatures and gods that were ambiguous, inconsistent, unpredictable, intriguing and unknowable had arrived. To use a distinction made by E. M. Forster when talking about people in novels, the world now went from flat characters to rounded characters – to the development of personalities whose actions could surprise. The fun began.

The Muses

One of the original Titans, Mnemosyne (Memory), was mother by Zeus to nine highly intelligent and creative daughters, the Muses, who lived at various times on Mount Helicon (where the Hippocrene fountain later played), on Mount Parnassus above Delphi, and in Pieria in Thessaly where the Pierian Spring, the metaphorical source of all the arts and sciences, flowed.*

We think of the Muses today as patron saints of the arts in general, and private sources of inspiration in particular. 'O

---

* The PIERIDES came from Pieria too. They were nine sisters who made the mistake of challenging the Muses, only to be turned into birds for their troubles. Alexander Pope refers to Pieria as the fount of all wisdom and knowledge in this well-known couplet from his *Essay on Criticism*:

> A *little Learning* is a dang'rous Thing;
> Drink deep, or taste not the *Pierian* Spring . . .

for a Muse of fire!' cries the Chorus at the opening of Shakespeare's *Henry V.* He or she is 'my muse' we might say of those who fire our creativity and spur us on to greatness. The Muses can be found in 'music', 'amusements', 'museums' and general 'musings'. W. H. Auden believed that the image of a capricious goddess whispering ideas in the poet's ear was the best way of accounting for the maddening unreliability of creative inspiration. Sometimes she gives you gold, sometimes you read back what she has dictated and see that it is dross. The Muses' mother might be Memory, but their father is Zeus, whose faithless inconstancy is the subject of many stories yet to come.

But let us meet these nine sisters, each of whom represents and stands patron to their own particular art form.

Calliope

Rather an undignified linguistic end meets CALLIOPE, the Muse of epic poetry. Somehow she became a steam-powered organ commonly played in fairgrounds, which are just about the only places where you will hear her name spoken today. To the Roman poet Ovid she was the chief of all the Muses. Her name means 'beautiful voice' and she gave birth to ORPHEUS, the most important musician in all Greek history. The finest poets, Homer, Virgil and Dante included, invoked her aid when embarking on their great epics.

Clio

Now relegated to a model of Renault motorcar and a series of awards in the advertising industry, CLIO or *Kleio* (famous) was the Muse of history. She was responsible for proclaiming, for noising abroad and making famous the deeds of the great. America's oldest debating union, founded in Princeton by

James Madison, Aaron Burr and others, is called the Clio-sophical Society in her honour.

Erato

ERATO was the Muse of lyric and love poetry. Her name is related to Eros and the erotic and she has sometimes been represented in art with a golden arrow to suggest the connection. Turtle doves and the myrtle are common symbols associated with her, as is the lute.

Euterpe

The Muse of music itself, the 'delightful' and 'joyous' EUTERPE bore, by the river god STRYMON, the Thracian king RHESUS who went on to play a very minor part in the Trojan War. Whether he gave his name to the monkeys that in turn went on to describe types of human blood factor is not agreed upon.

Melpomene

The tragic Muse, MELPOMENE (whose name derives from a Greek verb meaning 'to celebrate with dance and song') represented originally the chorus and then the whole of tragedy – a very important fusing of music, poetry, drama, mask, dance, song and religious celebration. Tragic actors wore a type of thick-soled boot,* called a 'buskin' in English and the *cothurnus* in Greek; and Melpomene is usually depicted either holding or wearing these, as well as, of course, the famous tragic masque with its unhappy down-curved lips. Along with her sister Terpsichore, she was a mother to the Sirens, whose time will come.

---

* To give the actors added height, and with it metaphorical stature too.

Polyhymnia

Hymnos is the Greek for 'praise' and POLYHYMNIA was the Muse of hymns, of *sacred* music, dance, poetry and rhetoric as well as – slightly randomly one might think – agriculture, pantomime, geometry and meditation. I suppose today we would call her 'the Muse of mindfulness'. She is usually portrayed as a rather serious figure, finger held pensively to her mouth in an attitude of solemn rumination. She is another contender, along with Calliope, for mother of the hero Orpheus.

Terpsichore

Cheese Shop Owner: Oh, I thought you were complaining about the bouzouki player.
Customer: Oh, heaven forbid. I am one who delights in all manifestations of the Terpsichorean muse.

This dialogue from Monty Python's immortal 'Cheese Shop Sketch' introduced many, myself included, to TERPSICHORE, the Muse of dance.

Thalia

The finest, funniest, friendliest Muse of all, THALIA supervised the comic arts and idyllic poetry. Her name derives from the Greek verb for 'to flourish'.* Like her tragic counterpart Melpomene she sports actors' boots and a mask (hers being the cheerful smiling one of course), but she is wreathed in ivy and carries a bugle and a trumpet.

---

* Which also gave us (via the word for a flourishing green shoot) the element thallium, a favourite of crime writers and criminal poisoners.

URANIA derives her name from Ouranos, the primal god of the heavens (and a great-grandfather of the nine sisters); she is the Muse who presides over astronomy and the stars. She is also considered a figure of Universal Love, a kind of Greek version of the Paraclete, or Holy Spirit.

Threesomes

The three times three Muses remind me to introduce more triads. Gaia and Ouranos gave birth, as we know, to three Hecatonchires, three Cyclopes and four times three Titans. We have already encountered the three Erinyes, also called the Eumenides – those vengeful Furies who sprang from the blood-soaked earth at the moment of the castration of Ouranos. Three seems to have been a very magic number to the Greeks.

The Charites

During the course of the ten-year Titanomachy, apocalyptic as it was, Zeus always found time to fulfil his desires. Perhaps he saw it as discharging his duty to populate the earth. It is certainly the case that Zeus liked to discharge.

One day Zeus's eye fell on the most beautiful of all the Oceanids – EURYNOME, daughter of Oceanus and Tethys. Hidden in a cave while the battle roared outside, Eurynome bore Zeus three ravishing daughters, AGLAEA (which means 'splendour'), EUPHROSYNE also known as EUTHYMIA (glee, merriment, mirth) and THALIA* (cheerfulness). Together they were known as the CHARITES or, to the Romans, the

---

* Sharing her name with the Muse of comedy.

GRATIAE. We call them the Three Graces, favoured throughout history by sculptors and painters seeking an excuse to render perfect female nudes. Their sweetness of nature gave the world something to counteract the horrible malice and cruelty of the Erinyes.

Horai

The HORAI, or Hours, consisted of two sets of triplet sisters. These daughters of THEMIS (the embodiment of law, justice and custom) originally personified the seasons. There seem to have been two to begin with, summer and winter, AUXESIA* and CARPO. The classical first triad of Horai was made up by the later addition of THALLO (FLORA to the Romans), bringer of flowers and blossoms, the embodiment of spring. The Horai's most valuable quality derived from their mother: their gift of the propitious moment, the benign relationship between natural law and the unfolding of time – what you might call 'divine serendipity'.

The second set of Horai was responsible for a more worldly kind of law and order. They were EUNOMIA, goddess of law and legislation, DIKÉ goddess of justice and the moral order (the Roman equivalent was JUSTITIA) and EIRENE, the goddess of peace (PAX to the Romans).

Moirai

The three MOIRAI, or Fates, were named CLOTHO, LACHESIS and ATROPOS. These daughters of Nyx are to be thought of as sitting round a spinning wheel: Clotho spins the thread that represents a life, Lachesis measures out its length and Atropos (the relentless, remorseless one, literally the 'un-turning') chooses when to

---

* Sometimes just Auxo.

shear the thread and cut the life short.* I picture them as sunken-cheeked crones, clothed in black rags, sitting in a cave cackling and nodding as they spin, but many sculptors and poets represented them as pink-cheeked maidens, dressed in white robes and smiling demurely. Their name derives from a word that means 'portion' or 'lot', in the sense of 'that which is allotted to you'. 'It was not her portion to be loved', or, 'It was his lot to be unhappy', are the kinds of phrases Greeks employed to describe attributes or destinies apportioned by the Moirai. Even the gods had to submit themselves to the Fates' cruel decrees.†

Keres

These carrion daughters of Nyx were the vile and rapacious spirits of violent death. Like the Valkyries of Norse and Germanic myth they collected the souls of warriors killed in battle. Unlike those benevolent warrior goddesses however, the Keres did not escort their heroic souls to the reward of a Valhalla. They flew from bleeding body to body, greedily sucking up the blood that flowed from them; then, when each corpse was thoroughly drained, they threw it over their shoulders and moved on to the next.

Gorgons

The primordial sea god Pontus had by Gaia a son, PHORCYS, and a daughter, CETO. The progeny of this brother and sister were three island-dwelling sisters, the Gorgons STHENO, EURYALE and MEDUSA. With hair of writhing venomous snakes, intense staring eyes, hideous fixed smiles, boar's tusk

---

* Atropine, the poison derived from mandrakes and *Atropa belladonna* (deadly nightshade), gets its name from this last and most terrible of the sisters.

† Later Greeks considered the Fates to be not daughters of Night, but of Necessity – ANANKE. They bear a very strong resemblance to the Norns of Norse mythology.

teeth, clawed hands of brass and taloned feet, and scaly golden bodies, these monstrous sisters appeared frightful enough to freeze the blood. But anyone who caught a Gorgon's eye – exchanged looks with her for just one fleeting second – would quite literally be turned instantly to stone. The word for that is 'petrified', which has come to mean scared *stiff*.

Spirits of Air, Earth and Water

These threesomes were not the only significant beings to spring into life at this time. All over the world, as the Titanomachy raged around them, nature sprites and spirits of all kinds began to multiply and claim their areas of sovereignty. One pictures them scampering for shelter and trembling behind bushes while the rocks and thunderbolts fly through the air and the earth shakes with the violence of war. Somehow these often fragile beings survived and thrived, to enrich the world with their beauty, dedication and charm.

Perhaps the best known of them are the NYMPHS, a major class of minor female deities, divided into clans or sub-species according to their habitats. The OREADS held court in the mountains, hills and grottoes of Greece and its islands, while the Nereids (like the Oceanids from whom they descended) were denizens of the deep. NAIADS, their fresh-water counterparts, were found in lakes and streams of running water, or in the reeds that fringed them and on river-banks. Over time some water nymphs began to associate themselves with ever more specific realms. Soon there were PEGAEAE, who looked after natural springs, and POTAMEI-DES, who dwelt in and around rivers.* On land the

---

* The TAGIDES were nymphs associated within just one river, the Tagus, but now that I've mentioned them we can forget all about them as we shan't meet them ever again.

AULONIADES kept to pastures and groves, while the LEI-MAKIDES lived in meadows. Woodland spirits included light-winged DRYADS and the HAMADRYADS, sylvan nymphs whose lives were tied to the trees they made their home. When their tree died or was cut down, they died too. More specialist wood nymphs populated just apple trees or laurels. The Meliae, nymphs of the sweet manna-bearing ash tree, we have already met.

The fate of the hamadryads shows that nymphs could die. They never aged or fell prey to diseases, but they were not always immortal.

And so, while the natural world ripened, rippled and replicated in this prodigiously bravura manner, seeding itself with ever more marvellous demigods and immortals, the earth trembled and shook with the violence and terror of war. But this proliferation ensured that, when the smoke and dust of battle at last cleared, the victors would rule a world filled with life, colour and character. The triumphant Zeus was set to inherit an earth, sea and sky infinitely richer than the ones into which he had been born.

Disposer Supreme and Judge of the Earth

Zeus now moved to make sure the defeated Titans could never rise again to threaten his order. His strongest and most violent opponent in the war had not been Kronos but ATLAS, the brutally powerful eldest son of Iapetus and Clymene.* Atlas had been at the centre of every battle, rousing his fellow

---

* Atlas's brother MENOETIUS, whose name means 'doomed might', had been a furiously powerful and terrible opponent too, but Zeus had destroyed him with one of the very first thunderbolts.

Titans into combat, shouting for one last supreme effort even as the Hecatonchires were battering them into submission. As punishment for his enmity, Zeus sentenced him to hold up the sky for eternity. This killed two birds with one stone. Zeus's predecessors, Kronos and Ouranos, had been forced to waste much of their energy in separating heaven from earth. At a stroke Zeus relieved himself of that draining burden and placed it, quite literally, on the shoulders of his most dangerous enemy. At the junction of what we would call Africa and Europe the Titan strained, the whole weight of the sky bearing down upon him. Legs braced, muscles bunched, his mighty body contorted itself with this supreme and agonizing effort. For aeons he groaned there like a Bulgarian weightlifter. In time he solidified into the Atlas Mountains that shoulder the skies of North Africa to this day. His straining, squatting image is to be found on copies of the very first maps of the world, which in his honour we still call 'atlases'.* To one side of him lies the Mediterranean and to the other the ocean still named 'the Atlantic' after him, where the mysterious island kingdom of Atlantis is said to have flourished.

As for Kronos – the dark unhappy soul who had once been Lord of All, the brooding and unnatural tyrant who ate his own children out of fear of prophecy – his punishment, just as his gelded father Ouranos had foretold, was ceaselessly to travel the world, measuring out eternity in inexorable, perpetual and lonely exile. Every day and hour and minute was his to be marked out, for Zeus doomed Kronos to count infinity itself. We can see him everywhere even today, the gaunt sinister figure with his sickle. Now given the cheap and humiliating nickname

---

* These later images, however, show him holding up not the sky but the world.

'Old Father Time', his sallow, drawn features tell us of the inevitable and merciless ticking of Cosmos's clock, driving all to their end days. The scythe swings and cuts like a remorseless pendulum. All mortal flesh is as grass beneath the cruel sweep of its mowing blade. We find Kronos in all things 'chronic' or 'synchronized', in 'chronometers', 'chronographs' and 'chronicles'.* The Romans gave this saturnine, sallow husk of a defeated Titan the name SATURN. He hangs in the sky between his father Uranus and his son Jupiter.†

Not all the Titans were banished or punished. To many Zeus showed magnanimity and mercy, while on those few who had sided with him in the war he showered favours.‡ Atlas's brother Prometheus was chief amongst those who had had the prescience to fight for the gods against their own kind.§ Zeus rewarded him with his companionship, taking ever more delight in the young Titan's presence until one day which was to have massive consequences for humankind, consequences we feel even now. The story of that friendship and its tragic end will be told soon.

During the war, the Cyclopes had, as mentioned, given Zeus in respectful homage the weapon with which he is always associated: the thunderbolt. Their brothers the Hecatonchires, whose tremendous strength had secured

---

* To some mythographers Kronos (the Titan) and Chronos (Time) are quite separate entities. I prefer the versions that unite them.

† Astronomers consult classical scholars when they name the heavenly bodies in our solar system. The numerous moons of Saturn include Titan, Iapetus, Atlas, Prometheus, Hyperion, Tethys, Rhea and Calypso. Then there are the Rings of Saturn. Perhaps they signify time, like the rings of a tree.

‡ Some of the Titanides were very attractive and – as lustful, highly sexed and prone to falling in love as any being that has ever lived – Zeus already had designs on one or two of the more appealing ones.

§ And 'prescience' or 'forethought' is just what the name Prometheus means . . .

victory, were rewarded by being sent back to Tartarus – not as prisoners this time, but as guardians of the gates to those imponderable depths. The Cyclopes' reward was to be appointed by Zeus his personal artificers, armourers and smiths.

THE THIRD ORDER

The shattered world was still smoking from the savagery of war. Zeus saw that it needed to heal and he knew that his own generation, the Third Order of divine beings, must manage better than the first two had done. It was time for a new order, an order purged of the wasteful bloodlust and elemental brutality that had marked earlier times.

To the victors, the spoils. Like a chief executive who has just completed a hostile takeover, Zeus wanted the old management out and his people in. He allotted each of his siblings their own domain, their areas of divine responsibility. The President of the Immortals chose his cabinet.

For himself, he assumed overall command as supreme leader and emperor, lord of the firmament, master of weather and storms: King of the Gods, Sky Father, Cloud-Gatherer. Thunder and lightning were his to command. The eagle and the oak were his emblems, symbols then as now of fierce grace and unopposable might. His word was law, his power formidably great. But he was not perfect. He was very, *very* far from being perfect.

Hestia

Of all the gods, Hestia – 'First to be devoured and the last to be yielded up again' – is probably the least well known to us, perhaps because the realm that Zeus in his wisdom apportioned to her was the hearth. In our less communal age of central heating and separate rooms for each family member, we do not lend the hearth quite the importance that our ancestors did, Greek or otherwise. Yet, even for us, the word stands for something more than just a fireplace. We speak of 'hearth and home'. Our word 'hearth' shares its ancestry with 'heart', just as the modern Greek for 'hearth' is *kardia*, which also means 'heart'. In ancient Greece the wider concept of hearth and home was expressed by the *oikos*, which lives on for us today in words like 'economics' and 'ecology'. The Latin for hearth is *focus* – which speaks for itself. It is a strange and wonderful thing that out of words for a fireplace we have spun 'cardiologist', 'deep focus' and 'eco-warrior'. The essential meaning of centrality that connects them also reveals the great significance of the hearth to the Greeks and Romans, and consequently the importance of Hestia, its presiding deity.

Refusing offers of marriage from the other gods, Hestia devoted herself to perpetual maidenhood. Placid, contented, kind, hospitable and domestic, she tended to stay away from the everyday power struggles and political machinations of the other gods.* A modest divinity, Hestia is usually depicted in a plain gown offering up flame in a bowl or sitting on a coarse woollen cushion on a simple wooden throne. It was the custom in Greece to say a grace to her before every meal.

The Romans, whose name for her was VESTA, considered her so important that they had a school of priestesses devoted to her, the celebrated Vestal Virgins. Their responsibility, aside from life-long celibacy, was to make sure that the flame

---

* Hospitality, or *xenia*, was so extraordinarily esteemed in the Greek world that Hestia shared the care of it with Zeus himself, who was on occasion given the name Zeus Xenios. Sometimes the gods tested human 'guest friendship', as we shall see in the story of Philemon and Baucis. This was known as *theoxenia*. *Xenophobes*, of course, do not extend the hand of friendship to strangers . . .

representing her was never extinguished. They were the original guardians of the sacred flame.

You can imagine then that there are not many great stories about this gentle and endearing goddess. I only know one, which we will hear before long. Naturally she comes out of it very well.

The Lottery

Zeus turned next to his dark and troublesome brothers, Hades and Poseidon. They had acquitted themselves with equal skill, bravery and cunning in the war against the Titans and he thought it only fair that they should draw lots for the two most important unassigned provinces – the sea and the underworld.

You will recall that Kronos had wrested control of all things in, under and over the sea from Thalassa, Pontus, Oceanus and Tethys. Now, Kronos was gone and the salt-water realm was in Zeus's gift. As for the underworld – which included Tartarus, the mysterious Meadows of Asphodel (of which more later) and the subterranean darkness controlled by Erebus – it was time for those also to be subject to a sole presiding deity, one of Zeus's generation.

Hades and Poseidon had no love for each other, and when Zeus put his hands behind his back and brought them out before him in closed fists, they hesitated. In cases of fraternal dislike each brother will usually want what the other wants.

'Does Hades hope for the sea or the underworld?' Poseidon wondered. 'If he wants the underworld then I want that too, just to infuriate him.'

Hades thought along the same lines. 'Whichever I choose,' he said to himself, 'I will shout in triumph, just to annoy that prick Poseidon.'

In each of Zeus's outstretched fists lay concealed a precious stone: a sapphire as blue as the sea in one and a piece of jet as black as Erebus in the other. Poseidon did a jig of delight when he touched the back of Zeus's right hand and saw it open to reveal the winking blue sapphire. 'The oceans are mine!' he roared.

'That means – *yes*!' cried Hades with a mighty fist-pump. 'That means I have the underworld. Ha ha!'

Secretly, inside, he was sickened. Gods are such children.

Hades

This was the last time Hades was ever seen to laugh. From that moment on, any merriment or sense of fun deserted him. Perhaps the duties of King of the Underworld slowly ground away any youthful zest or lightness of touch that may once have been his.

Down to the depths he went to carve out his kingdom. While his name will always be associated with death and the afterlife, and the whole realm of the underworld (which shares his name) with pain, punishment and perpetual suffering, Hades also came to symbolize riches and opulence. The jewels and precious metals that are mined deep underground and the priceless crops of grain, vegetables and flowers that germinate beneath the earth are all reminders that from decay and death spring life, abundance and wealth. The Romans called him PLUTO and words like 'plutocrat' and 'plutonium' tell of this great opulence and power.*

Under Hades' personal command came Erebus and Nyx

---

* You will sometimes see the name DIS (a Latin word for 'rich') used for him or his Judaeo-Christian descendant, LUCIFER. Dante in his *Inferno* called the city of hell Dis. Today only cryptic crossword setters use the name with any frequency.

and their son Thanatos (Death himself). A system of river deities, too dark and dreadful to flow in the open air, wound their way through this underworld. The principal was Styx (hate), a daughter of Tethys and Oceanus whose name and 'stygian' attributes are invoked to this day whenever we want to describe something dark, menacing and gloomy, something hellishly black and brooding. Into her seeped PHLEGETHON, the flaming river of fire, ACHERON, the river of woe, LETHE, the waters of forgetfulness, and COCYTUS, the stream of lamentation and wailing. Styx's brother Charon was appointed ferryman, and for the time being he waited, leaning on his pole, by the banks of the Styx. He had dreamed that one day souls by the thousand would come to the shores of the river and pay him the price of transport across. One day soon.

Space was given by Hades to the Furies, the earth-born Erinyes, to live within the darkest heart of his kingdom. From there the three of them could fly to all corners of the world to exact their revenge on those transgressors whose crimes were foul enough to merit their violent attentions.

In time Hades acquired a pet, a gigantic snake-tailed, three-headed dog, offspring of those monstrous children of Gaia and Tartarus, Echidna and Typhon. His name was KERBEROS (although he answered to his Roman name, CERBERUS, too). He was the original hound of hell, the fearsome and tireless watchdog and guardian of the underworld.

At Lerna, a lake that could be used as one of the entrances to the underworld, Hades posted HYDRA, another child of Tartarus and Gaia. I mentioned before the frightening mutations possible when monsters mate, and the difference between Cerberus and his sister Hydra offers a striking example. On the one hand, a dog with a more or less manageable three heads and an elegantly snaky tail to wag; and on the other, his sister, a many-headed water-beast who was almost impossible to kill. Chop off one of her heads and she could grow back ten more in its place.

Despite these zoological atrocities Hades was for the time being a quiet place, ruled over by a god with little to do. In order for hell to be busy, mortal beings are needed. Creatures that die. So we will leave Pluto for the time being, seated on his cold infernal throne, brooding darkly, as hostile, chilly and remote as the planet that bears his name,* and secretly cursing the good fortune that had given rule of the seas to his hated brother.

Poseidon

Poseidon was a very different kind of god to Hades. He could be as truculent, stormy, vain, capricious, inconsistent, restless, cruel and unfathomable as the oceans he commanded. But he could be loyal and grateful too. In common with his brothers and some of his sisters, he was also to exhibit urgent bodily lust, deep spiritual love and every feeling in between. Like all the gods, he was greedy for admiration, sacrifice, obedience and adoration. Once your friend, always your friend. Once your enemy, always your enemy. And he was ambitious for more than burnt offerings, libations and prayers. He always kept an eager, avaricious eye on the youngest of his brothers, the one who now called himself 'eldest' and 'king'. Should the great Zeus make too many mistakes, Poseidon would be there to topple him from his throne.

---

* Or 'dwarf planet' as it is now disrespectfully designated. The moons of Pluto are Styx, Nyx (or Nix), Charon, Kerberos and Hydra.

The Cyclopes, just as they had forged thunderbolts for Zeus, now created a great weapon for Poseidon too – a trident. This massive three-pronged fishing spear could be used to stir up tidal waves and whirlpools – even to make the earth tremble with earthquakes, which gave Poseidon the soubriquet 'Earth Shaker'. His desire for his sister Demeter caused him to invent the horse to impress and please her. He lost his passion for Demeter, but the horse remained sacred to him always.

Under what we would now call the Aegean Sea, Poseidon built a vast palace of coral and pearl in which he installed himself and his chosen consort, AMPHITRITE, a daughter of Nereus and Doris, or (some say) of Oceanus and Tethys. As a wedding gift, Poseidon presented Amphitrite with the very first dolphin. She bore him a son, TRITON, a kind of merman, usually depicted sitting on his tail and blowing with bulging cheeks into a large conch shell. Amphitrite, if truth be told, seems to have been rather colourless and appears in few stories of any great interest. Poseidon spent almost all his time pursuing a perfectly exhausting quantity of beautiful girls and boys and fathering by the girls an even greater number of monsters, demigods and human heroes – Percy Jackson and Theseus to name but two.

Poseidon's Roman equivalent was NEPTUNE, whose giant planet is surrounded by moons that include Thalassa, Triton, Naiad* and Proteus.†

---

* Which is strange, as naiads, of course, were freshwater nymphs, unlike the salty Nereids and Oceanids. Perhaps the astronomers in this case failed to consult a classicist before allocating names.

† PROTEUS, the shape-shifting Old Man of the Sea, herded sea-beasts and knew much. To get information from him you had to wrestle him, which was tricky as he could quickly and frustratingly change himself into any number of new shapes – from lizard to leopard, from dolphin to dormouse. From this slippery ability we get the word 'protean'.

Demeter

The next of Kronos's children to be apportioned her divine duties was Demeter. Hair the colour of ripe wheat, skin like cream and eyes bluer than cornflowers, she was as richly dreamily beautiful as any of the goddesses, except perhaps . . . well, the question of who was the most beautiful goddess would turn out to be the most vexed, thorny and ultimately cataclysmic one ever asked.

So lovely was Demeter that she attracted the unwanted attention of her brothers Zeus and Poseidon. To avoid Poseidon she transformed herself into a mare, and to chase her he turned into a stallion. The issue of that union was a colt, ARION, who grew into an immortal horse magically endowed with the power of speech.* By Zeus she had a daughter, PERSEPHONE, whose story comes along later.

Zeus gave Demeter responsibility for the harvest and with it sovereignty over growth, fertility and the seasons. Her Roman name was CERES, from which we get our word 'cereal'.†

Like Hestia, Demeter is one of the divinities less clear in our minds today as a personality than others of her passionate and charismatic family. But, as with Hestia, her domain was of paramount importance to the Greeks; shrines and cults dedicated to her far outlasted those devoted to the more superficially glamorous gods. The one great story devoted to Demeter, her daughter and the god Hades is as beautiful as it is dramatic, far-reaching and true.

---

* Not to be confused with ARION the singer songwriter, whom we will meet later.

† *De-meter* is often translated as 'barley mother' or 'corn mother', although it is now thought more likely that it originally signified 'earth mother', showing just how thoroughly Zeus's generation of gods had wrested the reins from Gaia.

Hera

Hera came out of Rhea second to last.* Words that are still applied to her, and which would have maddened her greatly, include 'proud', 'imperious', 'jealous', 'haughty' and 'vengeful'. In art and common reference she is often saddled with the extra indignity of three upsetting '-esques': statuesque, Ruben-esque and – courtesy of her Roman appellation – Junoesque.

Fate and posterity have been unkind to the Queen of Heaven. Unlike Aphrodite or Gaia she has no planet named in her honour,† and she must bear the burden of a reputation that portrays her as more reactive than active – reactive always to the errant infidelities of her husband-brother Zeus.

It is easy to dismiss Hera as a tyrant and a bore – jealous and suspicious, storming and ranting like the very picture of a scorned harridan wife (one imagines her hurling china orna-ments at feckless minions), exacting spiteful revenge on nymphs and mortals who have displeased her, failed to burn enough animals on her altars or, most fatally of all, committed the crime of consorting with Zeus (whether they had been willing or unwilling she never forgave them and could hold a grudge for lifetimes). But, ambitious, snobbish, conservatively protective of hierarchy and impatient of originality and flair as she certainly was – the archetype of many a literary aunt and cinematic dowager dragon – Hera was never a bore.‡ The force and resolution with which she faced up to a god who

---

* Anagrammatically 'Rhea' does indeed come out of 'Hera'; at least so I *hear*, but we won't chase that *hare*.

† We shouldn't forget that Gaia is a planet too: she is our home world. Latinized as *Tellus* or *Terra Mater* she is Saxonized for us as 'Earth' (cognate with the Germanic goddess *Erde*, *Erda*, *Joeth* or *Urd*).

‡ I would suggest that Marie Dressler, Lady Bracknell and Aunt Agatha, to name three great examples, can all trace their lineage back to Hera.

could disintegrate her with one thunderbolt shows self-belief as well as courage.

I am very fond of her and, while I am sure I would stammer, blush and swallow awkwardly in her presence, she finds in me a devoted admirer. She gave the gods gravity, heft and the immeasurable gift of what the Romans called *auctoritas*. If that makes her seem a spoilsport, well, sometimes sport needs to be spoiled and the children called in from the playground. Her special province was marriage; the animals associated with her were the peacock and the cow.

Over the course of the war against the Titans she and Zeus developed into a natural couple, and it became apparent to him that she was the only one with enough presence, dignity and command to stand as his consort and bear him new gods.

Crackling with tension, impatience and distrust, theirs was nonetheless a great marriage.

A New Home

Zeus's ambition for a new era, a new dispensation for the cosmos, encompassed more than the simple distribution of powers and provinces amongst his brothers and sisters. Zeus imagined something more enlightened, and rationally constituted than the bloody and brutal tyrannies that had gone before.

He envisioned an assembly of twelve major gods – a *dodecatheon* as he Greekly put it to himself.* So far we have met

---

* Since Zeus took that decision the number twelve seems to have taken on important properties. It is divisible by two, three, four and six of course, making it twice as composite as the stupid number ten. The dozen can still be seen around us in the Zodiac, the day's hours, in months and inches and pennies (well, when I was a boy, it was twelve pennies to the shilling, anyway) not to mention the Tribes of Israel, Disciples of Jesus, Days of Christmas and the Asian twelve-year cycle. It's a duodecimal world.

six, the children of Kronos and Rhea. There was already another deity to call upon of course, one who was older than any of them – foam-born Aphrodite. The moment the Titanomachy erupted, Zeus collected Aphrodite from Cyprus, aware that she would constitute a great prize if kidnapped, ransomed or recruited by the Titans. For the last ten years she had contentedly been living amongst them and thus the gods now numbered seven.*

As the Titans had made Othrys their mountain home, so Zeus now chose for his headquarters Mount Olympus, Greece's highest peak. He and his gods would be known as the OLYMPIANS and they would rule as no divine beings ruled before or since.

The Runt

Hera was pregnant when the gods moved to Olympus. She could not have been more satisfied. Her ambition was to bear Zeus children of such majestic power, strength and beauty that her place as Queen of Heaven would be assured for eternity. She knew that Zeus had a roving eye and she was determined not to let any other parts of him rove either. First she would give birth to the greatest of the gods, a boy whom she would call HEPHAESTUS, and then Zeus would marry her properly and submit himself for ever to her will. This was her plan. The plans of the immortals, however, are as subject to the cruel tricks of Moros as are the plans of mortals.

When her time came, Hera lay down and Hephaestus was

---

* The gods were – if you think it through – Aphrodite's nephews and nieces. They were born of Kronos and she was the direct issue of the ejaculate of Ouranos.

born. To her dismay the child turned out to be so swarthy, ugly and diminutive that, after one disgusted glance, she snatched him up and hurled him down the mountainside. The other gods watched the wailing baby bounce once off a cliff and then disappear into the sea. There was a terrible silence.

We will find out what happened to Hephaestus soon enough, but for the moment let us stay on Olympus, where Hera soon became pregnant by Zeus again. This time she took every care to look after herself, eating healthy foods and exercising gently but regularly, in accordance with all the approved precepts and practices of pregnancy and parturition. She wanted a *proper* son, not a runt fit only to be thrown away.

It's War

In due time Hera was indeed delivered of the lusty, strong and handsome child she had set her heart on.

ARES, for so she called him, was from the beginning a pugnacious, violent and aggressive boy. He picked quarrels with everyone and thought of nothing but the clash of arms and horses, chariots, spears and martial arts. It was natural that Zeus, who disliked him from the first, should appoint him god of war.

Ares – MARS to the Romans – was unintelligent of course, monumentally dense and unimaginative for, as everyone knows, war is stupid. Nevertheless even Zeus acknowledged with grudging consent that he was a necessary addition to Olympus. War may be stupid, but it is also inevitable and sometimes – dare one say it? – necessary.

As Ares grew swiftly to manhood he found himself irresistibly attracted to Aphrodite – as which gods weren't? More perplexingly perhaps, she was equally drawn to him. She loved him, in fact; his violence and strength appealed to some deep part of her. He in turn grew to love her, so far as such a violent brute was capable of the emotion. Love and war, Venus and Mars, have always had a strong affinity. No one quite knows why, but plenty of money has been made trying to find an answer.

The Enchanted Throne

To cement her position as the universally recognized Queen of Heaven and undisputed consort of Zeus, Hera felt the need to institute a nuptial feast, a grand public ceremony that would for ever bind her in wedlock to Zeus.

Hera's twin impulses of propriety and ambition motivated almost everything she did. She had been pleased to see her son falling for Aphrodite, yet she did not trust the goddess. If Aphrodite agreed to make a public commitment to Ares, as Zeus was to do to Hera, then that would make everything binding and official, setting a permanent seal on her triumph. The world's first wedding would therefore solemnize two marriages.

A date was set and invitations sent out. Presents began to arrive, the most spectacular of which, all agreed, was a marvellous golden chair addressed personally to Hera. Never had so glorious and gorgeous an object been seen. Whoever the anonymous sender might be, it was obvious, Hera declared, that he or she had the most exquisite taste. Smiling with satisfaction, she lowered herself onto the throne. Instantly its arms came to life and sprang inwards, enclosing her in a tight embrace. Struggle as she might she could not escape, the arms had locked themselves around her and she was trapped. The screams were appalling.

The Lame One

There is doubt, disagreement and speculation about what happened to Hephaestus after he had been cast down from heaven. Some say the infant god was cared for by the Oceanid Eurynome and either the Titaness Tethys, Eurynome's mother, or perhaps by THETIS, a Nereid (daughter of Nereus and Doris) who was to give birth to ACHILLES many years later. It seems certain, though, that Hephaestus grew up on the island of Lemnos, where he learned how to forge metal and make exquisite, intricate objects. He quickly showed a remarkable talent for the fashioning of useful, ornamental and even magical artefacts, which – allied to his strength with the bellows and apparent immunity from scorching in the intense heat of the forges – combined to make him the greatest of smiths.

In bouncing off the Olympian mountainside he had damaged his foot, which left him with a permanent limp. With his awkward gait, slightly contorted features and disordered black curls, he was a fearful sight. His later reputation, however, was for faithfulness, kindness, good humour and equable temper. Greek myth is replete with infants cast into the wilderness or abandoned on mountaintops to die, either because some prophecy foretold they would one day bring disaster on their parents, tribe or city, or because they were considered accursed, ugly or malformed. Such outcasts seemed always to survive and return to fulfil the prophecy or win back their birthright.

Hephaestus longed to come back to Olympus, which he knew to be his home by right, but he was aware that he could not do so without bitterness or on proper terms unless he allowed himself one measured act of revenge, which would prove his strength of personality, his right to divinity and serve as his calling card to heaven.

So, as Hephaestus learned his trade and worked his bellows, his quick and clever mind devised the plan that his quick and clever fingers would turn into startling reality.

The Hand of Aphrodite

Bound fast on the golden throne, Hera howled with rage and frustration. Neither her power, nor even that of Zeus himself had been able to release her from its curse. How could she invite the immortal world to a feast in which she sat pinioned like a criminal in the stocks? It would be grotesque and undignified. She would be laughed at. What magic was at work here? Who had done this to her? How could she be released from the spell?

The hapless Zeus, bombarded by a shrieked fusillade of questions and complaints, turned to the other gods for help. Whoever managed to release Hera, he proclaimed, could take Aphrodite's hand in marriage, the greatest matrimonial prize there was.

Ares was loudly annoyed by this peremptory decree. Was it not understood that *he* was to wed Aphrodite?

'Calm yourself,' said Zeus. 'You are stronger than all the other gods put together. Your union is safe.'

Aphrodite was confident too and pushed her lover forward with encouraging words. But none of Ares' pulling and pushing and kicking and swearing had the slightest effect. If anything, it seemed that the more he strained, the tighter the throne's hold on Hera became. Poseidon (despite already having Amphitrite as his consort) made a spirited attempt that likewise came to nothing. Even Hades rose up from the underworld to try his hand at freeing Hera from her increasingly embarrassing predicament. All to no avail.

As Zeus himself tugged frantically and uselessly at the arms of the throne, enduring yet more insults from the humiliated and enraged Hera, a polite but insistent cough cut through the commotion. The assembled gods turned.

In the very hall of heaven, a gentle smile on his lopsided face, stood Hephaestus.

'Hello, mother,' he said. 'Having problems?'

'Hephaestus!'

He limped forward. 'I understand that there is some sort of reward . . . ?'

Aphrodite looked at the ground, chewing her lip. Ares growled and started forward, but Zeus held him back. The other gods parted to let the ugly little creature hobble through to where Hera sat imprisoned in her throne of gold. At one touch of his fingers the arms of the golden throne swung open and Hera was free.* She rose to her feet, adjusted her gown and straightened herself in a manner that told the world the whole situation had been under control the whole time. Colour flew to Aphrodite's cheek. This could not be!

It was a moment of sweet revenge for Hephaestus, but his essential good nature kept him from gloating. Despite – or

---

* An important principal is demonstrated here, one that we will encounter many times. No god can undo the spells, transformations, curses or enchantments of another.

perhaps because of – the pangs of rejection he had endured all his life, he was motivated not by anger or resentment but only by a desire to please, to make himself useful and give delight. He knew that he was ugly and he knew Aphrodite did not love him. He knew that if he claimed her as his prize she would betray him and slip often into the bed of his brother Ares. But he was simply happy to be home.

As for Hera – rather than acknowledge that she had been paid back for her cruel and unnatural betrayal of the maternal instinct, she maintained a dignified and frosty silence. Secretly the better part of her was rather proud of her elder boy, and in time she grew genuinely fond of him, as did all Olympus.

Hephaestus would make gifts for Aphrodite and for all the gods and prove himself a worthy member of the twelve. He was given one whole valley of the mountain for his own forge. It was to become the greatest and most productive workshop in the world. For assistants he chose the Cyclopes, themselves craftsmen of the highest order, as we have seen. Anything Hephaestus did not yet know they could teach him, and together, working to his designs, they would fashion remarkable objects that would change the world.

Hephaestus – god of fire, and of blacksmiths, artisans, sculptors and metalworkers – was home. His Roman name is VULCAN, which lives on in volcanoes and vulcanized rubber.*

---

* Vulcan the planet and its people – notably Commander Spock – are not connected, so far as I can establish. The Romans sometimes referred to Vulcan as MULCIBER, smelter, in recognition either of his power to soften metal for working or his ability to soothe the anger of volcanoes.

The Wedding Feast

Fresh invitations to the marriage of Zeus and Hera, hastily amended to include the wedding of Aphrodite and Hephaestus, were now sent out. All who were summoned to the double wedding accepted with excited pleasure. Such a thing had never been known in all creation, but then creation had never known a goddess like Hera, with her great sense of propriety and intense feeling for order, ceremony and familial honour.

Nymphs of the trees, rivers, breezes, mountains and oceans talked of nothing but the wedding for weeks. The wood spirits too – the lustful fauns as well as the tough barky dryads and hamadryads – made their way to Olympus from every forest, copse and spinney. In celebration of the nuptials Zeus went so far as to pardon some of the Titans. Not Atlas, of course, nor the long exiled Kronos; but the least threatening and violent, Iapetus and Hyperion amongst them, were forgiven and allowed their freedom.

To add zest to an already frenziedly anticipated occasion, Zeus issued a challenge: whoever could devise the best and most original wedding dish could ask any favour of him. The lesser immortals and animals went wild with excitement at this chance to shine. Mice, frogs, lizards, bears, beavers and birds all put together recipes to bring before Zeus and Hera. There were cakes, buns, biscuits, soups, eel-skin terrines, porridges made of moss and mould. All things sweet, salty, bitter, sour and savoury were placed on small trestle tables for the King and Queen of the Gods to judge.

But first the marriages took place. Aphrodite and Hephaestus were wed, then Hera and Zeus. The service was conducted with charming simplicity by Hestia, who anointed each of the four with aromatic oils, wafting perfumed smoke and singing in a low musical voice hymns to companionship, service and mutual respect. Family and guests looked on, many of them sniffing and blinking back tears. A faun who made the tactless error of declaring between gulping sobs that Aphrodite and Hephaestus made a lovely couple was given a swift and violent kick in the backside by a glowering Ares.

That official business over, it was time to find the winner of the great culinary competition. Zeus and Hera walked slowly up and down, sniffing, tapping, prodding, tasting, sipping and licking their way round the entries like professional food critics. The competitors behind the trestle tables held their breath. When Zeus nodded approvingly at a wobbling hibiscus, beetle and walnut jelly, its creator, a young heron called Margaret, gave a single shriek of excitement and fainted clean away.

But hers was not the prize. The winner was the seemingly modest submission of a shy little creature named MELISSA. She offered up for the gods a very small amphora filled almost to the top with a sticky, amber-coloured goo.

'Ah yes,' said Zeus, dipping his finger in with a knowledgeable and approving nod. 'Pine resin.'*

But it was not pine resin in the little jar, it was something quite other. Something new. Something gloopy without being unguent, slow-moving without being stodgy, sweet without being cloying, and perfumed with a flavour that drove the senses wild with pleasure. Melissa's name for it was 'honey'. It seemed to Hera that when she took a spoonful the scent of the loveliest meadow flowers and mountain herbs

---

* The Greeks still add pine resin to wine, call it *retsina* and offer it to visitors. No one knows why a normally kind and hospitable people should do such a thing. It tastes like what it essentially is, the kind of turpentine artists use to thin their oil paints. I love it.

danced and hummed inside her mouth. Zeus licked the back of the spoon and mmm-ed with delight. Husband and wife glanced at each other and nodded. No more consultation was needed.

'Um, the . . . er . . . standard has been . . . has been agreeably high this year,' said Zeus. 'Well done all. But Queen Hera and I are agreed. This . . . ah . . . *honey* takes first place.'

The other creatures, trying to hide their disappointment, put on sporting expressions of pleasure as they formed a large semicircle and watched Melissa zip forward to claim her prize – a wish that was to be granted by the King of the Gods himself.

Melissa was very small and looked even smaller as she approached the winner's podium. She flew (for she could fly, despite looking as if she might be too bulky and bulgy in the wrong places to be able to) as close to Zeus's face as she dared and buzzed to him these words:

'Dread lord, I am pleased that you like my delicacy, but I must tell you it is quite extraordinarily hard to make. I have to zoom from flower to flower to collect the nectar deep inside. Only the smallest amount can be sucked up and carried. All day, for as long as Aether grants me light to see by, I must sip, search and return to the nest, sip, search and return to the nest, often travelling huge distances. Even then, at day's end, I will only have the tiniest possible fraction of nectar to convert – using my secret process – into the confection that has so pleased you. Just that little amphora you are holding took me four and a half weeks to fill, so you can see that this is a most laborious business. The smell of honey is so intense, so ravishing and so irresistible that many come to raid my nest. They do so with impunity, for I am small, and all I can do is buzz angrily at them and urge them to leave. Imagine, a whole week's work can be lost with just one swipe of a weasel's paw or one lick of a bear cub's tongue. Only let me have a *weapon*, your majesty. You have equipped the scorpion, who makes no foodstuffs, with a deadly sting, while the snake, who does nothing but bask in the sun all day, him you granted a venomous bite. Give me, great Zeus, such a weapon. A fatal one, that will kill any who dare to steal my precious stock of honey.'

Zeus's eyebrows gathered in a dark and troubled frown. There was a rumbling in the sky and black clouds began to bank and billow above. The animals fidgeted, watching in alarm as the light dimmed and frets of wind flapped the festive tablecloths and ruffled the goddesses' shimmering gowns.

Zeus, like most busy and important beings, had no patience with fussiness or self-pity. This silly, flighty dot of a creature was demanding a mortal sting, was she? Well, he would show *her*.

'Wretched insect!' he thundered. 'How dare you demand so monstrous a prize? A talent like yours should be shared out, not jealously hoarded. Not only shall I deny your request –'

Melissa broke in with a high-pitched drone of displeasure. 'But you gave your word!'

There was a gasp from the whole assembly. Could she really have dared to interrupt Zeus and question his honour?

'I beg your pardon, but I think you'll find that I proclaimed . . .' growled the god with an icy self-restraint that was far more terrifying than any outburst of temper '. . . that the winner could *ask* any favour. I made no promise that such a request would be *granted*.'

Melissa's wings drooped in disappointment.*

---

* Of course, this is not the last time we shall witness Zeus playing with oaths and wriggling out of commitments.

78

'However,' Zeus said, raising his hand, 'from this moment forward the gathering of your honey will be made easier by my decree that you shall not labour alone. You will be queen of a whole colony, a whole swarm of productive subjects. Furthermore, I *shall* grant you a fatal and painful sting.'

Melissa's wings pricked up perkily.

'But,' Zeus continued, 'while it will bring a sharp pain to the one you sting, it is to *you* and your kind that it will bring death. So let it be.'

Another rumble of thunder and the sky began to clear.

Immediately Melissa felt a strange movement inside her. She looked down and saw that something long, thin and sharp like a lance was pushing its way out of the end of her abdomen. It was a sting, as finely pointed as a needle but ending in a wicked and terrible barb. With a wild twitch, a buzz and a final droning wail she flew away.

Meliss is still the Greek word for the honeybee, and it is true that its sting is a suicide weapon of last resort. If it should try to fly away after the barb has lodged in the pierced skin of its victim, a bee will tug out its own insides in the effort of freeing itself. The much less useful and diligent wasp has no such barb and can administer its sting as many times as it likes without danger to itself. But wasps, annoying as they are, never made selfish, hubristic demands of the gods.

It is also true that science calls the order of insects to which the honeybee belongs *Hymenoptera*, which is Greek for 'wedding wings'.

Food of the Gods

Perhaps it was more than just temper and impatience that caused Zeus to punish Melissa – whose honey really was quite marvellously delicious – with such severity. Perhaps it had been policy. The whole assembled world of immortals was there to witness the moment. It had been a lesson for them in the implacability of the King of the Gods.

The silence that now fell on the wedding feast was as dark and forbidding as the storm clouds that had massed earlier. Zeus raised the amphora of honey high above his head.

'For my queen and my beloved wife, I bless this amphora. It shall never empty. Eternally shall it feed us. Whosoever tastes its honey shall never grow old or die. It shall be the food of the gods and, when mixed with the juice of fruits, it shall be the drink of the gods.'

A great cheer went up, doves flew overhead, the clouds and the silence were dispelled. The Muses Calliope, Euterpe and Terpsichore stepped forward and clapped their hands. Music played, hymns of praise were sung and the dancing began. Many plates were broken in ecstasy, a tradition that is carried on to this day wherever Greeks gather to eat, celebrate and earn tourist money.

The Greek for 'immortal' is *ambrotos* and 'immortality' itself is AMBROSIA, which became the name of the specially blessed honey. Its fermented drinkable form, a kind of mead, they called NECTAR in honour of the flowers whose sweet gift it was.

Bad Zeus

Hera's cup was running over – literally, at the moment, for an attentive naiad was filling her goblet with nectar up to and over the brim – but figuratively too. Her oldest son had made a brilliant marriage and Zeus had sworn oaths of fidelity and fealty to her before all who mattered in the world.

She did not notice that, even now, her insatiable lord was watching with lustful eyes the dancing of LETO, a most beautiful nymph from the island of Kos.* Leto was a daughter of the Titans Phoebe and Coeus, themselves grateful recipients of Zeus's recent amnesty and present at the feast.

A voice murmured in Zeus's ear. 'You are thinking that my cousin Leto owes you her life and should therefore be willing to share her bed with you.'

Zeus looked up into the wise, humorous eyes of his tutor Metis, the Oceanid whose wit, guile and insight were unmatched anywhere. Metis, whom he still loved and who he was sure loved him. His blood, already warmed by nectar and ambrosia, had been heated further by the dancing and the music.† The spark that had always jumped between him and Metis threatened to burst into a great fire.

She saw this and raised a hand. 'Never, Zeus, never. I have been like a mother to you. Besides, this is your wedding day – are you lost to all sense of decency?'

All sense of decency was exactly what Zeus was lost to. He touched Metis under the table. Alarmed, she moved away. Zeus got up and followed her. She quickened her pace, turned a corner and darted down the mountainside.

Zeus ran in pursuit, transforming himself first into a bull, then a bear, next a lion and then an eagle. Metis hid behind a pile of boulders deep in a cave, but Zeus, turning himself into a snake, managed to slither through a gap in the rocks and wrap his coils around her.

Metis had always loved Zeus and, both worn down and

---

* Or Cos, home of the type of romaine lettuce that bears its name and is one of the essential ingredients of a Caesar salad.

† Actually the gods did not have blood in their veins but a beautiful silvery-gold liquid called ICHOR. It was a paradoxical fluid because, while it retained all the eternal life-giving qualities of ambrosia and nectar, it was lethally and instantaneously poisonous to mortals.

touched by his persistence, she finally consented. Yet even as they came together something bothered Zeus. A prophecy he had heard from Phoebe. Something about a child of Metis rising to overcome the father.

Afterwards, as playful pillow talk, they fell into a conversation on the subject of transformations – *metamorphoses* as they are called in Greek. How a god or Titan might be able to turn others, or themselves, into animals, plants and even solid objects, just as Zeus had done as he had chased Metis. She congratulated him on his skill at this art.

'Yes,' said Zeus, with some self-satisfaction. 'I pursued you as bull, bear, lion and eagle, but it was as a snake that I captured you. You have a reputation for cunning and guile, Metis, but I outsmarted you. Admit it.'

'Oh, I'm sure I could have beaten you. Why, if I had turned myself into a fly you could never have caught me, could you?'

Zeus laughed. 'You think not? How little you know me.'

'Go on, then,' Metis taunted. 'Catch me now!' With a buzz and whizz she turned into a fly and darted about the cave. In a twinkle Zeus transformed himself into a lizard and with a quick flick of a long sticky tongue Metis (along with any possible child of Zeus's that even now might be forming in her womb) had been safely transferred to his interior. His father Kronos's unkind habit of eating anyone prophesied to conquer him seemed to have been passed down to Zeus.

When he slipped back to Olympus in his own shape, congratulating himself at how much cleverer than the supposedly cunning Metis he was, the music and dancing were in full swing and his wife didn't seem to have noticed a thing.

The Mother of All Migraines

The King of the Gods had a headache. Not a hangover from the wedding feast, nor a headache in the sense of an annoying problem that needed solving – as a leader he always had plenty of those – but a headache in the sense of a real ache in the head. And what an ache. Each day the pain grew until Zeus was in the most acute, searing, blinding, pounding agony that had ever been suffered in the history of anything. Gods may be immune from death, ageing and many of the other horrors that afflict and affright mortals, but they are not immune from pain.

Zeus's roars, howls and screams filled the valleys, canyons and caves of mainland Greece. They rang around the grottoes, cliffs and coves of the islands until the world wondered if the Hecatonchires had come up from Tartarus and the Titanomachy had started all over again.

Zeus's brothers, sisters and other family members clustered concernedly about him on the seashore, where they had found him begging his nephew Triton, Poseidon's eldest, to drown him in seawater. Triton declined to do any such thing, so everyone racked their brains and tried to think of another solution while poor Zeus stamped and yelled in torment, squeezing his head in his hands as if trying to crush it.

Then Prometheus, Zeus's favourite young Titan, came up with an idea which he whispered to Hephaestus, who nodded eagerly before limping back to his smithy as fast as his imperfect legs could carry him.

What was happening inside Zeus's head was rather interesting. It was no wonder that he was suffering such excruciating pain, for crafty Metis was hard at work inside his skull, smelting, firing and hammering out armour and weaponry. There was enough iron and other metals, minerals, rare earths and trace elements in the god's varied, healthy and balanced diet to allow her to find in his blood and bones all the ingredients, all the ores and compounds, she needed.

Hephaestus, who would have approved of her rudimentary but effective metalworking, returned to the crowded beach carrying a huge axe, double-bladed in the Minoan style.

Prometheus now persuaded Zeus that the only way to alleviate his agony was to take his hands away from his temples, kneel down and have faith. Zeus muttered something about the trouble with being the King of the Gods was that there was no one higher to pray to, but he dropped obediently to his knees and awaited his fate. Hephaestus spat cheerfully and confidently on his hands, gripped the thick wooden haft and – as the hushed crowd looked on – brought it down in one swift swinging movement clean through the very centre of Zeus's skull, splitting it neatly in two.

There was a terrible silence as everyone stared in stunned horror. The stunned horror turned to wild disbelief and the wild disbelief to bewildered amazement as they now witnessed, rising up from inside Zeus's opened head, the tip of a spear. It was followed by the topmost plumes of a russet crest. The onlookers held their breaths as slowly there arose into view a female figure dressed in full armour. Zeus lowered his head – whether in pain, relief, submission or sheer awe nobody could be certain – and, as if his bowed head had been a ramp or gangway let down for her convenience – the glorious being stepped calmly onto the sand and turned to face him.

Equipped with plated armour, shield, spear and plumed helmet, she gazed at her father with eyes of a matchless and wonderful grey. A grey that seemed to radiate one quality above all others – infinite wisdom.

From one of the pines that fringed the shoreline an owl flew out and perched on the shining she-warrior's shoulder. From the dunes an emerald and amethyst snake slid forward and coiled itself about her feet.

With a slightly unpleasant slurping sound Zeus's head closed up its wound and healed itself.

It was clear at once to all present that this new goddess was endowed with levels of power and personality that raised her above all the immortals. Even Hera, who realized that the newcomer could only be the issue of an adulterous affair that must have taken place very close to her wedding day, was nearly tempted to bend her knee.

Zeus gazed at the daughter who had caused him so much pain and smiled a warm smile. A name came to him and he spoke it.

'Athena!'

'Father!' she said, smiling gently in return.

Athena

The qualities that ATHENA* embodied were ones that would become the paramount virtues and accomplishments of the great city state that would bear her name: Athens. Wisdom and insight were inherited from her mother, Metis. Handicraft, warcraft and statecraft were hers. Law and justice too. She took a share in what had been uniquely Aphrodite's domains of love and beauty. Athena's kind of beauty was

---

* Also Athene – there doesn't seem to be any shade of meaning attached to the variant spelling.

expressed in aesthetics, in the apprehension of its *ideal* in art, representation, thought and character, rather than in the more physical, obvious and perhaps superficial kinds that would always be the business of Aphrodite. The love that Athena stood for had a less heated and physical emphasis too; it was the kind that would later become known as 'Platonic'. The Athenians were to prize these attributes of Athena above all others, just as they prized her, their patroness, over all existing immortals. I say 'existing' for – as we shall discover – two other Olympian deities, as yet unborn, would soon play their part in defining what it was to be an Athenian and a Greek.

In later years Athena and Poseidon would vie for the special patronage of the city of Cecropia. He struck his trident into the high rock on which they stood and produced a spring of seawater; an impressive trick, but its saltiness rendered it more or less useless as anything more than a picturesque public fountain. Athena's simple gift was the first olive tree. The citizens of Cecropia in their wisdom saw the manifold benefits of its fruit, oil and wood and chose her as their presiding deity and protectress, changing the name of their city to Athens in her honour.*

In Rome she was worshipped as MINERVA, but without really that special personal connection that the Greeks felt for her. Her favoured animals were the owl, that dignified symbol of watchful wisdom, and the serpent – in which guise her father had won her mother. The olive tree, whose

---

* Sea power, and the trade that it allowed, was to be the saving of Athens (it won them a startling victory over the Persians at Salamis). But the cultivation of the olive and the other crafts, arts and techniques that were the domain of Athena were arguably of even greater importance.

soft and versatile fruit proved to be such a blessing to Greece, was sacred to her also.*

The apparent gentleness of those grey eyes belied a new kind of ideal, one which combined physical power with strength of character and strength of mind. It was not wise to anger her. Besides, if you crossed Athena, you crossed Zeus. He was besotted with his daughter and she could do no wrong in his eyes. Ares, his least favourite child, made an interesting contrast to his new half-sister. They were both gods of war, but Athena's interests lay in planning, tactics, strategy and the intelligent art of war, while Ares was a god of battles, combat and all forms of fighting. He understood only violence, force, aggression, conquest and coercion. It is distressing but essential to recognize that neither was as powerful when not allied with the other.

Athena was often given the forename PALLAS, and as Pallas Athena she protected her city Athens. The symbol of her guardianship was called the *palladium*, a word that has somehow found its way into the naming of theatres as well as giving us the element Pd. The original Pallas was a daughter of the sea god Triton and a dear childhood friend of Athena's. They would play semi-serious war games together. On one occasion, when Pallas was winning against Athena, Zeus (ever watchful and protective of his darling) intervened and, setting one of his thunderbolts to stun, knocked Pallas unconscious.

---

* Besides her armour, Athena was always depicted with an AEGIS. No one is quite agreed as to precisely what an aegis looked like. It is sometimes described as an animal skin (originally goat: *aiga* is a word for 'goat' in Greek), though pelts of lion or leopard can later be seen in sculpture and ceramic representations. Zeus's aegis is generally held to have been a shield, perhaps covered with goatskin and often showing the face of a Gorgon. Human kings and emperors keen to suggest semi-divine status would throw an aegis over their shoulders as a mark of their right to rule. The word these days suggests a badge of leadership or authority. Acts are performed and proclamations made 'under the aegis' of such and such a person, principle or institution.

Athena, in the heat of the moment, administered the *coup de grâce* and killed her friend. For ever after she bore Pallas's name as a sorrowful token of her enduring affection and remorse.

Athena, like Demeter, remained untouched by man.* Her childless, single life and her youthful relationship with Pallas have led some to maintain that she should stand as a symbol of feminine same-sex love.

Metis Within

When Zeus had tricked Athena's mother into becoming a fly in order to use his lizard tongue to reel her in, Metis had been uncharacteristically foolish. Or so it seemed.

In fact she had not been tricked at all. She had done the tricking. *Metis* means 'craft' and 'guile' after all. She had quite deliberately allowed herself to be consumed by Zeus – more than that, she had duped him into doing so. She saw that, if she sacrificed her freedom and remained inside him always, she could assume the role of a wise counsellor, a kind of consigliere, for ever able to whisper advice to him. Whether he liked it or not.

Those who speak truth to power usually end up in chains or an early grave, but inside Zeus's head Metis could never be silenced. She would be a prudent check on the reckless excesses and headlong passions that often threatened to get the god of thunder into trouble. His storms of temper, lust and jealousy needed to be balanced by her calm voice, a voice that could urge his instincts into more rational and enlightened channels.

Whether Metis sacrificed her freedom out of a sense of

---

* *Parthenos*, the Greek word for virgin, was often attached to her name – hence 'the Parthenon', her temple on the Acropolis.

duty and responsibility, or out of love for the Zeus whom she had always adored, I cannot conclusively state. I like to think it was a mixture of the two. It was, as a Greek might say, her *moira* both to serve and to love.

Combined with Zeus's other positive characteristics – charisma,* heart, native guile and (usually) a strong sense of justice, fairness and right – the shrewd inner guidance of Metis helped raise him into a great ruler whose attributes far outshone those of his father and grandfather, Kronos and Ouranos. In fact so much a part of him did Metis become that Homer sometimes referred to Zeus as *Metieta* – 'wise counsellor'.

Seeking sanctuary

Wisdom, in the form of Metis, may have whispered to Zeus in one ear, but in the other he always heard the hot urgings of passion. When beautiful girls and women – and sometimes youths – crossed his path, nothing could stop him from chasing them from one end of the earth to the other, even if he had to transform himself into any number of animals to do it. Once the lustful fit was on him, Metis could no more control him than a whisper can quieten a tempest, while Hera's wild shrieks of jealous rage had no more power to call him back than the wingbeats of a butterfly can blow a ship off course.

I have mentioned that Zeus's passionate glance had already fallen once on Leto, demure daughter of the Titans Phoebe and Coeus. I should imagine that 'demure' is an annoying

---

* We are permitted the use of that tired word here – it is Greek after all and allows us to picture Athena as embued with the grace of the Charities.

word for a woman to hear applied to herself (one rarely hears of demure men after all), but Leto was to become a kind of minor deity representing precisely the quality of modest dignity that the word 'demure' evokes.* Nevertheless Zeus soon chased her down and had his way with her.

An unshowy Titaness, Leto (LATONA to the Romans) was later worshipped as a goddess of motherhood as well as a paragon of modesty. Probably this was in honour of a pregnancy which, once Zeus had finished with her, turned out to be a most courageous triumph over adversity. For when Hera found out that her husband had got Leto with child, she commanded her grandmother Gaia to deny Leto any land on which to give birth. It was maddening enough to Hera that the baseborn Athena should have taken precedence in Zeus's affections over her noble and darling sons Hephaestus and Ares (she seemed to have forgotten in her sudden burst of maternal feeling for her firstborn that she had once hurled him down from heaven), and she was not about to let another bastard godling come muscling in to disturb Olympus's proper order. There is much about Hera that brings to mind the Roman emperor Augustus's wife Livia or the wives of certain English kings and mafia dons. Always looking to the dynasty and the bloodlines, always prepared to do anything for honour and family, lineage and legacy.

Denied landfall, poor pregnant young Leto sailed the seas looking for somewhere to give birth. She tried to find shelter with the wild Hyperboreans, who dwelt beyond the North

---

* I looked it up in a thesaurus and was offered: 'unassuming, meek, mild, reserved, retiring, quiet, shy, bashful, diffident, reticent, timid, shrinking, coy; decorous, decent, seemly, ladylike, respectable, proper, virtuous, pure, innocent, chaste; sober, sedate, staid, prim, goody-goody, strait-laced'. I don't suppose many women would jump up and down in delight if those words were used of them.

Wind,* but fearing the wrath of Hera they would not let her stay. At sea in every sense, Leto cast up prayers to Zeus, who had got her into this dreadful pickle in the first place; but, as King of the Gods, his authority rested on accepting and endorsing the other gods' right to rule their own spheres and exercise their own will. He could not interfere and countermand Hera's edict or undo her awful spell. Leaders, kings and emperors always complain that they are the least free of their subjects, and there is some truth to this. Certainly Zeus, for all his might and majesty, was always constrained by the cabinet government principles of consensus and collective responsibility that allowed him to rule.

The best that he could manage for Leto now was to persuade his brother Poseidon to cause an upswell of waves to guide her boat to Delos, a small uninhabited island floating in the eddies and swirl of the Cyclades, unanchored to the seabed and therefore immune from Hera's curse.

Twins!

Leto made an exhausted landfall on the hospitable floating island of Delos with barely enough strength to crawl up beyond the dunes to shelter beneath a straggling line of pine trees that fringed the shore. The few pine nuts and grasses she could eat there would not feed the active life she felt kicking inside her and so she made her way to a green valley that she could see in the distance. There, beneath Mount Cynthos, she subsisted for a month on fruits and seeds, living like a wild creature but safe from the curse of Hera. Her stomach swelled so much during this time that she feared

---

* In today's Thrace, bounded by Greece, Bulgaria and Turkey.

she was carrying a monster or giant. But still she foraged, ate and rested, foraged, ate and rested.

One day the pangs of hunger gave way to new and sharper stabs of pain. Alone and unaided Leto gave birth to a girl, the most lovely baby yet.* Leto gasped out the name ARTEMIS for her. Strong, endowed with a most astonishing silvery quickness and supple strength, the infant girl found herself put to immediate and miraculous work even on this, her first day alive. For Leto now understood why her pregnancy had been so hard and so heavy – there was another child inside her, and this younger twin had become lodged sideways in the birth canal, causing her terrible agonies. Artemis proved to have an instinctive sense of how a baby should most easily be delivered and assisted with the birth of a glorious twin brother.

Mother and daughter cried out with joyful surprise when the boy gave his first choking cries. For the hair on his head was not jet black like his sister's or mother's, it was blond – an inheritance from his maternal grandmother, the shining Phoebe. Leto named the child APOLLO. 'Delian Apollo', he was sometimes called in honour of his birthplace, and 'Phoebus Apollo' in deference to his Titaness grandmother and his own radiant, golden beauty, for Phoebus means 'shining one'.

Artemis

Zeus loved Artemis almost as much as he loved Athena and took great pains to protect her from the wrath of Hera, who

---

* Aphrodite and Athena, who equalled her in beauty, were neither of them in the strict sense *born*, so the claim is good.

could not bear to look upon yet another child of adultery, especially one whom she loftily characterized as a hoydenish tomboy and a disgrace to the dignity of feminine divinity.

One afternoon, when Artemis was still a very young girl, Zeus found her playfully catching and releasing mice and frogs in the undergrowth down at the base of Mount Olympus. He sat on a rock beside her and hoisted her onto his knee.

She tugged at his beard for a while before she asked, 'Father, do you love me?'

'Artemis, what a question! You know I do. You know I love you with all my heart.'

If you are the child of a faithless reprobate of a father there is almost nothing you cannot get him to agree to. Artemis now twisted Zeus around her fingers just as she twisted the hairs of his beard.

'Do you love me enough to grant me a wish?'

'Of course, my dear.'

'Hm. Come to think, that's nothing. You grant wishes to the smallest and least significant nymphs and water sprites. Would you grant me *several* wishes?'

Inwardly Zeus groaned. The whole world seemed to believe that being the all-powerful one, sitting upon the throne of Olympus and commanding the heavens and the earth, was the easiest job there was. What did they know of paternal guilt, sibling rivalry, power struggles and jealous wives? Please one member of the family and you maddened another.

'Several wishes? Goodness! Surely you have everything a girl could want? You are immortal and once you reach your moment of greatest beauty you will never age. You are strong, clever, swift and – ow!' This last exclamation was in reaction to a hair that had been plucked with some violence from his chin.

'They aren't difficult wishes, daddy. Just the smallest things.'

'Very well, let's hear them.'

'I never ever want to have a boyfriend or husband or have a man touch me, you know, in that way –'

'Yes, yes . . . er . . . I fully understand.'

This may have been the first time Zeus ever blushed.

'Also, I want lots of different names, like my brother has. "Appellations", they're called. Also a bow, which I notice *he* has a whole collection of but I don't because I'm a girl which is totally unfair. I'm the older twin after all. Hephaestus can make me a really special one as a birth present just like he did for Apollo, a silver bow with silver arrows please. And I want a knee-length tunic for hunting in, because long dresses are stupid and impractical. I don't want dominion over towns or cities, but I do want to rule mountainsides and forests. And stags. I like stags. And dogs, hunting dogs anyway, not lap dogs which are useless. And, if you'd be very *very* kind, I'd like a choir of young girls to sing my praises in temples and a group of nymphs to walk the dogs and look after me and help protect me from *men*.'

'Is that it?' Zeus was almost giddy at this recitation.

'I think so. Oh, and I'd like the power to make childbirth easier for women. I've seen how painful it is. In fact it is actually quite sincerely gross and I want to help make it better.'

'Goodness me. You don't ask for the moon, do you?'

'Oh, what a good idea! The moon. Yes, I'd love the moon, please. That will be all. I'll never ask for anything ever again ever.'

Zeus granted every wish. How could he not?

Goddess of the chase and the chaste, of the untutored and the untamed, of hounds and hinds, of midwives and the moon, Artemis duly became. The queen of archers and huntresses grew to value her independence and her celibacy above all things. The kindness with which she expressed her sympathy for women in childbirth was countered by the ferocity with which she pursued game and punished any man who presumed to come too near. Feared, admired and adored across the ancient world, she was sometimes known, in honour of the mountainside of her birth, as CYNTHIA. The Romans called her DIANA. Her special tree was the cypress. Inasmuch as Athena was goddess of things cultivated, made, crafted and thought through, Artemis – in her dominion over the natural, instinctive and wild – stood as her opposite. They shared, however – along with Hestia – a passion for their own chastity.

Apollo

If Artemis was silver, her twin Apollo was all gold. If Artemis was the moon, he was the sun. His radiant features captivated all who beheld them. His proportions and lineaments remain to this day the very ideal of a certain kind of male beauty. I say 'a certain kind', for Apollo was striking not only in his fair complexion but in his beardless face and hairless chest, a rarity amongst Greeks or their gods. Like Jacob in the Bible he was a smooth man, but no less manly for that.

Apollo was lord of mathematics, reason and logic. Poetry and medicine, knowledge, rhetoric and enlightenment were his realm. In essence he was the god of harmony. The idea that the base material world and its ordinary objects had divine properties and could resonate with the heavens, this was Apollonian, whether expressed in the magical properties of squares, circles and spheres or in the perfect modulation and rhythms of a voice or a chain of reasoning. Even meaning and destiny themselves can be read in ordinary things, if you have the gift. Apollo had it in abundance, allied to an inability ever to lie. This made him a natural choice for taking charge of oracles and prophecy too. The python was sacred to him, of course, and the laurel. His particular animals were the dolphin and the white raven.*

It would be a fool who mistook Apollo's golden beauty for a sign of weakness. He was a supreme archer and when necessary as fierce and fiery a warrior as any on Olympus: like all his close relations he was capable of cruelty, meanness, jealousy and spite. Unusually for a god he was worshipped by the Romans under his Greek name without any alterations. Apollo was Apollo wherever you went in the ancient world.

The Wrath of Hera

On the floating island of their birth, the newborn twins Apollo and Artemis had found themselves the focus of the Queen of Heaven's continuing fury. Hera had done everything possible to prevent the birth of these living reminders of Zeus's infidelity and her frustrated rage at her failure knew no bounds. So she tried again.

When the twins were just days old she sent the snake Python to consume them. You remember the magnetite stone the pregnant Rhea had duped Kronos into

---

* Why Apollo turned the raven black, and why the laurel also became sacred to him, we shall discover later on.

swallowing instead of the infant Zeus? The one that he had later vomited up and which Zeus cast far from Othrys? Well, it had landed at a place called Pytho on the slopes of Mount Parnassus. Lodged fast in the earth it would in time become the Omphalos or navel-stone of Greece – the Hellenic belly-button, its spiritual centre and point of origin. From exactly the spot where it fell, at the command of Gaia, for whom this place was already sacred, there had emerged out of the ground a huge dragon-like serpent to serve as the stone's guardian. Taking the name of his birthplace he was called Python, as have been many snakes in his honour since.

Hera in her anger now sent Python to the isle of Delos to kill Leto and her children. Zeus took the risk of incensing Hera even further by secretly whispering this news to the wind, which passed it on to the infant Apollo, who in turn sent a desperate message to Hephaestus, begging for the best bow and arrow his half-brother could fashion. Hephaestus toiled at the forge for seven days and seven nights, at the end of which time a matchlessly beautiful and powerful weapon and a set of golden arrows were despatched to Delos, just in time for Apollo to take delivery of them, conceal himself behind the dunes and await the great serpent's arrival. The moment Python emerged from the sea and slithered onto the sand Apollo stepped from his hiding place and shot him through the eye with an arrow. He sliced the dead body into pieces there on the beach and sent up a great cry of triumph to the sky.

You might think Apollo had every justification to protect his sister, his mother and himself from such a deadly creature, but Python was chthonic – he sprang from the earth – making him a child of Gaia and as such under divine protection. Zeus knew that he must punish Apollo for the slaying of the serpent or lose all authority.

In truth, the punishment he chose for Apollo was not so very harsh. Zeus exiled the young god for eight years to the snake's birthplace beneath Mount Parnassus to atone for his crime. As well as replacing the snake-monster Python as guardian of the Omphalos, Apollo was tasked with organizing a regular athletics tournament there. The Pythian Games were duly held every four years, two either side of the Olympic meeting.*

Apollo also established at Pytho (whose name he changed to Delphi†) an oracle where anyone could come to ask the god or his appointed priestess (known sometimes as a SIBYL or the PYTHIA) questions about the future. In a trance-like state of prophetic ecstasy the priestess would sit out of sight of her interrogator, above a chasm in the ground which channelled down to the womb of the earth itself, and call her ambiguous prognostications up into the chamber above where the anxious petitioner awaited her proclamation. In this way Apollo and the Sibyl were seen to draw their oracular powers in part from Gaia herself, Apollo's great-grandmother. Vapours were said to rise from beneath the ground that many took to be Gaia's actual breath.‡ The spring of Castalia bubbles up here, whose waters are said to

---

* Along with the regular Nemean and Isthmian Games, the Pythian and Olympic meetings made up the four so-called 'Panhellenic Games'. The prizes do not really compare with today's lucrative purses and endorsements. An olive wreath for the winners of the Olympics, laurel for the Pythian, pine for the Isthmian and – most thrilling of all – wild celery for the lucky victor of the Nemean Games.

† The name 'Delphi' is thought to derive from *delphys*, meaning 'womb'. Of course it might be from *adelphi*, which means 'siblings' (because they come from the same womb). So perhaps the sacred place is named after Apollo the twin, perhaps after the womb of Gaia. There is another theory that suggests Apollo arrived at Pytho on a dolphin, *delphis* in Greek. A dolphin is, after all, a fish with a womb. But how he could have travelled so far over land on a dolphin I can't quite say.

‡ When the Pythia prophesied she was possessed by the god Apollo, the Titaness Themis or the goddess Gaia. Or perhaps all three. The Greek for 'divine possession' is *enthusiasmos* – enthusiasm. To be enthused or enthusiastic is to be 'engodded', to be divinely inspired.

inspire poetry in those who drink them or hear their whispers.*

So Delian Apollo became Delphic Apollo too. People still travel to Delphi to ask him about their future. I have done so myself. Apollo never lies, but nor does he ever give a straight answer, finding it amusing to reply with another question or a riddle so obscure as only to make sense when it is too late to act upon it.

To atone for his grievous assault on the proper way of things and to allow the slain Python to sleep the eternal sleep of death in the arms of his mother Gaia, Zeus finally fixed the serpent's resting-place, the island of Delos, to the earth. While it no longer floats free, those who visit the island can testify to this day that it is tough to sail to, being beset by violent Etesian winds and treacherous *meltemi* currents. Anyone who travels there is likely to suffer the most awful sea-sickness. It is as if Hera has still not forgiven Delos for the part it played in the birth of the LETOIDES, the glorious twins Artemis and Apollo.

Maia Maia

How many Olympians were there now? Let's do a quick headcount.

Zeus sat on the throne, with Hera at his side, that's two. Around them were ranged Hestia, Poseidon (who liked to come inland and keep an eye on Zeus), Demeter, Aphrodite, Hephaestus, Ares, Athena, Artemis and Apollo – that's

---

* Some say that steam hissed out from the subterranean Castalian spring, which delighted the local goats, apparently. Perhaps this reminded people of a dolphin's blowhole, offering yet another explanation for the change of the name from Pytho to Delphi. Castalia, incidentally, is the name of the future world in Hermann Hesse's novel *The Glass Bead Game*.

eleven. Hades doesn't count because he spent all his time in the underworld and had no interest in taking a seat in the dodecatheon. Eleven. One more then, before Olympus reaches its quorum of twelve.

Hardly had the dust settled, and the shrieking recriminations from the Python debacle abated to sulks and glowers, than Zeus saw the path of his duty clear before him. He must father the twelfth and final god. Or, to put it another way, his sex-crazed glance fell on yet another appetizing immortal.

During the Titanomachy, Atlas, the most ferocious champion of the Titans, had fathered seven daughters by the Oceanid PLEIONE. In her honour the Seven Sisters were known as the PLEIADES, although sometimes, out of respect for their father, they might be addressed as the ATLANTIDES too.

The eldest and loveliest of these dark-eyed sisters was called MAIA. She lived as a shy and happy oread on the pleasant Corinthian slopes of Mount Cyllene in Arcadia.* Happy, that is, until the night the great god Zeus appeared to her and got her with child. With great stealth – for word of Hera's attitude to Zeus's bastard children had got out and struck fear into every beautiful girl in Greece and beyond – Maia in due time gave birth in a remote and hidden cave to a healthy boy, whom she named HERMES.

The Infant Prodigy

Hermes proved himself to be the most extraordinarily pert and precocious baby that ever drew breath. Within a quarter hour of his birth he had crawled from one side of the cave to

---

* Today's Mount Kyllini.

the other, throwing out comments to his startled mother as he did so. Five minutes later he had requested a light so that he might better examine the cave's walls. Being offered none he struck two stones together over twists of straw and kindled a flame. This had never been done before. Now standing upright (and still not half an hour old), this remarkable infant announced that he was going for a walk.

'The close confines of this cramped cavern are occasioning me uncomfortably acute claustrophobia,' he said, inventing both alliteration and the family of '-phobia' words as he spoke. 'I shall see you presently. Get on with your spinning or knitting or whatever it is, there's a good mother.'

As he ambled down the slopes of Mount Cyllene this singular and sensational prodigy began to hum to himself. His humming turned into tuneful singing, which the nightingales in the woods around him immediately began to copy and have been trying to recapture ever since.

After he had travelled he knew not how far he found himself in a field where he was met by the wondrous sight of a herd of pure white cattle cropping the grass and lowing gently in the moonlight.

'Oh!' he breathed, entranced. 'What beautiful moo-moos.' For all his precocity he was still not above baby-talk.

Hermes looked at the cows and the cows looked at Hermes.

'Come here,' he commanded.

The cows stared for a while then lowered their heads and continued to graze.

'Hm. So it's like that is it?'

Hermes thought quickly and gathered up long blades of grass which he plaited together into something like a bovine version of horseshoes, attaching one to each hoof of every cow. Around his own tiny plump feet he wrapped laurel leaves. Finally he snapped off a branch of young willow and stripped it down into a long switch with which he easily and expertly tickled and stung the cows into a tight and manoeuvrable herd. As an extra precaution he drove them backwards, all the way up the slope and back to the mouth of the cave, where his astonished and alarmed mother had been worriedly standing ever since he had wandered so very calmly away.

Maia had had no experience of motherhood before this, but she was certain that the striking style and eccentric behaviour of her son were not usual – even amongst gods. Apollo, she knew, had defeated Pytho while still an infant, and Athena of course had been born fully armed, but creating fire out of nothing but stones? Driving cattle? And what was this he was dangling before her eyes – *a tortoise*? Was she dreaming?

'Now, mother,' said Hermes. 'Listen. I've had an idea. I'd like you to stun the tortoise, scoop out the flesh and cook it. I expect it will make a delicious soup. I'd recommend adding plenty of wild garlic if I were you and perhaps a suspicion of fennel? And then there'll be beef for mains, which I shall see to now. I'll just borrow this knife and be with you again before you know it.'

With those words he disappeared to the back of the cave, off whose stone walls rang the appalling screams of a cow having its throat cut by a plump-fisted baby.

After what Maia had to confess was a truly delicious supper she summoned up the courage to ask her son what he might be up to now, for he was hanging out stringy lines of cow gut in front of the fire. While he waited for these foul-smelling strips to dry he busied himself with boring little holes along the edges of the tortoiseshell.

'I've had an idea,' was all he would tell her.

Hermes may or may not have known it, but on his first night on earth he had travelled quite a distance. All the way from his birthplace on Mount Cyllene north through the fields of Thessaly and as far as Pieria, where he had found and rustled the cattle. And back again. In baby steps that is quite a distance.

What Hermes certainly could not have known was that the white cattle belonged to Apollo, who prized them highly. When news reached the god of their disappearance he set off in fury to Pieria in order to follow what he assumed was a vicious gang of thieves to their lair. Wild dryads or fauns gone to the bad, he imagined. They would regret taking property from the god of arrows. He lay down in the cattle's field to examine the ground with all the thoroughness of an experienced tracker. To his astonishment the brigands had left no useful traces at all. All he could see were random brush marks, meaningless whorls and swirls and – unless he was going mad – one tiny infant footprint. Any impressions that might have been formed by cow's hoofs seemed to be heading, not away from the field, but *towards* it!

Whoever had stolen the cattle was mocking Apollo. They were practised and expert thieves, that much was clear. His sister Artemis was the most skilled hunter he knew: would she dare? Perhaps she had devised some cunning way to conceal her tracks. Ares didn't have the wit. Poseidon wouldn't be interested. Hephaestus? Unlikely. *Who* then?

He noticed a thrush preening on a branch not far away and in one smooth action drew his bow and brought the creature down. Slitting open its crop the god of oracles and augury peered forward to read the entrails.

From the colouration in the lower intestine, the kink in the right kidney and the unusual disposition of the thymus gland it was clear at once that the cattle were somewhere in Arcadia, not far from Corinth. And what was that clot of blood on the liver saying to him? Mount Cyllene. And what else? So! It *had* been a baby's footprint after all.

Apollo's usually smooth brow was drawn into a frown, his blue eyes blazed and his rose-red lips compressed themselves into a grim line.

Revenge would be his.

Half-Brothers

By the time Apollo arrived at the foot of Mount Cyllene his temper had frayed almost to breaking point. The world knew the cows were sacred to him. It was obvious that they were a rare and valuable breed. Who would *dare*?

A hamadryad drooping herself from the branches of her aspen could offer no clue but informed him that further up an assorted gaggle of nymphs had gathered around the mouth of Maia's cave. Maybe he would find his answer there? She would go herself if only she could leave her tree.

When Apollo reached the top of the mountain he saw that the whole population of Cyllene had congregated at the cave. As he drew nearer he became aware of a sound emerging from it – a sound such as he had never heard before. It was as if sweetness and love and perfection and all that was beautiful had come to life and were gently coursing through his ears and into his very soul. Just as the scent of ambrosia enticed a god to table and made him sigh with glorious anticipation, just as the sight of a comely nymph caused the hot ichor in his veins to sing and fizz until he felt he could burst, just as the warm touch of skin on skin thrilled him to his deeps – so now these invisible noises seduced and bewitched the god until he thought he might go mad with joy and desire. If only he could pluck them from the air and absorb them into his breast, if only . . .

The magical sound abruptly stopped and the spell was broken.

The crowd of naiads and dryads and other spirits that had clustered around the cave's entrance now dispersed, shaking their heads in wonder as they went, as if emerging from a trance. Shouldering through them, Apollo saw that, beside the mouth of the cave, on piles of stone, two vast sides of beef were on display, sliced into neat steaks. His furious outrage resurfaced.

'Now you will pay!' he roared as he rushed inside. 'Now you will –'

'Sh!'

Apollo's cousin, the oread Maia, was sitting in a basket chair sewing. She put a finger to her lips and inclined her head in the direction of a crib by the fire in which a rosy-cheeked baby gurgled in its sleep.

Apollo was not to be put off. 'That demonic child stole my cattle!'

'Are you mad?' said Maia. 'My little angel is not so much as a day old.'

'Little angel my foot! I know how to read a thrush's entrails. Besides, I can hear the beasts stamping and lowing in the back. I'd know their moo anywhere. That baby is a thief and I demand –'

'You demand *what*?' Hermes had sat up and was now staring at Apollo with a quelling eye. 'Can't a boy get a wink of sleep? I had a heavy night of it transporting cattle and the last thing I need is for –'

'You admit it!' yelled Apollo, striding towards him. 'By Zeus, I'll strangle the life out of you, you little –'

But as he picked Hermes up, ready to do who knows what to him, a strange device made of wood and tortoiseshell fell from the crib. In falling it made a noise that instantly recalled the magical sound that had so transfixed Apollo when he stood outside the cave.

He dropped Hermes back into his cot and snatched up the device. Two thin bars of wood had been attached to the tortoiseshell and lines of cattlegut strung tightly across them. Apollo picked at one string with his thumb and again the marvellous sound came to him.

'How . . . ?'

'What, this old thing?' said Hermes, raising his eyebrows in surprise. 'Just a little nonsense I put together last night. I call it a "lyre". You can get some interesting effects from it though. If you pluck it just right. Or you can strum if you like. You press down on a couple of strings and – here, give it me, I'll show you.'

They were soon picking, plucking, slapping, strumming, twanging and swapping new chords like excited teenagers. Hermes was in the process of demonstrating the principle of natural harmonics when Apollo, entranced as he was by the feelings stirred in him by this extraordinary device, came to himself. 'Yes, that's all very well,' he said, 'but what about my bloody cattle?'

Hermes eyed him quizzically. 'You must be, let me see . . . don't tell me . . . Apollo, right?'

Not to be recognized was a new experience for Apollo and one that he found he didn't quite like. Being spoken to in superior tones by a day-old baby was another on his list of least favourite experiences. He was about to crush this cocky little squirt with a cutting remark and possibly a swift right hook to the chin when he found himself facing a dimpled outstretched hand.

'Put it there, Pol. Delighted to meet you. Hermes, latest addition to the divine roster. You'll be my half-brother, I think? Mother Maia here took me through the family tree last night. What a nutty bunch we are, eh? Eh?'

Another new sensation for Apollo was being playfully poked in the ribs. He felt he was losing control of the situation.

'Look, I don't care who you are, you can't go round stealing my cattle and not expecting to pay for it.'

'Oh, I'll pay you back, don't worry about that. But I just had to have them. Best quality guts. If I was going to make a lyre for my beloved half-brother I wanted only the finest strings.'

Apollo looked from Hermes to the lyre and from the lyre to Hermes. 'You mean . . . ?'

Hermes nodded. 'With my love. Yours are the lyre and the art that lies behind it. I mean you're already god of numbers, reason, logic and harmony. Music fits into that portfolio rather well, don't you think?'

'I don't know what to say.'

'You can say, "Thank you, Hermes," and, "By all means keep the cattle, brother mine." '

'Thank you, Hermes! And by all means, yes, keep the cattle.'

'Kind of you, old man, but I actually only needed two. You can have the rest back.'

Apollo pressed a bewildered hand to his perspiring brow. 'And why did you need only two?'

Hermes hopped down onto the floor. 'Maia told me how

gods love to be worshipped, you see, and how much animal sacrifices mean to them. So I butchered two of the cattle and offered up eleven slices of burning meat from one of them to Olympus. Mum and I shared the twelfth steak last night. There's some left over if you'd like it cold? Very good with a preparation of mustard-seed paste I've developed.'

'Thank you, no,' said Apollo. 'It was thoughtful of you to send up smoke to the gods like that,' he added. Apollo loved a votive offering as much as the next god. 'Very proper.'

'Well,' said Hermes, 'let's see if it's worked, shall we?' Without warning he leapt up into Apollo's arms, gripping him by the shoulders.

This remarkable baby's lightning fast mind, body and manner were making Apollo dizzy. 'See if what has worked?'

'My plan to ingratiate myself to our father. Take me up to Olympus and introduce me around,' said Hermes. 'That vacant twelfth throne has got my name on it.'

The Twelfth God

Everything about Hermes was quick. His mind, his wit, his impulses and his reflexes. The gods of Olympus, already flattered by the fine savoury smoke that had risen to their nostrils the previous night from Mount Cyllene, were entranced by the newcomer. Even Hera presented a cheek to be kissed and declared the child enchanting. He was on Zeus's lap and pulling at his beard before anyone had noticed. Zeus laughed and all the gods laughed along with him.

What were to be this god's duties? His fleetness of mind and foot suggested one immediate answer – he should become the messenger of the gods. To make Hermes even faster, Hephaestus fashioned what would become his signature footwear, the *talaria* – a pair of winged sandals that allowed him to zip from one place to another more swiftly than an eagle. Hermes was so unaffectedly delighted with them, and clasped Hephaestus to him with such warm and grateful affection, that the god of fire and forges immediately limped back to his workshop and, after a day and a night's furious work, returned with a winged helmet with a low crown and a flexible brim to go with the *talaria*. This lent Hermes a touch of grandeur and showed the world that this pert and handsome youth represented the dread majesty of the gods. For extra élan and glamour Hephaestus presented him with a silver staff topped with wings and entwined with two snakes.*

The stories of Hermes' exploits tickled Zeus greatly, then and thenceforward. The guile and duplicity he had shown in stealing Apollo's cattle made Hermes a natural choice for god of rascals, thieves, liars, conmen, gamblers, hucksters, jokers, story-tellers and sportsmen. The grander side to liars, jokers and story-tellers gave him a share in literature, poetry, oratory and wit too. His skill and insight allowed him to hold sway in the fields of science and medicine.† He became the god of commerce and trade, of herdsmen (of course) and of travel and roads. Despite music being his invention he did, as promised, present the divine responsibility for it as a gift to Apollo. Apollo simplified the lyre's structure by replacing

---

* Hermes' natty headgear is known as the *petasus*. His staff, the *kerykeion* – or *caduceus* to the Romans – often appears as a worldwide symbol of medicine and ambulances, either as an alternative to or a confusion with the staff of ASCLEPIUS (of whom, more later).

† Medieval and Renaissance alchemists called him Hermes *Trismegistus* (Hermes the Thrice Majestic). Since he is said to have been able magically to seal glass tubes, chests and boxes, a seventeenth-century invention called the Magdeburg Hemispheres (which employed the power of atmospheric pressure and a vacuum to create an incredibly strong seal) was described as 'hermetically sealed', a phrase still much in use today.

the tortoiseshell with the elegant bracketed frame of gold with which we associate the classic instrument.

In the same way that I suggested Artemis and Athena might be considered to represent opposites (wild *v*. cultivated, impulsive *v*. considered, etc.) so the mutability, swiftness and energetic impulses of traffic and exchange personified by Hermes might be said to present an exact counter to the serenity, permanence, order and centred domestic sufficiency of Hestia.

Aside from the staff, hat and winged sandals that Hephaestus fashioned for Hermes, his symbols included the tortoise, the lyre and the cockerel. The Romans called him MERCURY and worshipped him with almost as much fervour as the Greeks. He was smooth of skin like his favourite half-brother Apollo (they were now the firmest of friends) and like him he was a deity of light. His light was not golden like Apollo's, but silver – quicksilver. Indeed the element named 'mercury' after him is still sometimes called 'quicksilver', and all things mercurial remind us of this most delightful of gods. Later, Hermes would take on perhaps his most important divine responsibility, but for the moment we will seat him in the twelfth chair and survey the grandeur of Megala Kazania*, the great stage at the summit of Mount Olympus.

The Olympians

Two great thrones face ten smaller ones. Each is now occupied by a god or goddess. Zeus reaches out his left hand for Hera to take.

Megala Kazania, the amphitheatre scooped out of Olympian rock by the Hecatonchires during their great battering

---

* This is its modern name – meaning literally 'large kettles' and to this day a rewarding sight for mountaineers who dare scale the heights of Olympus.

of the Titans, is spread out before the gods.* A great cheer goes up from the crowd of immortals gathered there to witness this great occasion, Zeus's supreme moment.

The Queen of Heaven takes his hand. She is content. She and her wayward husband have had a Conversation. There are to be no new gods. There will be no more seduction and impregnation of nymphs or Titanesses. The dodecatheon is complete and Zeus will now turn to the serious business of establishing his rule in perpetuity. She, Hera, will always be there to support and guide him, to uphold order and decorum.

As he surveys the ten smiling gods ranged in front of them Zeus feels Hera squeezing his hand and understands just what that firm pressure means. He salutes the crowd of pardoned Titans and swooning nymphs massed below. Cyclopes, Gigantes, Meliae and Oceanids jostle each other to get a good view. The Charites and Horai shimmer shyly. Hades, the Erinyes and other dark creatures of the underworld bow low. The three hundred hands of the Hecatonchires wave their fierce loyalty.

Now, to signify the start of the Reign of the Twelve, Hestia steps down from her throne and sets light to the oil in a great gleaming bowl of beaten copper. A huge cheer rings around the mountain. An eagle flies overhead. Thunder rumbles across the sky.

Hestia returns to her throne. Zeus watches her calmly smoothing the skirt of her gown and transfers his gaze to the others, one by one – Poseidon. Demeter. Aphrodite. Hephaestus. Ares. Athena. Artemis. Apollo. Hermes. These gods and all creation are bowing down before him. All his enemies are scattered, destroyed, imprisoned or tamed. He

---

* It was either the action of the Hecatonchires or of glacial moraines. No one can say for absolute certain.

has created an empire and a rule the like of which the world has never seen. He has won. Yet he feels nothing.

He looks up and on the far edge of the mountain sees silhouetted against the sky a figure whose dark clothes billow in the wind. His father Kronos has come. The blade of his scythe catches the light of the flames below as he slowly swings it back and forth like a pendulum. Although even Zeus cannot possibly make it out so far away in such poor light he is sure that there is a cruel, taunting grimace on his father's gaunt and ravaged face.

'Wave, Zeus. And for heaven's sake, smile!' Hera's hissed undertone jerks him away. When he looks back the dark silhouette of his father has gone. Perhaps he only imagined it.

More cheers arise. To the growl of thunder is added a rumble from the earth itself. Gaia and Ouranos are adding their congratulations. Or perhaps their warnings. The cheering will not stop. Everything alive worships and adores him. This should be the happiest day of his life.

Something is missing. *Something* . . . he frowns and thinks. Suddenly a great lightning bolt stabs down from the sky and strikes the ground, sending up a violent puff of smoke and burnt dust.

'Don't do that, dear,' says Hera.

But Zeus isn't listening. He has had an idea.

THE TOYS OF ZEUS

PART ONE

PROMETHEUS

I have mentioned Prometheus, son of Iapetus and Clymene, before. This far-sighted young Titan had all the attributes that charm. He was strong, almost distressingly good-looking, faithful, loyal, discreet, modest, humorous, considerate, well mannered and altogether the most engaging and captivating company. Everybody liked him, but Zeus liked him best. When Zeus's packed schedule allowed, the pair would go rambling over the countryside together, talking of everything and nothing – of fortune, friendship and family, of war and destiny and of many silly and inconsequential things besides, as friends will.

In the days leading up to the inauguration of the dodecatheon, Prometheus – who was as fond of Zeus as Zeus was of him – had begun to notice a change in his friend. The god seemed moody and irritable, less inclined to go for walks, less silly and playful and more prone to sulks and outbursts of petulance that were unworthy of the kingly, humorous and self-controlled god that Prometheus knew and loved. He put it down to nerves and kept out of his way.

One morning, a week or so following the great ceremony, Prometheus, who had taken to sleeping in the long grass somewhere in the fragrant meadows of Thrace, felt himself being jerked awake by a persistent tweaking of his toes. He opened his eyes to see a lively and rejuvenated King of the Gods bouncing up and down in front of him like an impatient child on their birthday morning. The gloom had melted away like mist from a mountaintop and all the signature joviality had returned tenfold.

'Up, Prometheus! Up and at 'em!'

'Hwuh?'

'We're going to do something remarkable today, some-thing that the world will shout about for aeons. It will ring down the ages, it will be the –'

'Hunting for bears, are we?'

'Bears? I have had the most extraordinary idea. Come *on*.'

'Where are we going?'

Zeus gave no answer, but putting an arm round Prometheus he led him forcefully across the fields in a silence punctuated only by occasional barks of excited laughter. If Prometheus hadn't known his friend better he might have thought him drunk on nectar.

'This idea,' he prompted. 'Perhaps you could start at the beginning?'

'Good, yes. The beginning. That's right. The beginning is exactly where we should start. Sit there.' Zeus indicated a fallen tree and paced up and down while Prometheus inspected the bark for ants before seating himself. 'Now. Consider how everything began. *En arche en Chaos.* In the beginning was Chaos. Out of Chaos came the First Order – Erebus, Nyx, Hemera and their generation – followed by the Second Order, our grandparents Gaia and Ouranos, yes?'

Prometheus gave a cautious nod.

'Gaia and Ouranos, who then unleashed upon creation the catastrophic aberration of you people, the Titans –'

'Hey!'

'– and next came all those nymphs and spirits, endless minor deities and monsters and animals and what have you, and finally the culmination. Us. The gods. Heaven and earth perfected.'

'After a long and bloody war against my race. Which I helped you win.'

'Yes, yes. But the end result – all is well. Peace and prosperity have broken out everywhere. And yet . . .'

Zeus left such a long silence that Prometheus felt obliged to break it.

'You surely can't mean that you miss the war?'

'No, it's not that . . .' Zeus continued pacing up and down in front of Prometheus, like a teacher lecturing a class of one. 'You must have noticed I've been out of sorts lately. I'll tell you why. You know how sometimes I like to soar over the world in the form of an eagle?'

'Scouting for nymphs.'

'This world,' Zeus went on, affecting not to hear, 'is quite extraordinarily beautiful. Everything in its place – rivers, mountains, birds, beasts, oceans, groves, plains and canyons . . . But you know, when I look down, I find myself sorrowing at how empty it is.'

'*Empty?*'

'Oh Prometheus, you have absolutely no idea how boring it is to be a god in a complete and finished world.'

'*Boring?*'

'Yes, boring. For some time I've realized that I'm bored and I'm lonely. I mean "lonely" in the larger sense. In the cosmic sense. I am cosmically lonely. Is this how it's going to be for ever and ever now? Me on a throne on Olympus, thunderbolt on lap, while everyone bows and scrapes, sings praises and begs favours? In perpetuity. Where's the fun in that?'

'Well . . .'

'Be honest, you'd hate it too.'

Prometheus compressed his lips and thought for a while. It was true that he had never envied his friend the imperial throne and all its bothers and burdens.

'Suppose,' said Zeus, 'suppose I were to start a new race.'

'In the Pythian Games?'

117

'No, not a running race. A race as in a *species*. A new order of beings. Like us in every particular, upright, on two legs –'

'One head?'

'One head. Two hands. Resembling us in every particular, and they would have – you're the intellectual, Prometheus, what's the name for that aspect of us that raises us above the animals?'

'Our hands?'

'No, the part that tells us that we exist, that makes us aware of ourselves?'

'Consciousness.'

'That's the one. These creatures would have *consciousness*. And language. They wouldn't be a threat to us, of course. They'd live down here on the land, use their wit to farm and feed and fend for themselves.'

'So . . .' Prometheus frowned in concentration as he tried to form a coherent picture in his mind. 'A race of beings like us?'

'Exactly! But not as big as us. And they'd be my creation. Well, our creation.'

'*Our* creation?'

'You're good with your hands. Another Hephaestus. My idea is that you would model these creatures out of . . . out of clay, for example. They should be shaped in our image, anatomically correct in every detail, but on a smaller scale. Then we could animate them, give them life, replicate them and release them into nature to see what happens.'

Prometheus pondered this idea.

'Would we engage with them, speak to them, move about with them?'

'That would be exactly the point. To have an intelligent – well, semi-intelligent – species to praise and worship us, to play with us and amuse us. A subservient, adoring race of little miniatures.'

'Male and female?'

'Oh, good heavens no, just male. You can imagine what Hera would say otherwise . . .'

Prometheus could indeed imagine what Hera's reaction might be if the world were suddenly filled with more females for her errant husband to involve himself with. He saw that Zeus was very excited by his grand scheme. Once he was set upon a course, Prometheus knew, even one as novel and strange as this, not even the Hecatonchires and Gigantes combined could sway his friend from it.

Not that Prometheus was against the idea. It was an exciting experiment, he decided. Playthings for the immortals. When you came to think of it, it was really rather an enchanting notion. Artemis had her hounds, Aphrodite her doves, Athena her owl and serpent, Poseidon and Amphitrite their dolphins and turtles. Even Hades kept a dog – albeit a perfectly disgusting one. It was only fitting that the chief of gods should design his own special kind of pet, more intelligent, loyal and endearing than the others.

Kneading and Firing

History does not agree on exactly where Prometheus and Zeus went to find the best clay for realizing the plan. Early sources, like the traveller Pausanias in the second century AD, claimed that Panopeus in Phocis was the place. Later scholars say that the pair journeyed east of Asia Minor, all the way down to the fertile lands that lie between the rivers Tigris and Euphrates.* The most recent scholarship

---

* The Greek for 'between rivers' is *Mesopotamia*, which is how that area was always known to the Greeks.

maintains that the search took them right down past Nilus, crossing the Equator and ending up in East Africa.

Wherever it was, they found at last what Prometheus pronounced to be the perfect spot: a river whose slimy banks oozed with just the kind of mud and minerals he wanted for consistency, texture, durability and colour.

'This is good clay,' he told Zeus. 'No, don't settle down. I need to work in peace and free of all distraction. But before you go I shall require some of your saliva.'

'Excuse me?'

'If these creatures are to live and breathe they will need something of you in the composition.'

Zeus saw the justice of this and was happy enough to hawk up and fill a dried out waterhole with his divine spittle.

'I'll need to line up my little clay figures one by one on the riverbank to be baked in the heat of the sun,' said Prometheus. 'So be back by evenfall and they should be nicely ready.'

Zeus would have liked to watch, but he knew enough about the artistic temperament to leave Prometheus to it. Leaping upwards in the form of an eagle he flew away, leaving his friend alone with his art.

Prometheus began tentatively, first rolling out sausages of clay, each roughly four *podes* long.* On top of these he stuck a ball of spit-moistened clay for a head. It was then a question of teasing, twisting and tweaking, mushing, moulding and massaging, pulling, prising and pinching, until something like a small version of a god or Titan appeared. The more he worked, the more excited he became. Zeus had not been exaggerating when he compared Prometheus to Hephaestus – he did possess real skill. In fact what he exhibited now as he pressed and shaped was more than skill, it was artistry.

---

* See Appendix on p. 401.

Mixing the clay with different pigments he built up a diverse and colourful array of life-like masculine creatures. His first effort had been a small being whose skin closely matched the sun-kissed complexions of the gods. Next he made one in shining black, then another who was more a creamy ivory tinged with pink, then came figures of amber, yellow, bronze, red, green, beige, vivid purple and the brightest blue.

A Reduced Set

As evening fell Prometheus stood and stretched with a yawn and that special groan of weariness and satisfaction that follows a long session of concentrated labour.

The afternoon sun had warmed his work into the supple, malleable consistency known in the world of ceramics as 'cheese-ware'. This was perfect timing on Prometheus's part, for if the finished creations had been exposed to fiercer midday heat they would have dried into 'biscuit-ware', rendering them too friable and frangible for any of the last-minute modifications that his royal and divine patron would be sure to demand. Longer ears, twice the number of genitals, that kind of thing. Gods are nothing if not capricious.

And here, unless his own ears deceived him, came the King of the Gods now, crashing through the thicket in loud conversation with someone. Prometheus could make out an answering voice, female, low and measured. Zeus had brought along Athena, his favourite child.

'Your father the emperor god, the world knows,' Prometheus could hear him saying. 'Zeus the all-powerful, yes. Zeus the all-conquering, certainly. Zeus the all-knowing, of course. Zeus the –'

'Zeus the all-modest?'

'– Zeus the *creator*, though. Doesn't that have a ring?'

'Quite a ring.'

'Now then, the riverbank should be just over there. Let's call him. Oh, *Prometheus*!'

Roosting weaver-birds rocketed into the air, squawking in alarm. '*Promeeeetheus!*'

'Over here,' Prometheus called. 'But be careful because –'
Too late!

Breaking out through the trees into the clearing Zeus had, in his excitement, stepped onto the row of exquisitely fashioned figures drying on the bank. With a cry of fury and despair Prometheus hurried forward to survey the damage.

'You clumsy oaf!' he cried. 'You've destroyed them. Look!'

No one else in creation could get away with talking to Zeus like that. Athena was astonished to see her father bow his head in meek apology.

On inspection things were not quite as bad as Prometheus had feared. Only three of the figures were beyond repair. He prised these from the mud, the squashed clay still bearing the imprint of Zeus's enormous toes.

'Oh good,' said Zeus cheerfully, 'the rest are fine, that's plenty. Let's get on, shall we?'

'But look at these!' said Prometheus holding up the squashed and ruined statuettes. 'The little green, violet and blue creatures were just about my favourites.'

'We've still got the black, brown, ivory, yellow, reddish and what have you. That's enough, surely?'

'I really *loved* that shade of cobalt blue.'

Athena was looking down at the intact figures which lay glowing in the dying rays of the sun. 'Oh Prometheus, they're perfect,' she said in the mild voice that commanded more attention than the roars and screams of the other Olympians.

Prometheus cheered up at once. Praise from Athena meant everything.

'Well, I did pretty much put my heart and soul into them.'

'Fine job, really fine,' said Zeus. 'Formed by a great Titan from Gaia's clay, they are held together by my royal saliva and fired by the sun and shall be brought to life by the gentle breath of my daughter.'

It was Metis, always inside Zeus, who had sparked the thought in him that it should be Athena who brought these creatures to life. She would breathe into each one, literally *inspiring* them with some of her great qualities of wisdom, instinct, craft and sense.

A Name Is Found

Kneeling down on the bank of the river Athena breathed her warm sweet breath into each of the little statues. When she had finished she stood to join Prometheus and her father, looking on to see what would transpire.

It all happened quite slowly.

At first one of the darker figures gave a twitch and let out a kind of gasping moan.

At the other end of the row a yellow one wriggled, sat up and gave a small cough.

Within seconds all the little beings were alive and moving. Just moments later they were trying out their limbs, eyes and other senses, looking at each other, smelling the air, chattering and shouting. Before long they were standing and even taking their first wobbling steps.

Zeus took Prometheus by both his hands and danced him round and round.

'Look!' he shouted. 'Look! Aren't they beautiful! They're wonderful, quite wonderful!'

Athena raised a finger to her lips. 'Sh! You're frightening them.' She pointed down at the tiny men who were now staring up with looks of fear and consternation on their faces. The tallest of them didn't quite come up to the level of her knees.

'It's alright, little ones,' said Zeus stooping down and addressing them in what he hoped was a soothing voice. 'There's no need to be afraid!'

But the colossal booming sound that emerged seemed to alarm the little creatures further and they began to flail and whirl about in alarm.

'Let's reduce ourselves to their size,' said Prometheus. As he spoke he shrank himself down so that he was only a foot or so taller than his creations. Zeus and Athena did the same.

With embraces, smiles and soft words, the scared and bewildered beings were slowly pacified and befriended. They clustered around the three immortals, bowing and prostrating themselves.

'There's no need to bow,' said Prometheus, touching one of them and marvelling at the texture and life he could feel pounding within. Athena's breath had turned the clay into such quick, warm flesh. The eyes of them all were bright with life and energy and hope.

'Excuse me,' said Zeus, 'there is *every* need to bow. We are their gods and they are not to forget it.'

'I'm not their god,' said Prometheus, gazing down on them with an intense feeling of love and pride. 'I am their friend.' He knelt so that he was lower than them. 'I shall teach them how to farm, how to mill wheat and rye so that they can make bread. How to cook and forge tools and –'

'No!' Zeus gave a sudden roar that sent the startled creatures milling in panic again. Zeus's roar was answered by a great rumble of thunder in the sky. 'You can befriend them as much as you like, Prometheus, and I have no doubt that Athena and all the other gods will do so too. But one thing they are not to have. Ever. And that is fire.'

Prometheus stared at his friend in astonishment. 'But . . . but why ever not?'

'With fire they could rise up to challenge us. With fire they could think themselves our equals. I feel it and know it. They must never be given fire. I have spoken.'

A long peal of thunder in the distance affirmed his words.

'But,' Zeus smiled now, 'everything else in the world is theirs to enjoy. They may travel to every corner. They can sail Poseidon's oceans, seek Demeter's help in sowing seeds and growing food, learn from Hestia the arts of keeping a home, discover how to keep animals for their milk, fur and labour, and they can learn the arts of hunting from Artemis. Hermes can teach them guile, Apollo can instruct them in the arts of music and knowledge. Athena will teach them how to be wise and contented. And Aphrodite will share with them the arts of love. They will be free and happy.'

'What shall we call them?' Athena asked.

'"That which is below",' said Zeus after some thought. '*Anthropos*.'*

He clapped his hands and the huddle of hand-crafted humans became a hundred and the hundred became a horde

---

* That is one theory as to the origin of the word *anthropos*, which does strictly mean 'man'. It is unfortunate that many words for our species *seem* to refer only to the male. 'Human', for example, is cognate with *homo*, the Latin for 'man'. Thus 'humanity' rudely leaves out half the species. 'Folk' and 'people' aren't so specific. It is worth bearing in mind, however, that 'man' is actually connected to *mens* (mind) and *manus* (hand), and was in fact gender neutral until perhaps a thousand years ago.

and the horde, spreading ever outwards, became a multitude, until the human population, numbering now in the hundreds of thousands, was on its way to finding a home in every corner of the world.

And so the early race of man came to be. Gaia, Zeus, Apollo and Athena might be said to be its progenitors as much as Prometheus, who fashioned humanity from the four elements: Earth (Gaia's clay), Water (the spittle of Zeus), Fire (the sun of Apollo) and Air (the breath of Athena). They lived and thrived, exemplifying the best of their creators. But something was missing. Something very important.

The Golden Age

Alma Mater, the bountiful Mother Earth, made fertile and fruitful by Demeter, was a sweet paradise for the first men. They knew no disease, poverty, famine or war. Life was an idyll of innocence and light pastoral duties. It was a time of happy worship of, and familiarity and even friendship with, the deities who moved amongst them in easy, unfrightening shapes and dimensions. It gave Zeus and the other gods, Titans and immortals great pleasure to mingle with the charming, child-like homunculi that Prometheus has shaped from clay.

Perhaps we only imagined these first days of beautiful simplicity and universal kindness so that we could have a high point of paradisal sublimity against which to judge the low, degraded times that came after. The later Greeks certainly believed that the Golden Age had truly existed. It was ever present in their thinking and poetry and gave them a dream of perfection to aspire to, a vision more concrete and realized than our own vague ideas of early man grunting in caves. Platonic ideals and perfect forms were perhaps the intellectual expression of that wistful race memory.

It was natural that, of all the immortals, the one who loved humankind best should be their artist-creator Prometheus. He and his brother Epimetheus now spent more time living with man than they spent on Olympus in the company of their fellow immortals.

It saddened Prometheus that he had only been allowed to create male people, for he felt that this cloned single-sex race lacked variety both in its outlook, disposition and character and in its inability to breed and create new types. His humans were happy, yes; but to Prometheus such a safe, unchallenged and unchallenging existence had no zest to it. To approach the godlike status that his creation deserved, mankind needed something more. They needed *fire*. Real hot, fierce, flickering, flaming fire to enable them to melt, smelt, roast, toast, boil, broil, fashion and forge; and they needed an inner creative fire too, a *divine* fire, to enable them to think, imagine, dare and do.

The more he watched over and mingled with his creation, the more Prometheus became convinced that fire was exactly what they needed. And he knew where to find it.

The Fennel Stalk

Prometheus surveyed the twin crowns of Olympus towering above him. The tallest peak, Mytikos, reached nearly ten thousand *podes* high into the clouds. Next to it, two or three hundred or so feet lower but much harder to climb, reared the rocky face of Stefani. To the west loomed the heights of Skolio. Prometheus knew that the dying rays of the evening sun would shield that climb – the toughest of all – from the gods enthroned above, and so he began the perilous ascent confident that he could reach the summit unseen.

Prometheus had never disobeyed Zeus before. Not in anything big. In games and races and wrestling matches and competitions to win the hearts of nymphs he had freely teased and taunted his friend, but he had never defied him outright. The hierarchy of the pantheon was not something any being could disrupt without real consequences. Zeus was a beloved friend, but he was, above all, Zeus.

Yet Prometheus was determined on his course of action. Much as he had always loved Zeus, he found that he loved mankind more. The excitement and resolution he felt were stronger than any fear of divine wrath. He hated to cross his friend, but when it came to a choice, there was no choice.

By the time he had scaled Skolio's sheer wall, the western gates had closed upon Apollo's chariot of the sun and the whole mountain was shrouded in darkness. Crouching low, Prometheus made his way around the jagged outcrop that crested the bowl-like amphitheatre of Megala Kazania. Looking ahead he could see the Plateau of the Muses beyond, flickering with dancing licks of light thrown by the fires of Hephaestus's forge several hundred *podes* or so further off.

Around the other side of Olympus the gods were supping. Prometheus could hear Apollo's lyre, Hermes' fluting syrinx, the raucous laugh of Ares and the snarling of Artemis's hounds. Hugging the outer walls of the forge the Titan edged along to its forecourt. He was startled, as he rounded the corner, to see stretched out naked on the ground the huge figure of Brontes snoring by the fire. Prometheus hung back in the shadows. He knew that the Cyclopes assisted Hephaestus, but that they might sleep on the premises was more than he had bargained for.

1. Gaia, a primordial goddess and the personification of Earth, brought into being at the dawn of creation.

2. Themis, the Titan goddess who became the embodiment of law, justice and order. She is shown here seated on the Delphic tripod, holding a cup in one hand and a sprig of laurel in the other.

3. The Cyclopes had a single, orb-shaped eye in the middle of their forehead.

4. Hypnos, the personification of sleep. He would father Morpheus, who shaped and formed dreams.

5. Kronos (Cronus) uses a scythe to mutilate his father, Ouranos (Uranus).

6. Botticelli's *Birth of Venus* shows Aphrodite as she makes landfall in Cyprus.

7. Kronos devouring one of his sons.

8. Kronus receives the Omphalos stone from Rhea.

9. The infant Zeus being fed by nymphs and the she-goat Amalthea on Crete.

10. Two giants battling the gods during the Gigantomachy.

11. Zeus aims a thunderbolt at the winged and snake-legged monster, Typhon.

12. The Muses: nine sisters, each of whom represents and stands patron to her own particular art form.

13. The three Moirai, or Fates. Clotho spins the thread that represents a life, Lachesis measures out its length and Atropos chooses when to cut the life off.

14. The gods battle the Titans during the ten-year conflict known as the Titanomachy.

15. The triumphant gods of Olympus.

At the very mouth of the forge he saw a narthex plant, sometimes called the laserwort or giant fennel (*Ferula communis*) – not quite the same bulbous vegetable we use today to impart a pleasant aniseedy flavour to fish, but a near enough relation. Prometheus leaned forward and picked a long, vigorous specimen. Tightly packed within there was a thick, lint-like pith. Stripping the stem of its outer leaves Prometheus stretched out and pushed the stalk across the forecourt, over Brontes' slumbering, mumbling form and towards the fire. The heat emanating from the furnace was enough to cause the end of the stalk to catch at once. Prometheus pulled it back in with as much care as he could, but he could not prevent a spark from falling from its sputtering end straight down onto Brontes' torso. The skin on the Cyclops's chest sizzled and hissed and he awoke with a roar of pain. As Brontes looked groggily down at his chest, trying to understand where this pain was coming from and what it could mean, Prometheus hauled in the stalk and fled.

The Gift of Fire

Prometheus clambered back down Olympus, the fennel stalk clenched between his teeth, its pith burning slowly. Every five minutes or so he would take it from his mouth and blow gently, nursing its glow. When he at last reached the safety of the valley floor he made his way to the human settlement where he and his brother had made their home.

You may say that Prometheus could surely have had the wit to teach man to strike stones together, or rub sticks, but we have to remember that what Prometheus stole was fire from heaven, divine fire. Perhaps he took the inner spark that ignited in man the curiosity to rub sticks and strike flints in the first place.

When he showed men the leaping, dancing darting demon they initially cried out in fear and backed away from its flames. But their curiosity soon overcame their fear and they began to delight in this magical new toy, substance, phenomenon – call it what you will. They learned from Prometheus that fire was not their enemy but a powerful friend which, once tamed, had ten thousand thousand uses.

Prometheus moved from village to village demonstrating techniques for the fashioning of tools and weapons, the firing of earthen pots, the cooking of meat and the baking of cereal doughs, all of which quickly let loose an avalanche of advantages, raising man above the animal prey that had no answer to metal-tipped spears and arrows.

It was not long before Zeus chanced to look down from Olympus and saw points of dancing orange light dotting the landscape all around. He knew at once what had happened. Nor did he need to be told who was responsible. His anger was swift and terrible. Never had such almighty, such tumultuous, such apocalyptic fury been witnessed. Not even Ouranos in his mutilated agony had been so filled with vengeful rage. Ouranos was brought low by a son he had no regard for, but Zeus had been betrayed by the friend he loved most. No betrayal could be more terrible.

THE PUNISHMENTS

The Gift

Zeus's wrath was so overwhelming that all Olympus feared Prometheus would be blasted with such power that his atoms would never reassemble. It is possible that just such a fate might have befallen the once-favoured Titan had not the wise and stabilizing presence of Metis inside Zeus's head counselled a subtler and more dignified revenge. The intensity of his rage was in no way dimmed, but rather it was now focussed, channelled into clearer lines of retribution. He would leave Prometheus for the time being and unleash his cosmic fury upon man, puny impudent man, the creature he had taken such delight in and for whom now he felt nothing but resentment and cold contempt.

For a whole week, watched by a grave and concerned Athena, the King of the Gods paced up and down in front of his throne considering how best humans should pay for daring to appropriate fire, for presuming to ape the Olympians. A voice within him seemed to whisper that one day, no matter what vengeance he took, mankind would reach ever upwards until they came level with the gods – or, perhaps more terribly, until they no longer *needed* the gods and felt free to abandon them. No more worship, no more prayers sent up to heavenly Olympus. The prospect was too blasphemous and absurd for Zeus to entertain, but the fact that such a scandalous idea could even enter his mind served only to fuel his rage.

Whether the magnificent scheme that was finally put into operation was his or Metis's or even Athena's is unclear, but it was, Zeus believed, a screamer of a plan. There was a golden symmetry to it that appealed to his very Greek mind. He would show Prometheus and, by heaven, he would show mankind.

First he commanded Hephaestus to do as Prometheus had done, to shape a human being from clay moistened by his spittle. But this was to be the figure of a young *female*. Taking his wife Aphrodite, his mother Hera, his aunt Demeter and his sister Athena as models, Hephaestus lovingly sculpted a girl of quite marvellous beauty into whom Aphrodite then breathed life and all the arts of love.

The other gods joined together to equip this girl uniquely for the world. Athena trained her in the household crafts, embroidery and weaving, and dressed her in a glorious silver robe. The Charites were put in charge of accessorizing this with necklaces, brooches and bracelets of the finest pearl, agate, jasper and chalcedony. The Horai plaited flowers around her hair until she was so beautiful that all who saw her caught their breath. Hera endowed her with poise and self-possession. Hermes schooled her in speech and the arts of deception, curiosity and cunning. And he gave her a name. Since each of the gods had conferred upon her a notable talent or accomplishment, she was to be called 'All-Gifted', which in Greek is PANDORA.*

Hephaestus bestowed one more gift upon this paragon, which Zeus presented himself. It was a container filled with . . . secrets.

Now, you probably think I am going to say the container was a box, or perhaps a chest of some description, but in fact

---

* It is a subtler name than that, for *pan-dora* can mean 'all-giving' as well as 'all-given'.

it was the kind of glazed and sealed earthenware jar that is known in Grecian lands as a *pithos*.*

'Here you are, my dear,' said Zeus. 'Now, this is purely decorative. You are never ever to open it. You understand?'

Pandora shook her lovely head. 'Never,' she breathed with great sincerity. 'Never!'

'There's a good girl. It is your wedding gift. Bury it deep below your marriage bed, but you must not open it. Ever. What it contains . . . well, never mind. Nothing of interest to you at all.'

Hermes took Pandora by the hand and transported her to the little stone house where Prometheus and his brother Epimetheus lived, right in the centre of a prosperous human town.

The Brothers

Prometheus knew that Zeus would seek some kind of retribution for his disobedience and warned his brother Epimetheus that, while he was away teaching the newly sprung up villages and towns how to use fire, he should on no account accept any gift from Olympus, no matter in what guise it presented itself.

Epimetheus, who always acted first and considered the consequences later, promised to obey his more perspicacious brother.

Nothing could prepare him for Zeus's gift, however.

Epimetheus answered a knock at the door one morning to see the cheerful smiling face of the messengers of the gods.

---

* It is said to have been Erasmus of all people, the great sixteenth-century scholar and Prince of Humanists, who misread Pandora's *pithos* (jar) into *pyxis* (box).

'May we come in?' Hermes stepped nimbly aside to reveal, cradling a stoneware jar in her arms, the most beautiful creature Epimetheus had ever seen. Aphrodite was beautiful, of course she was, but too remote and ethereal to be considered as anything other than a subject of veneration and distant awe. Likewise Demeter, Artemis, Athena, Hestia and Hera. Their loveliness was majestic and unattainable. The prettiness of nymphs, oreads and Oceanids, while enchanting enough, seemed shallow and childish next to the blushing sweetness of the vision that looked up at him so shyly, so winningly, so adorably.

'May we?' repeated Hermes.

Epimetheus gulped, swallowed and stepped backwards, opening the door wide.

'Meet your wife to be,' said Hermes. 'Her name is Pandora.'

When It's a Jar

Epimetheus and Pandora were soon married. Epimetheus had an inkling that Prometheus – who was far away teaching the art of casting in bronze to the people of Varanasi – would not approve of Pandora. A quick wedding before his brother returned seemed a good idea.

Epimetheus and Pandora were very much in love. That could not be denied. Pandora's beauty and attainments were such as to delight him every day, and in return his facile ability to live always for the moment and never to fret about the future gave her a sense of life as a light and lovely adventure.

But one little itch tickled her, one little fly buzzed around her, one little worm burrowed inside.

That jar.

She kept it on a shelf in their bedroom. When Epimetheus had asked about it she laughed. 'Just a silly thing that Hephaestus made to remind me of Olympus. It's of no value.'

'Pretty though,' said Epimetheus, giving it no further thought.

One afternoon, when her husband was away practising the discus with his friends, Pandora approached the jar and ran her finger round the rim of its sealed lid. Why had Zeus even *mentioned* that there was nothing interesting inside it? He would never have said such a thing if truly there weren't. She pieced the logic of it together in her mind.

If you give a friend an empty jar you would never concern yourself with *mentioning* that the jar was empty. Your friend might look inside one day and see that for themselves. So why should Zeus take the trouble to repeat that this jar contained nothing of any interest? There could be only one explanation. There was something of *great* interest inside. Something of value or power. Something either enchanting or enchanted.

But, no – she had sworn never to open it. 'A promise is a promise,' she told herself, and straight away felt very virtuous. She believed it her duty to resist the spell of the jar which now, really, seemed almost to be singing out to her in the most alluring way. It was excessively vexing to have an object so bewitching in her bedroom where it could taunt and tempt her every morning and every night.

Temptation loses much of its power when removed from sight. Pandora went to the small back garden and – next to a sundial that a neighbour had given them as a wedding gift – she dug a hole and buried the jar deep in the ground. She patted the earth flat and wheeled the heavy sundial on its plinth over the hiding place. There!

For the next week she was as gay and skittish and happy as

a person had ever been. Epimetheus fell even more in love with her and invited their friends over to feast and hear a song he had written in her honour. It was a happy and successful party. The last festival that the Golden Age was ever to know.

That night, perhaps a little flushed with the praise that had flowed so freely in her direction, Pandora found it hard to sleep. Through the window of her bedroom the moonlight shone down on the garden. The sundial's gnomon gleamed like a silver blade and once again she thought she heard the music of the jar.

Epimetheus was sleeping happily beside her. The moonbeams danced in the garden. Unable to stand it any longer Pandora leapt from her matrimonial bed and was out in the garden, unrolling the base of the sundial and scrabbling at the earth, before she had time to tell herself that this was the wrong thing to do.

She pulled the jar from its hiding place and twisted at the lid. Its waxen seal gave way and she pulled it free. There was a fast fluttering, a furious flapping of wings and a wild wheeling and whirling in her ears.

Oh! Glorious flying creatures!

But no . . . they were not glorious at all. Pandora cried out in pain and fright as she felt something leathery brush her neck, followed by a sharp and terrible prick of pain as some sting or bite pierced her skin. More and more flying shapes buzzed from the mouth of the jar – a great cloud of them chattering, screaming and howling in her ears. Through the swirling fog of these dreadful creatures she saw the face of her husband as he came outside to see what was happening. It was white with horror and fright. With a great cry Pandora summoned up the courage and strength to close the lid and seal the jar.

On the garden wall, in the shape of a wolf, Zeus looked on, smiling the most terrible and wicked smile as, like a cloud of locusts, the shrieking, wailing creatures clawed the air and circled the garden below them in a great vortex before flying up and away over the town, over the countryside and around the world, settling like a pestilence wherever man had habitation.

And what were they, these shapes? They were mutant descendants of the dark and evil children of both Nyx and Erebus. They were born of Apate, Deceit; Geras, Old Age; Oizys, Misery; Momos, Blame; Keres, Violent Death. They were the offshoots of Ate, Ruin, and Eris, Discord. These were their names: PONOS, Hardship; LIMOS, Starvation; ALGOS, Pain; DYSNOMIA, Anarchy; PSEUDEA, Lies; NEIKEA, Quarrels; AMPHILOGIAI, Disputes; MAKHAI, Wars; HYSMI-NAI, Battles; ANDROKTASIAI and PHONOI, Manslaughters and Murders.

Illness, Violence, Deceit, Misery and Want had arrived. They would never leave the earth.

What Pandora did not know was that, when she shut the lid of the jar so hastily, she for ever imprisoned inside one last daughter of Nyx. One last little creature was left behind to beat its wings hopelessly in the jar for ever. Its name was ELPIS, Hope.*

The Chest, the Waters and the Bones of Gaia

And so the Golden Age came to a swift and terrible end. Death, disease, poverty, crime, famine and war were now an inevitable and eternal part of humanity's lot.

---

* See Appendix, p. 398.

But the Silver Age, as this epoch was to be known, wasn't all despair. It differed from our own in that gods, demigods and monsters mingled with mankind, interbred with us and fully involved themselves in our lives. With fire on man's side, and now women to allow propagation as well as a full sense of family and completeness, some of the evils of Pandora's jar were offset. Zeus looked down and saw this. Inside him the voice of Metis seemed to whisper that nothing he could do would stop humanity from one day standing on its own two feet, in more than just the obvious sense. This troubled him deeply.

For the meantime, people were duly in awe of the gods and used their new-found affinity with fire to send burnt offerings up to Olympus as a mark of their obedience and devotion.

Pandora, the first woman, bore several children by Epimetheus, including a daughter PYRRHA. Prometheus too fathered a child, a son called DEUCALION, possibly by Prometheus's own mother, Clymene, or, if other sources are to be believed, by HESIONE, an Oceanid.

And so the race of men and women multiplied.

Prometheus, whose gift of foresight never deserted him,* was keenly aware that Zeus's anger had yet to be assuaged. He brought Deucalion up to be prepared for the worst kinds of divine retribution. When the boy was old enough he taught him the art of building in wood. Together they constructed an enormous chest.

The brother Titans were overjoyed when their children Pyrrha and Deucalion fell in love and married. Prometheus and Epimetheus could now think of themselves as patriarchs of a new, independent human dynasty. Yet always there

---

* Foresight, but not prophecy . . .

lurked the threat from the Thunderer, brooding on his Olympian throne.

Time passed and humanity continued to breed and spread, in Zeus's eyes more like a plague than the beloved playthings he had once adored. The excuse he needed to visit a second punishment on mankind was furnished by one of their first rulers, LYCAON, King of Arcadia – son of the Pelasgos who gave the Pelasgians their name. This Pelasgos had been one of the original clay figures formed by Prometheus and animated by Athena. Pelasgos was what we would consider ethnically Hellenic, with brownish skin, hair and eyes. Later Greeks regarded these people, their language and practices, as barbaric; and, as we shall see, this first race was not fated to populate the Mediterranean for long.

Lycaon, either to test Zeus's omniscience and discrimination or for other brutal reasons, killed and roasted the flesh of his own son NYCTIMUS which he served to the god, who had come as a guest to a feast at his palace. Zeus was so revolted by this unspeakably gross act that he brought the boy back to life and turned Lycaon into a wolf.* Nyctimus had little time to reign in his father's stead, however, as his forty-nine brothers ravaged the land with such violence and behaved so disgustingly that Zeus decided it was time for the whole human experiment to be brought to a close. To that end he gathered the clouds into a storm so intense that the land was flooded and all the people of Greece and the Mediterranean world were drowned.

All, save Deucalion and Pyrrha who – thanks to the perspicacity of Prometheus – survived the nine days of high water aboard their wooden chest, which floated safely on the flood. Like good survivalists they had kept their chest well

---

* Another English word for a werewolf is *lycanthrope*, Greek for 'wolf-man'.

provisioned with food, drink and a few useful tools and arte-facts, so that when the deluge finally receded and their vessel was able to settle on Mount Parnassus they could survive in the post-diluvian mud and slime.*

When the world had dried enough for Pyrrha and Deuca-lion (who is said to have been eighty-two years old at this time) to travel safely down the mountainside, they made their way to Delphi, which lies in the valley below Parnassus. There they consulted the oracle of Themis, the prophetic Titaness whose special quality was an understanding of the right thing to do.

'O Themis, Mother of Justice, Peace and Order, instruct us, we beseech you,' they cried. 'We are alone in the world now and too advanced in years to fill this empty world with offspring.'

'Children of Prometheus and Epimetheus,' the oracle intoned. 'Hear my voice and do as I command. Cover your head and throw the bones of your mother over your shoulder.'

Not a word more could the perplexed couple induce the oracle to utter.

'My mother was Pandora,' said Pyrrha, sitting on the ground. 'And I must presume she is drowned. Where could I find her bones?'

'My mother is Clymene,' said Deucalion. 'Or, if you believe variant sources, she is the Oceanid Hesione. In either case they are both immortals and therefore alive and surely unwilling to give up their bones.'

'We must think,' said Pyrrha. '*The bones of our mother.* Can that have another meaning? *Our mother's bones.* Maternal bones . . . Think, Deucalion, think!'

---

* According to Ovid at least. Other sources suggest Mount Etna or Mount Athos. Round about the same time Noah was landing on Mount Ararat. Archaeology confirms, it seems, that there really was a Great Flood.

Deucalion covered his head with a folded cloth, sat down next to his wife, whose head was already covered, and pondered the problem with creased brow. Oracles. They always paltered and prevaricated. Moodily he picked up a rock and sent it rolling down the hillside. Pyrrha grabbed his arm.

'Our mother!'

Deucalion stared at her. She had started slapping the ground with the palms of her hands. '*Gaia!* Gaia is mother of us all,' she cried. 'Our Mother Earth! *These* are the bones of our mother, look . . .' She started to gather up rocks from the ground. 'Come on!'

Deucalion got to his feet and scrabbled around, collecting rocks and stones. They made their way across the fields below Delphi, casting them over their shoulders as instructed, but not daring to look back until they had covered many *stadia*.

When they turned the sight that greeted them filled their hearts with joy.

From out of the ground where Pyrrha's stones had landed sprang girls and women, hundreds of them, smiling and healthy and fully formed. From the earth where Deucalion's stones had fallen boys and men grew up.

So it was that the old Pelasgians drowned in the Great Deluge, and the Mediterranean world was repopulated by a new race descended through Deucalion and Pyrrha from Prometheus, Epimetheus, Pandora and – most importantly of course – from Gaia.*

And that is who we are, a compound of foresight and impulse, of all gifts and of the earth.

---

* See Appendix on p. 395.

Death

Our human race, now satisfactorily comprised equally of males and females, bred and spread about the world building cities and establishing nation states. Ships and chariots, cottages and castles, culture and commerce, merchants and markets, farming and finance, weapons and wheat. In short, civilization began. It was an age of kings, queens, princes and princesses, of hunters, warriors, shepherds, potters and poets. An age of empires, slaves, warfare, trade and treaties. An age of votive offerings, sacrifices and worship. Towns and villages chose their favourite gods and goddesses to be guardian deities, patrons and protectors. The immortals themselves were not shy to come down in their own forms, or in the forms of humans and animals, to have their way with such humans as appealed to them or to punish those that aggravated them and reward those that most fawned on them. The gods never tired of flattery.

Perhaps most importantly the plague of sorrows that had flown from Pandora's jar ensured that from this point onwards humanity would have to face the inevitability of death in all its forms. Sudden death, slow lingering death, death by violence, death by disease, death by accident, death by murder and death by divine decree.

The god Hades found, to his great delight – or the closest to delight that gloomy god could ever manage – that the shades of more and more dead humans began to arrive at his subterranean kingdom. Hermes was assigned a new role – that of Arch Psychopomp, or 'chief conductor of souls' – a duty he discharged with his customary sprightliness and puckish humour. Though, as the human population grew, only the most important dead were granted the honour of a personal escort by Hermes, the rest were taken by Thanatos, the grim, forbidding figure of Death.

The instant that human spirits departed their bodies, Hermes or Thanatos would lead them to the underground cavern where the River Styx (Hate) met the River Acheron (Woe). There the grim and silent Charon held out his hand to receive his payment for ferrying the souls across the Styx. If the dead had no payment to offer they would have to wait on the bank a hundred years before the disobliging Charon consented to take them. To avoid this limbo it became a custom amongst the living to place some money, usually an *obolus*, on the tongue of the dying to pay the ferryman and assure safe and swift passage.* When he had taken his fee, Charon would pull the dead soul aboard and pole his rust-coloured punt or skiff over the black, Stygian waters to the disembarkation stage, hell's muster point.† Once dead, no mortal could go back to the upper world. Immortals, if they tasted so much as a morsel of food or drink in Hades, were fated to return to the infernal kingdom.

And what was their final destination? It seems that this rather depended on the kind of life they had led. At first Hades himself was the arbiter, but in later years he delegated the Great Weighing Up to two sons of Zeus and EUROPA – MINOS and RHADAMANTHUS who, after their own deaths, were appointed, along with their half-brother AEACUS, Judges of the Underworld. They decided whether an individual had lived a heroic, average or punishably wicked life.‡

The heroes and those deemed exceedingly righteous (as well as the dead who had some divine blood in them) found

---

* Charon was also happy to receive a *danake* or *danace*, the Persian equivalent, later incorporated into ancient Greek currency.
† Virgil's description of Aeneas's visit to the underworld tells of the colour of Charon's boat.
‡ The story of how Zeus seduced Europa will be told a little later on.

themselves transported to the Elysian Fields, which lay somewhere on the archipelago known as the Fortunate Isles, or Isles of the Blessed. There is no real agreement as to where this might actually be. Perhaps they are what we now call the Canaries, perhaps the Azores, the Lesser Antilles or even Bermuda.* Later descriptions place the Elysian Fields within the kingdom of Hades itself.† In these accounts souls who reincarnated three times, on each occasion leading a heroic, just and virtuous life, then earned themselves a transfer from Elysium to the Isles of the Blessed.

The blameless majority, whose lives were neither especially virtuous nor especially vicious, might expect to be parked for eternity in the Meadows of Asphodel, whose name derived from the white flowers that carpeted its fields. These souls were guaranteed a pleasant enough afterlife: before they arrived they drank of the waters of forgetfulness from the River Lethe so that a blithe and bland eternity could be passed, untroubled by upsetting memories of earthly life.

But the sinners – the debauched, blasphemous, wicked and dissolute – what of them? The least of them flitted in the halls of Hades, eternally without feeling, strength or any real consciousness of their existence, but the most profane and unpardonable were taken to the Fields of Punishment, which lay between the Meadows of Asphodel and the abysmal depths of Tartarus itself. Here tortures that fitted their crimes with diabolical exactness were inflicted on them for all eternity. We will meet some of the more celebrated of these sinners at a later date. Names like SISYPHUS, IXION and TANTALUS still ring through the ages.

---

* The Canaries were Byron's candidate for the Isles of the Blessed in his *Don Juan*.

† But not in France, despite the name of Paris's grand thoroughfare, the Champs Elysées.

While Homer describes the spirits of the departed as keeping the faces and appearance they had in life, alternative accounts tell of a hideous demon called EURYNOMOS who met the dead and, like the Furies, stripped the flesh from their bones. Other poets suggest that the souls of the underworld were capable of speech and given to relating their life stories to each other.

Hades was the most jealous of all his jealous family. Not one soul could he bear to lose from his kingdom. Cerberus the three-headed dog patrolled the gates. Few, very few, heroes circumvented or duped Thanatos and Cerberus and managed to visit Hades' realm and return alive to the world above.

And so death became a constant in human life, as it remains to this day. But the world of the Silver Age, it should be understood, was very different from our own. Gods, demigods and all kinds of immortals still walked amongst us. Intercourse of the personal, social and sexual kind with the gods was as normal to men and women of the Silver Age as intercourse with machines and AI assistants is to us today. And, I dare say, a great deal more fun.

Prometheus Bound

With simmering fury Zeus watched the survival of Pyrrha and Deucalion and the rise of a new race of men and women from the stones of the earth. No one, not even the King of the Gods, could interfere with the will of Gaia. She represented an older, deeper, more permanent order than that of the Olympians and Zeus knew that he was powerless to prevent the repopulation of the world. But he could at least turn his attention to Prometheus. The day dawned when Zeus decided the Titan should pay for his betrayal. He looked down from Olympus and saw him in Phocis, assisting in the laying out of a new town, meddling as ever in the affairs of men.

Humankind had propagated in the twinkling of an immortal eye, which we would call the passage of several centuries. All this while Prometheus had, with titanic patience, encouraged the spread of civilization amongst Mankind 2.0 – once again teaching people all the arts, crafts and practices of agriculture, manufacture and building.

Adopting the form of an eagle Zeus swooped down and perched on the timbers of a half-built temple that was to be dedicated to himself. Prometheus, who had been carving scenes from the life of the young Zeus into the pediment, looked up and knew at once that the bird was his old friend. Zeus assumed his proper shape and inspected the carving.

'If that's supposed to be Adamanthea with me there, you've got the proportions all wrong,' he said.

'Artistic licence,' said Prometheus, whose heart was beating fast. It was the first time the two had spoken since Prometheus stole the fire.

'The time has come to pay for what you have done,' said Zeus. 'Now, I could call up the Hecatonchires to carry you forcibly to your destination, or you can choose to bow to the inevitable and come without fuss.'

Prometheus laid down his hammer and chisel and wiped his hands with a leather cloth. 'Let's go,' he said.

They did not speak or pause for rest or refreshment until they reached the foothills of the Caucasus Mountains, where the Black and Caspian Seas meet. Along the journey Zeus had wanted to say something, had longed to take his friend by the shoulder and embrace him. A weeping apology might have allowed him to forgive and make up. But Prometheus remained silent. Zeus's stinging sense of being wronged and ill-used flared up anew. 'Besides,' the god told himself, 'great rulers cannot be seen to exhibit weakness, especially when it comes to betrayal by those close to them.'

Prometheus shaded his eyes and looked up. He saw the three Cyclopes standing on a great sloping wall of rock that formed one side of the tallest mountain.

'I know you're good at climbing up the sides of mountains,' Zeus said with what he hoped was icy sarcasm, but which emerged even to his ears as something more like sulky muttering. 'So climb.'

When Prometheus reached the place where the Cyclopes were, they bound and fettered him and stretched him out on his back, hammering his shackles into the rock with mighty pegs of unbreakable iron. Two beautiful eagles swept down from the sky and glided close to Prometheus, blocking the sunlight. He could hear the hot wind ruffling their feathers.

Zeus called up to him. 'You will lie chained to this rock for ever. There is no hope of escape or forgiveness, not in all perpetuity. Each day these eagles will come to tear out your liver, just as you tore out my heart. They will eat it in front of your eyes. Since you are immortal it will grow back every night. This torture will never end. Each day the agony will seem greater. You will have nothing but time in which to consider the enormity of your crime and the folly of your actions. You who were named "foresight" showed none when you defied the King of the Gods.' Zeus's voice rang from the canyons and ravines. 'Well? Have you nothing to say?'

Prometheus sighed. 'You are wrong, Zeus,' he said. 'I thought my actions through with great care. I weighed my comfort against the future of the race of man. I see now that they will flourish and prosper independently of any immortals, even you. Knowing that is balm for any pain.'

Zeus stared at his former friend for a long time before speaking.

'You are not worth eagles,' he said with an awful coldness. 'Let them be vultures.'

The two eagles immediately changed into rank, ugly vultures who circled the outstretched body once before falling upon it. Their razor-sharp talons sliced open the Titan's side and with hideous screeches of triumph they began to feast.

Prometheus, mankind's chief creator, advocate and friend, taught us, stole for us and sacrificed himself for us. We all possess our share of Promethean fire, without it we would not be human. It is right to pity and admire him but, unlike the jealous and selfish gods he would never ask to be worshipped, praised and adored.

And it might make you happy to know that, despite the eternal punishment to which he was doomed, one day a hero would arise powerful enough to defy Zeus, unbind humanity's champion and set him free.

PERSEPHONE AND
THE CHARIOT

The world over which Zeus ruled as sovereign lord of heaven was a bountiful mother to mankind. Men, women and children helped themselves to the fruit of the trees, the grains of the grasses, the fish of the waters and the beasts of the fields without effort or much labour. Demeter, goddess of fertility and the harvest, blessed the natural world. If there was hunger or deprivation, it came about only as a result of human cruelty and the workings of those terrible creatures let loose from Pandora's jar, not as a result of divine neglect. All this was to change, however. Hades had a part in it and – who knows? – perhaps his plan all along was to hasten and increase death in the world and so increase the population of his kingdom. Intricate are the workings of Moros.

Demeter had a daughter, Persephone, by her brother Zeus. So beautiful and pure and lovely was she that the gods took to calling her KORE, or CORA, which means simply 'the maiden'. The Romans called her PROSERPINA. All the gods, especially the unattached Apollo and Hermes, fell dizzily in love with her and even offered marriage. But the protective (some might say overprotective) Demeter hid her away in the remote countryside, far from the hungry eyes of gods and immortals, honourable and dishonourable alike, intending for her to remain – like Hestia, Athena and Artemis – for ever virgin and unattached. There was one powerful god, however, who had laid his covetous eyes upon the girl and had no intention of respecting Demeter's wishes.

There was nothing the sweet and artless Persephone liked

to do more than commune with nature. Very much her mother's daughter, flowers and pretty growing things were her greatest source of joy. One golden afternoon, a little separated from the companions appointed by her mother to protect her, Persephone was chasing butterflies as they flitted from blossom to blossom in a sun-dappled, flowery meadow. Suddenly she heard a deep rending and roaring sound. It was like thunder yet seemed to be coming, not from the sky above, but from the ground beneath her feet. She looked about her in fear and bewilderment. The earth was shaking and the hillside in front of her split apart. From out of the opening there thundered a great chariot. Before the terrified girl had a chance to turn and run, the driver had scooped her up, swung the chariot round and driven it back through the cleft in the hillside. By the time Persephone's alarmed companions had reached the place, the opening had sealed itself up, leaving no sign that it had ever been there.

Persephone's disappearance was as inexplicable as it was sudden and complete. One minute she had been happily gambolling through the meadow, the next she had vanished from sight, leaving not a trace behind.

Demeter's despair can hardly be described. We have all lost something precious to us – animal, vegetable or mineral – and passed through the agonizing stages of grief, fright and anger that sudden dispossession can cause. When the loss is so personal, unforeseen, absolute and impossible to understand, those feelings are amplified to the most terrible degree. Although, as the days went by it became more and more difficult to believe that Persephone would ever be seen again, Demeter vowed that she would find her daughter if it took the eternity of her immortal span.

Demeter called upon her Titaness friend HECATE for aid. Hecate was a goddess of potions, keys, ghosts, poisons and all manner of witchcraft and enchantments.* She was the possessor of two torches that could illuminate all the corners of the earth. She and Demeter searched those corners, once, twice, a thousand times. They shone light into every cavern and dark place they could find. They scoured the world with no success.

Months passed. All this time Demeter neglected her responsibilities. The corn, the harvests, the ripening of fruit and the sowing of crops – all were abandoned, and in the earth nothing germinated. No seeds sprouted, no buds opened, no shoots grew and the world began to desertify.

The gods were safe on Olympus, but the cries of the famished and despairing people on earth reached the ears of Zeus. Only when he and the other gods, one night, were making much of the mystery of Persephone's disappearance did the sun Titan Helios speak up.†

'Persephone? Oh, I saw what happened to her. I see everything.'

'You saw? Then why didn't you say something?' demanded Zeus. 'Demeter has been dementedly wandering the earth looking for her, frantic with worry and the world is turning into a desert. Why the hell didn't you speak up?'

'No one asked me! No one ever asks me anything. But I know a lot. The eye of the sun sees all,' said Helios, repeating a line that Apollo had often used during his days in charge of the sun-chariot.

'What happened to her?'

'The earth opened and who should come out in his chariot and seize her but . . . Hades!'

'*Hades!*' chorused the gods.

---

* She features prominently in Shakespeare's *Macbeth*.

† Helios could be as dull and slow in the wits as he was bright and swift in the sun-chariot. How he came to take over these duties from Apollo will be revealed later.

The Pomegranate Seeds

Zeus immediately went down to the underworld to fetch Persephone back. But the King of the Underworld was in no mood to take orders from the King of the Overworld.

'She stays. She is my queen.'

'You dare to defy me?'

'You are my younger brother,' said Hades. 'My *youngest* brother in fact. You have always had everything you've ever wanted. I demand the right to keep the girl I love. You cannot deny me.'

'Oh, can't I?' said Zeus. 'The world is in famine. The cries of starving mortals keep us awake. Refuse to return Persephone and you will soon discover the force and reach of my will. Hermes will bring no more spirits of the dead to you. Not one single soul shall ever be sent here. All will be despatched to a new paradise, or perhaps never even die. Hades will become an empty realm drained of all power, influence or majesty. Your name will become a laughing stock.'

The brothers glared at each other. Hades was the first to blink.

'Damn you,' he growled. 'Give me one more day with her and then send Hermes to fetch her.'

Zeus travelled back up to Olympus well pleased.

The next day Hades knocked on the door of Persephone's chamber. You might be surprised that he knocked, but the fact is, in her dignified and assured presence, even such a power as Hades found himself uncertain and shy. He loved her with all his heart, and although he had lost the battle of wills with Zeus he was sure that he could not let her go. Besides, he detected in her something . . . something that gave him hope. A small flicker of returned love?

'My dear,' he said with a gentleness that would have astonished anyone who knew him. 'Zeus has prevailed upon me to send you back into the world of light.'

Persephone raised her pale face and gazed steadily at him.

Hades gazed earnestly back. 'I hope you do not think ill of me?'

She did not reply, but Hades thought he could detect a little colour flushing her cheeks and throat.

'Share some pomegranate seeds with me to show there is no ill-feeling?'

Listlessly Persephone took six seeds from his outstretched hand and sucked slowly at their sharp sweetness.

When Hermes arrived the trickster god found that he and Zeus had themselves been tricked.

'Persephone has eaten fruit from my kingdom,' said Hades. 'It is ordained that all who have tasted the food of hell must return. She has tasted six pomegranate seeds so she must come back to me for six months of every year.'

Hermes bowed. He knew that this was so. Taking Persephone by the hand he led her up out of the underworld. Demeter was so overjoyed to see her daughter that the world immediately began to spring into bloom. It was a joy that was to last for half the length of the year, for six months later, in accordance with ineluctable divine law, Persephone was forced to return to the underworld. Demeter's distress at this parting caused the trees to shed their leaves and a dead time to creep over the world. Another six months passed, Persephone emerged from Hades' domain and the cycle of birth, renewal and growth began again. In this way the seasons came about, the autumn and winter of Demeter's grieving for the absence of her daughter and the spring and summer of her jubilation at Persephone's return.

As for Persephone herself . . . well, it seems that she grew to love her time below as much as her time above. For six months she was no prisoner in Hades but the contented Queen of the Underworld, a loving consort who held imperious sway over the dominion of death with her husband. For the other six months she reverted to the laughing Kore of fertility, flowers, fruit and frolic.

The world had found a new rhythm.

Hermaphroditus and Silenus

As the men and women of the Silver Age became accustomed to the striving and toiling and suffering that seemed now to be their common lot, so the gods continued to breed. Hermes, who had grown swiftly into handsome but eternally youthful manhood, fathered the goat-footed nature god PAN by the nymph DRYOPE.* Behind the back of Hephaestus and Ares he also coupled with Aphrodite, a union blessed by the birth of a son of quite transcendent loveliness named – in honour of each parent – HERMAPHRODITUS.

This beautiful boy grew up in the shadow of Mount Ida, cared for by naiads.† When he reached the age of fifteen he left them to wander the world. Travelling in Asia Minor he met one bright afternoon a naiad called SALMACIS who was splashing in the clear waters of a spring near Halicarnassus. Hermaphroditus, who was as shy as he was lovely, became greatly confused and unhappy when this forward creature, stunned by his beauty, tried to seduce him.

---

* Although some say this, I tend to believe that Pan (FAUNUS to the Romans) was older than the Olympians. Perhaps as old as nature itself. We will encounter him from time to time as we move forward.
† There were two Mount Idas – the Cretan one, Zeus's birthplace, and another in Phrygia, Asia Minor – today's Turkish Anatolia. This was the one from which Hermaphroditus hailed.

Unlike most of her kind – modest, hard-working nymphs who attended with diligence to the maintenance of the streams, pools and water-courses over which they had charge – Salmacis had a reputation for vanity and indolence. She would rather swim lazily around admiring her own limbs in the water than hunt or exercise with the other naiads. But her peace and self-esteem were shattered by the beauty of this Hermaphroditus, and she exerted herself mightily to win him. The more she tried – revolving naked in the water, winningly rubbing her breasts, blowing coy bubbles under the surface – the less comfortable the boy became, until he shouted at her to leave him alone. She departed in a sulky surge, shocked and humiliated by the new and unwelcome experience of rejection.

It was a fine day, though, and Hermaphroditus, hot and sweaty from the excitement of fighting off this tiresome sprite and thinking she was safely out of the way, stripped off his clothing and plunged into the cool waters of the spring to refresh himself.

Almost immediately Salmacis, who had swum back under the cover of the reeds, leapt on him like a salmon and clung fast to his naked body. Revolted he wiggled and wriggled and jiggled to be set free, while she cried up to the heavens, 'O gods above, never let this youth and me part! Let us always be one!'

The gods heard her prayer and answered with the callous literalness that seemed ever to delight them. In an instant Salmacis and Hermaphroditus did indeed become one. The pair fused into a single body. One body, two sexes. No longer the naiad Salmacis and the youth Hermaphroditus, but now intersex, male and female coexisting in one form. Although the Romans were to regard this state of being as a disorder that threatened the strict militaristic norms of their society, the more open-minded Greeks prized, celebrated and even worshipped the hermaphrodite gender. Statuary and representations on pottery and temple friezes show us that what the Romans feared, the Greeks seemed to find admirable.*

In this new state Hermaphroditus joined the retinue of EROTES whose nature and purpose we will describe very soon.

By an unknown nymph, Hermes† also fathered the snub-nosed, donkey-tailed lecher SILENUS, who grew up to become a bearded, pot-bellied, pucker-browed old drunk, a popular subject in paintings, sculptures and carved drinking vessels, and whom we shall also encounter before too long.

As the gods bred, so man bred. But the divine fire that was now as much a part of our nature as the gods meant that we shared with them the capacity not just for lust, copulation and reproduction, but the capacity for *love*.

Love, as the Greeks understood, is complicated.

---

* The great museums of the world have hidden away treasures that represent intersex figures like Hermaphroditus. Many of these have only recently come to light, with exhibitions at the Ashmolean Museum in Oxford and other leading institutions setting a trend for rediscovery of this neglected area. It coincides with a greater, society-wide understanding of the fluidity of gender.

† Or possibly Pan.

CUPID AND PSYCHE

Erotes

The Greeks untangled love's complexity by naming each separate strand and providing divinities to represent them. Aphrodite, the supreme goddess of love and of beauty, was attended by a retinue of winged and naked godlings called Erotes. Like many deities (Hades and his underworld cohorts, for example) the Erotes suddenly found themselves with much to do once humanity established itself and began to flourish. Each of the Erotes had a special kind of amatory passion to promulgate and promote.

ANTEROS – the youthful patron of selfless uncondi-
tional love.*

EROS – the leader of the Erotes, god of physical love
and sexual desire.

HEDYLOGOS – the spirit of the language of love and
terms of endearment, who now, one assumes, looks
over Valentine cards, love-letters and romantic
fiction.

HERMAPHRODITUS – the protector of effeminate
males, mannish females and those of what we
would now call a more fluid gender.

* The well-known aluminium statue by Alfred Gilbert that forms the focus of the Shaftesbury Memorial in Piccadilly Circus, London, is actually not of Eros but of Anteros, deliberately chosen to celebrate the selfless love that demands no return. This was considered an appropriate commemoration of the seventh Earl of Shaftesbury's great philanthropic achievements in hastening the abolition of child labour, reforming lunacy laws, and so on.

HIMEROS – the embodiment of desperate, impetuous love, love that is impatient to be fulfilled and ready to burst.

HYMENAIOS – the guardian of the bridal-chamber and wedding music.

POTHOS – the personification of languorous longing, of love for the absent and the departed.

Of these the most influential and devastating was Eros, in his power and his capacity to sow mischief and discord. There are two stories concerning his origin and identity. In one telling of the birth of the cosmos he was hatched from a great egg laid by Nyx and sprang from it to seed all life in the universe. He could therefore be counted amongst the very first of the primordial spirits that kickstarted the cascade of creation. In a view perhaps more commonly held across the classical world, he was the son of Ares and Aphrodite. Under his Roman name of CUPID he is usually represented as a laughing winged child about to shoot an arrow from his silver bow, a very recognizable image to this day, making Eros perhaps the most instantly identifiable of all the gods of classical antiquity.

Cupidity and erotic desire are associated with him, as is the instant and uncontrollable falling in love that results from being pierced by his dart, the arrow that compels its victims to fall for the first person (or even animal) they see after being struck.* Eros can be as capricious, mischievous, random and cruel as love itself.

---

* Cupid draw back your bow
  And let your arrow go
  Straight to my lover's heart for me, for me . . .
  © Sam Cooke

Love, Love, Love

The Greeks had at least four words for love:

AGAPE – this was the great and generous kind that we would describe as 'charity' and which could refer to any holy kind of love, such as parents for their children or the love of worshippers for their god.*

EROS – the strain of love named after the god, or after whom the god is named. The kind that gets us into most trouble. So much more than affectionate, so much less than spiritual, *eros* and the erotic can lead us to glory and to disgrace, to the highest pitch of happiness and the deepest pit of despair.

PHILIA – the form of love applied to friendship, partiality and fondness. We see its traces in words like 'francophile', 'necrophilia' and 'philanthropy'.

STORGE – the love and loyalty someone might have for their country or their sports team could be regarded as storgic.

Eros himself, while later portrayed by Renaissance and Baroque artists in the manner I have described – a giggling, pert and dimpled cherub (sometimes wearing a blindfold to signify the wayward and arbitrary nature of his marksmanship) – was to the Greeks a fully grown young man of great accomplishment. An artist, an athlete (both sexual and sporting), he was regarded as a patron and protector of gay male love as well as a presiding presence in the gymnasium

---

* The King James Bible renders the conclusion of the thirteenth chapter of St Paul's first letter to the Corinthians (written in Greek of course) as: 'And now abideth faith, hope, charity, these three; but the greatest of these is charity.' In modern translations 'charity' is rendered simply as 'love'.

and on the running track. He was associated with dolphins, cockerels, roses, torches, lyres and, of course, that bow and quiverful of arrows.

Perhaps the best-known myth involving Eros and Psyche – Physical Love and Soul – is almost absurdly ripe for interpretation and explanation. I think, however, that it is best told like all myths, not as an allegory, symbolic fable or metaphor, but as a story. Just a story. It has many of the rhythms and plot turns we associate with later quest narratives and fairy tales,* perhaps because it comes down to us from what many regard as the strongest candidate for First Ever Novel: *The Golden Ass*, by the Roman writer Apuleius.† The story's influence on so much Western thought, folk literature and art – not to mention its charm – justify, I hope, its retelling in long form.

Psyche

Once upon a time, in a land whose name is now lost to us, lived a king and queen and their three beautiful daughters. We will call the king ARISTIDES and the queen DAMARIS. The two eldest girls, CALANTHE and ZONA, were lovely enough to be admired everywhere; but the youngest, whose name was PSYCHE, was so entirely beautiful that many in the kingdom abandoned the cult of Aphrodite and worshipped this young girl in her place. Aphrodite was a jealous and

---

* You might notice strong resemblances to *Beauty and the Beast* and *Cinderella*, for instance.

† Apuleius, who flourished in the second century AD, was from North Africa but wrote in Latin and so used the names Cupid (interchangeably with *Amor*) for Eros, Venus for Aphrodite and *Anima* for Psyche, a translation that conveys the word's sense not just of 'soul' but of 'breath of life' – 'that which animates'. If you were to translate Apuleius literally you would get a very allegorical tale indeed. 'Love said to Soul, you must not look at me', 'Soul fled from Love', etc.

vengeful goddess and could bear no rivalry, least of all from a mortal. She summoned her son Eros.

'I want you to find a pig,' she said to him, 'the ugliest and hairiest in all the land. Go to the palace where Psyche lives, shoot your arrow into her and make sure that the pig is the first thing she sees.'

Used to his mother's charming ways Eros set off on his errand cheerfully enough. He bought an especially bristly and foul-smelling boar from a swineherd who lived not far from the palace and led it that evening to the window of the room where Psyche slept. More clumsily than you might think of a slim athletic god, he tried to clamber through the window with the pig under his arm without making a noise.

A number of things happened very quickly.

Eros landed safely in the moonlit room.

Psyche slumbered peacefully on.

Eros wedged the pig firmly between his legs.

Eros reached behind his shoulder to pluck an arrow from his quiver.

The pig squealed.

A flustered Eros scratched his own arm with the point of his arrow as he drew the bow.

Psyche woke up with a start and lit a candle.

Eros saw Psyche and fell deeply in love with her.

What a business. The god of love himself lovestruck. You might imagine that the next thing he would do is fire an arrow at Psyche and that all would end happily. But here Eros comes out of the story rather well. So real, pure and absolute was his love that he could not think of cheating Psyche out of her own choice. He took one last longing look at her, turned and leapt out of the window and back into the night.

Psyche saw the pig running round in wild, snuffling

circles on her bedroom floor, concluded that she must be dreaming, blew out the candle and went back to sleep.

Prophecy and Abandonment

The next morning King Aristides was alarmed to be told by a servant that his youngest daughter seemed to have turned her bedroom into some kind of piggery. He and Queen Damaris had been worried enough already that, unlike her sisters Calanthe and Zona who had allied themselves to rich landowners, Psyche had stubbornly refused to marry. The news that she was now consorting with pigs made up his mind. He travelled to the oracle of Apollo to find out what the girl's future might be.

After the correct sacrifices and prayers had been offered up, the Sibyl made this answer. 'Garland your child with flowers and carry her to a high place. Lay her on a rock. The one that will come to take her for its bride is the most dangerous being of earth, sky or water. All the gods of Olympus fear its power. So it is ordained, so it must be. Fail in this and the creature will lay waste all your kingdom and discord and despair shall come in its train. You, Aristides, will be called the destroyer of your people's happiness.'

Ten days later a strange procession wound its way out of the town. Carried high on a litter, festooned with flowers and dressed in the purest white, sat a gloomy but resigned Psyche. She had been told of the oracle's pronouncement and had accepted it. Her so-called beauty had always been a source of irritation to her. She hated the fuss and stir it caused, how oddly it made people behave in her presence and how freakish and set apart it made her feel. She had planned never to marry, but if she had to then a rapacious beast would be no worse than a tedious fawning prince with mooncalf eyes. The agony of its attentions would at least be over quickly.

With piteous wails of grief and sorrow the crowd laboured up the mountainside until they came to the great basalt rock on which Psyche was to be laid for sacrifice. Her mother Damaris howled, shrieked and sobbed. King Aristides patted her hand and wished himself elsewhere. Calanthe and Zona, their dull, elderly but rich husbands at their sides, each tried their best to conceal the deep satisfaction they felt at the knowledge that they were soon to be the unchallenged fairest in the land.

As she was bound to the rock Psyche closed her eyes and breathed deeply, waiting for everyone to have done with indulging in their lamentations and shows of grief. Soon all suffering and pain would be over.

Singing hymns to Apollo the crowd wound its way down the hill, leaving Psyche alone on the rock. The sun shone down upon her. Larks called in the blue sky. She had pictured boiling clouds, shrieking winds, lashing rain and dreadful thunder as accompaniments to her violation and death, not this glorious idyll of late-spring sunshine and rippling birdsong.

Who or what could this creature be? If her father had reported the oracle correctly then even the high Olympians feared it. But she had heard of no such terrible monster in all the legends and rumours of legends on which she had been raised. Not even Typhon or Echidna had the power to alarm the mighty gods.

Suddenly a warm breath of wind ruffled her white ceremonial robes. The breath became a gust that pushed a cushion of air between her and the cold basalt on which she lay. To her great surprise Psyche felt herself being lifted up.

The wind seemed to be an almost solid thing – it supported her, holding her fast and carrying her up into the air.

The Enchanted Castle

Psyche was flying high above the ground, safe in the strong but gentle arms of ZEPHYRUS, the West Wind.

'This cannot be the beast we are all meant to fear,' she thought to herself. 'This wind must be the beast's messenger and herald. He is taking me to my doom. Well, at least it's a comfortable way to travel.'

She looked down on the city in which she had grown up. How small and neat and trim everything looked. So unlike the overgrown, ill-smelling and ramshackle township she knew and hated. Zephyrus gained speed and height and soon they were swooping over hills and along valleys, soaring over the blue ocean and flashing past islands, until they were in a country she did not recognize. It was fertile and densely wooded, and as they made a gradual descent she saw, set in a clearing, a magnificent palace, cornered by round towers and crowned with turrets. Gently and easily Psyche was lowered, until she landed with a gliding step on the flowered grass in front of a pair of golden gates. With a fizz and a sigh the wind flew away and she found herself alone. She heard no growls, roars or rapacious snarls, only a distant music floating from the palace's interior. As she made her tentative approach the gates swung open.

The royal palace in which Psyche grew up was – to the ordinary citizen of her country – ornate, opulent and overwhelming, but next to the gorgeous and fantastical edifice she was entering it was nothing but a crude hovel. As she made her way inside her amazed eyes passed over columns of gold, citron-wood and ivory, silver-relief panels carved with an intricacy and artistry she had never dreamed possible and marble statues so perfectly rendered that they seemed to move and breathe. The light glittered in the shimmering gold halls and passageways, the floor she stepped over was a dancing mosaic of jewels and the mysterious music grew louder and louder as she penetrated deeper inside. She passed fountains where crystal waters played in miraculous arcs, shaping and reshaping and quite defying gravity. She became aware of low female voices. Either she was dreaming or this palace was divine. No mortal, and surely no monster, could have ordained so fabulous a habitation.

She had arrived at a square central room whose painted panels showed scenes of the birth of the gods and the war with the Titans. The air was perfumed with sandalwood, roses and warm spices.

Voices, Visions and a Visitor

The whispers and music seemed to come from everywhere and nowhere, but all at once they ceased. In the loud silence left behind, a quiet voice called to her.

'Psyche, Psyche, don't be shy. Don't stare and twitch like a startled faun. Don't you know that all this is yours? All this beauty, all these gemstones, this grand palace and the lands around it – all yours. Go through that doorway and bathe yourself. The voices you hear are your handmaidens, here to do your bidding. When you are ready a great feast will be laid out. Welcome, beloved Psyche, welcome and enjoy.'

The dazed girl made her way into the next room, a vast chamber hung with tapestries and silks, lit by flaming torches in bronze brackets. At one end was a gleaming copper bathtub and in the centre a simply colossal bed whose myrtle-wound frame was of polished cypress and whose linen was strewn with rose petals. Psyche was so tired, so befuddled and so unable to make sense of things that she lay down on the bed and closed her eyes, in the confused hope that sleep might wake her up from this wild dream.

But when she awoke she was still inside the dream. She got up from the soft brocaded cushions and saw that there was steam rising from the bath. She stepped from her clothes into the water.

This is when things became entirely strange.

A silver flask by the side of the bath rose up, danced in the air and tipped its contents into the water. Before she had time to scream out her surprise a glorious cloud of unknown fragrances assailed her senses. Now an ivory-handled brush was scrubbing her back and a ewer of hot water was being emptied over her hair. Invisible hands kneaded, stroked, pummelled, teased and pressed. Psyche giggled like a little girl and allowed it all to happen. Whether this was a dream inside the real world or a moment of reality inside a dream no longer seemed important. She would enjoy the adventure and see where it took her.

Damasks, silks, satins and gossamer tissues flew from concealed closets and glided down onto the bed to shimmer beside her, rustling in anticipation of being chosen. She selected a chiffon gown of lapis blue – loose, comfortable and exciting.

The doors of her chambers opened and with shy uncertain steps she made her way back to the main hall. A great feast was laid out on the table. Unseen hands were moving backwards and forwards with platters of fruit, cups of fermented honey, dishes of exotic roast birds and plates of sweetmeats. Never had Psyche seen or imagined such a banquet. Beside herself with joy she dipped her fingers into dishes of such exquisite deliciousness that she could not help crying out in delight. The swine in the piggeries of her parents' farms did not snuffle and truffle at their wooden troughs with more uninhibited abandon than she did at the magical vessels of crystal, silver and gold that filled and refilled themselves as fast as she could empty them. Napkins flew up to dab her wine-stained lips and food-smeared chin. An invisible choir sang soft ballads and hymns to human love as she gorged and guzzled in ecstasy.

Finally she was done. A feeling of great warmth and well-being stole over her. If she was being fattened up for an ogre then so be it.

The candles on the table now rose up and led Psyche back to the bedchamber. The flickering torches and soft oil lamps had died down and the room was in almost complete darkness. The unseen hands pushed her gently to the bedside and her chiffon gown lifted up and away. Naked she lay back between the satin sheets and closed her eyes.

An instant later she gasped in shock. Someone or something had slipped into bed beside her. She felt her body being gently pulled towards this figure. Sweet warm breath mingled with hers. Her skin met the body, not of a beast, but of a man. He was beardless and – she knew this without being able to see him – beautiful. She could not see even the outline of him, only feel his heat and youthful firmness. He kissed her lips and they entwined.

Next morning the bed was empty and Psyche was bathed once more by the invisible handmaidens. As the long day passed she at last summoned the courage to ask them questions.

'Where am I?'

'Why, you are here, your highness.'

'And where is here?'

'Far from there but close to nearby.'

'Who is the master of this palace.'

'You are the mistress.'

Never a straight answer. She did not press. She knew that she was in an enchanted place and could sense that her hand-maidens were slaves to its rules and requirements.

That night, in pitch darkness, the beautiful young man came to her bed again. She tried to speak to him, but he placed a finger to her lips and a voice sounded inside her head.

'Hush, Psyche. Ask no questions. Love me as I love you.'

And slowly, as the days passed, she realized that she did love this unseen man very much. Every night they made love. Every morning she awoke to find him gone.

The palace was glorious and there was nothing Psyche's handmaidens would not do for her. She had everything she could ever want, the best to eat or drink and music to accompany her everywhere. But what long, lonely days stretched out between the evenings of delicious love, how hard she found it to pass the time.

The 'monster' with whom she slept every night was, you will have guessed, the god Eros whose self-inflicted dart had caused him to fall in love with Psyche, a love now magnified by their repeated nights of mutual bliss. The oracle had been right to say that Eros was a being whose powers frightened all the gods, for there was not one Olympian who had not been conquered by Eros at some time. Perhaps he was a monster after all. But he could be sensitive and sweet as well as capricious and cruel. He saw that Psyche was not entirely happy and one night, as they lay together in the darkness, he quizzed her tenderly.

'What ails you, beloved wife?'

'I hate to say this when you have given me so much, but I get lonely during the day. I miss my sisters.'

'Your sisters?'

'Calanthe and Zona. They believe me to be dead.'

'Only unhappiness can come from consorting with them. Misery and despair for them and for you.'

'But I love them . . .'

'Misery and despair, I tell you.'

Psyche sighed.

'Please believe me,' he said. 'It is for the best that you do not see them.'

'What about you? May I not see you? May I never look into the face of the one I love so well?'

'You must not ask me that. Never ask me that.'

The days passed and Eros saw that Psyche – for all the wine and food, for all the music and magical fountains and enchanted voices – was pining.

'Cheer up, beloved! Tomorrow is our anniversary,' he said.

A year! Had a whole year passed already?

'My present to you is to grant your wish. Tomorrow morning my friend Zephyrus will await you outside the palace and take you where you need to be. But please be careful. Do not allow yourself to become too involved in the lives of your family. And you must promise never to tell them about me. Not one word about me.'

Psyche promised and they fell into each others arms for a night of anniversary love. Never had she felt more passionate adoration or physical delight, and she sensed equal feelings of ardour and love in him too.

The next morning she awoke, as ever, to an empty bed. In a great fever of impatience she allowed herself to be dressed and served breakfast by the handmaidens before running excitedly to the great gate at the front of the palace. She had barely stepped out before Zephyrus swept down and flew her away in his strong, supportive arms.

Sisters

Meanwhile, back in the land of Psyche's birth, the populace had been marking the anniversary of her capture by the fabled unseen monster. King Aristides and Queen Damaris had led the procession of mourning up the hillside to the basalt slab on which their daughter had been bound – since named 'the Rock of Psyche' in her honour. Now there remained at the monument only the two princesses, Calanthe and Zona, who had loudly made it known to all that they wished to stay behind and lament in private.

Once the crowd died away they pulled back their mourning veils and began to laugh.

'Imagine what sort of creature it was that took her away,' said Zona.

'Winged like a Fury . . .' suggested Calanthe.

'With iron claws . . .'

'And fiery breath . . .'

'Great yellow fangs . . .'

'Snakes for hair . . .'

'A great tail that – *What was that?*'

A sudden gust of wind made them turn round. What they saw made them shout in fright.

Their sister Psyche was standing before them, radiant in a shimmering white gown edged with gold. She looked appallingly beautiful.

'But . . .' began Calanthe

'We thought . . .' stammered Zona.

And then both together: '*Sister!*'

Psyche came towards them, her hands held out and the sweetest smile of tender sisterly love lighting up her face. Calanthe and Zona each took a hand to kiss.

'You are alive!'

'And so . . . so . . .'

'This *dress* – it must have cost, that is to say it looks . . .'

'And *you* look . . .' said Zona, 'so . . . so . . . Calanthe, whatever is the word?'

'Happy?' suggested Psyche.

'Something,' her sisters agreed. 'You definitely look something.'

'But tell us, Psyche, dearest . . .'

'What happened to you?'

'Here we are mourning, *sobbing* our hearts out for you.'

'Who gave you that dress?'

'How did you get off the rock?'

'Is it real gold?'

'Did a monster come for you? A beast? An ogre?'

'And that material.'

'A dragon perhaps?'

'How do you keep it from creasing?'

'Did it take you to its den?'

'Who does your hair?'

'Did it try to chew your bones?'

'That can't be a real emerald can it?'

Laughing, Psyche held up a hand. 'Dear sisters! I will tell you everything. Better, I will show you everything. Come, wind, take us there!'

Before the sisters knew what was happening the three of them were lifted from their feet and were travelling swiftly through the air, safe in the arms of the West Wind.

'Don't fight it. Relax into it,' said Psyche as Zephyrus swept them up over the mountain. Zona's howls began to subside and Calanthe's muffled sobs softened to a whimper. Before long they were even able to open their eyes for a few seconds without screaming.

When the wind finally set them down on the grass in front of the enchanted palace Calanthe had decided that this was the only way to travel.

'Who needs a stupid horse pulling a rickety rackety old chariot?' she said. 'From now on I catch the wind . . .'

But Zona wasn't listening. She was staring transfixed at the walls, the turrets and the silver studded door of the palace, all glittering in the morning sun.

'Come in,' said Psyche. What an exciting feeling, to show her dear sisters around her new home. It was a pity they couldn't meet her darling husband.

To say that the girls were impressed would be criminally to understate the matter. Naturally therefore they sniffed, yawned, tittered, shook their heads and generally tut-tutted their way from golden apartment to golden apartment by silver-panelled corridors and jewel-encrusted passageways. Their tilted, wrinkled noses seemed to suggest that they were used to better.

'Just a *little* vulgar, don't we feel, darling?' Zona suggested. Inside she said to herself, 'This is the home of a god!'

Calanthe was thinking, 'If I just stop and pretend to fix the laces of my sandals I could break off one of the rubies encrusting that chair . . .'

When the invisible staff of stewards, footmen and hand-maidens began serving lunch the sisters found it harder to mask their wonder and astonishment. Afterwards they each took turns to be oiled, bathed and massaged.

Pressed for details of the castle's lord, Psyche remembered her promise and hastily made something up.

'He's a handsome huntsman and local landowner.'

'What's his name?'

'The kindest eyes.'

'And his name is . . . ?'

'He's so sorry to miss you. I'm afraid he always takes to the field with his hounds by day. He wanted so much to greet you personally. Perhaps another time.'

'Yes, but what's he called?'

'He – he doesn't really have a name.'

'What?'

'Well, he *has* a name. Obviously he has a name, everyone has a name, Zona, I mean really! But he doesn't use it.'

'But what is it?'

'Oh my goodness, quick! It'll be dark soon. Zephyrus won't fly you at night . . . Come, dear sisters, help yourselves to some little things to take home. Here's a handful of amethysts. These are sapphires. There's gold, silver . . . Be sure to take gifts for mother and father too.'

Loaded with precious treasures the sisters allowed themselves to be transported back to the rock. Psyche, who had stood and waved them off, was both relieved and sorry to see them go. While she welcomed their company and the chance to show them round and give them presents, her determination to keep the promise she had made to her husband had made the evasion of all their questions an exhausting business.

Back home the sisters – despite the fabulous treasures they now possessed – were eaten up with envy, resentment and fury. How could their younger sister, the stupid, selfish Psyche, now find herself in the position more or less of a goddess? It was so appallingly unfair. Spoiled, vain, ugly creature! Well, not ugly, perhaps. Possessed of a certain obvious and rather vulgar prettiness, but scarcely a match for their queenly beauty. It was all too monstrously unjust: there was almost certainly witchcraft and wickedness at the bottom of it. How could she not even know the name of her lord and master?

'My husband Sato's rheumatism,' said Calanthe, 'is getting so bad that every night I have to rub his fingers one by one, then apply plasters and poultices. It's disgusting and demeaning.'

'You think *your* life is hell?' said Zona. 'My Charion is as bald as an onion, his breath stinks and he has all the sex drive of a dead pig. While Psyche . . .'

'That selfish slut . . .'

The sisters clung to each other and sobbed their hearts out.

That night Psyche's lover Eros had momentous news for her. She was pouring out all her gratitude to him, and explaining how well she had managed to avoid describing him to her sisters, when he placed his finger on her lips.

'Sweet, trusting child. I fear those sisters and what they may do to you. But I am glad you are happy. Let me make you happier still.' She felt his warm hand slide down her front and gently stroke her belly. 'Our child is growing there.'

Psyche gasped and hugged him close, stunned with joy.

'If you keep this secret,' he said, 'the child will be a god. If you tell a living soul, it will be mortal.'

'I will keep the secret,' said Psyche. 'But before my condition becomes obvious let me at least see Calanthe and Zona one more time and say goodbye to them.'

Eros was troubled but could not see how he might deny so decent and sisterly a request, and so he assented.

'Zephyrus will send them a sign and they will come,' he said, leaning forward to kiss her. 'But remember, not a word about me or about our baby.'

A Drop of Oil

The next morning Calanthe and Zona awoke to feel the breath of Zephyrus ruffling at them like a hungry pet dog panting and pawing at the bedclothes. When they opened their eyes and sat up the wind departed, but their instinct, greed and inborn cunning told them what the signal meant, and they hurried to the rock to await their transport. This time they were determined to get to the bottom of the mystery of their sister's lover.

Psyche was there to welcome them when they were set down in front of the palace. Embracing her fondly the sisters hid the furious envy they felt at Psyche's good fortune, presenting instead a flurry of solicitous clucking and tutting, accompanied by much head-shaking.

'Whatever is the matter, Calanthe?' a puzzled Psyche asked as she sat them down to a great breakfast of fruit, cakes and honey-wine. 'Why so sorrowful, Zona? Are you not happy to see me?'

'Happy?' groaned Calanthe.

'If only,' Zona sighed.

'What can be worrying you?'

'Ah, child, child,' said Calanthe with a moan. 'You are so young. So sweet. So guileless.'

'So easy to take advantage of.'

'I don't understand.'

The sisters looked at each other as if weighing up whether to reveal harsh truths.

'How well – if at all – do you know this . . . this *thing* that comes nightly to visit you?'

'He's not a thing!' protested Psyche.

'Of course he's a thing. He's the monster foretold by the oracle.'

'Scaly, I'll bet,' said Zona. 'Or, if not scaly, hairy.'

'He's nothing of the sort,' said Psyche indignantly. 'He's young and beautiful and kind. Soft skin, firm muscles –'

'What colour are his eyes?'

175

'Well . . .'

'Is he blond or dark?'

'Darling sisters,' said Psyche, 'can you keep a secret?'

Calanthe and Zona craned in close and pawed their sister lovingly.

'Can we keep a secret? What a question!'

'The thing is,' said Psyche, 'well, the thing is I don't actually know *what* he looks like. I've never seen him, only . . . well . . . felt him.'

'What?' Calanthe was shocked.

'You mean you've never so much as looked upon his face?'

'He insists that I must not see him. He comes to me in the blackest black of night, slips between the sheets and we . . . well, we . . . you know . . .' Psyche blushed. 'But I can trace his outlines and what I feel is not the body of a monster. It is the body of a splendid and marvellous man. Just, in the morning, he's gone.'

'Oh, you silly *goose*!' tittered Zona. 'Don't you know –' She broke off here as if afraid to go on.

The sisters exchanged sorrowful and knowing glances.

'Oh dear . . .'

'Psyche *doesn't* know!'

Calanthe responded with a sound that was something between a titter and a sigh.

Psyche looked from one to the other in perplexity. 'Know what?'

Calanthe put her arms around her and explained, with Zona interposing her own observations and affirmations. The worst and most dreadful monsters – indeed the very kind that Apollo's oracle had predicted would devour her! – possessed powers – always have done, were known for having, were celebrated the world over for having them! – the power, for example, to *transform themselves*, to take on deceitful shapes – forms that might seem thrilling and attractive to the touch of a young girl – but this was only to win the trust of the innocent – the innocent and foolish! – so as one day to plant their demonic seed inside her – poor girl, she doesn't understand these things, but men can do this – and cause her to give birth to a new abomination, an even more terrible monster – a *mutation* – it's how they breed, how they propagate their vile species.

Psyche held up a hand. 'Stop! Please! I know you mean well, but you don't know how tender, how kind, how gentle . . .'

'That's their way! That's exactly their way!'

'Don't you see? If anything proves this monster's ferocious cruelty it's this very tenderness and gentleness!'

'A sure sign that it must be a hideous fiend.'

Psyche thought of the new life growing inside her and of her husband's insistence that she tell no one of it. And of his refusal ever to show himself. Oh dear. Perhaps her sisters were right.

They saw that she was wavering and they pounced.

'Here's what you do, my love. When he comes to you tonight you allow him to have his beastly way with you –'

'Ugh!'

'– and then let him fall asleep. But you must stay awake.'

'On all accounts, *stay awake*.'

'When you're satisfied that he's absolutely fast asleep you must rise and fetch a lamp.'

'And that razor that your handmaidens use to cut your hair.'

'Yes, you'll need that!'

'Light the lantern in the corner of the room and cover it so as not to wake him.'

'Then steal over to the bed . . .'

'Lift your lantern . . .'

'And slice his scaly dragon's neck . . .'

'Saw away at his knotty veins . . .'

'Kill him . . .'

'Kill the beast . . .'

'Then gather up all the gold and silver . . .'

'And the gemstones, that's most important . . .'

On and on the sisters talked until Psyche was fully persuaded.

And so that night it came about that, with Eros sleeping peacefully in the bed, Psyche found herself standing over him, a hooded lantern in one hand and a razor in the other. She raised the blinds from the lamp. Light fell on the curled-up naked form of the most beautiful being she had ever beheld. The warm glow danced on smooth, youthful skin – and on the most wonderful pair of feathered wings.

Psyche could not hold back a gasp of amazement. She knew at once whom she was looking at. This was no dragon or monster, no ogre or abomination. This was the young god of love. This was Eros himself. To think that she could have dreamed of harming him. How beautiful he was. His full, rosy lips were slightly parted and the sweetness of his breath came up to her as she leaned down to gaze more deeply. Everything about him was so perfect! The gentle heave and swell of muscles gave his youthful beauty a manly cast, but without that hard, bulging ungainliness she had seen on the bodies of her father's champion athletes and warriors. His tousled hair gleamed with a warm colour that lay between the gold of Apollo and the mahogany of Hermes. And those wings! Folded beneath his body they had the fullness and whiteness of a swan's. She reached out a trembling hand and ran her finger down the line of feathers. The soft fluttering whisper they returned hardly made a sound, yet it was enough to cause the sleeping Eros to shift and murmur.

Psyche pulled back and shaded the lantern, but within a

few moments an even rhythmic breathing reassured her that Eros was still deeply asleep. She unmasked the lantern again and saw that he was now turned away from her. She saw too that his movement had caused a curious object to be brought into view. The lamplight fell on a silver cylinder that lay beneath his wings. His quiver!

Hardly daring to breath Psyche leaned forward and pulled out a single arrow. Turning it in her hand she slowly fingered its shaft of shining ebony. The arrowhead itself was affixed by a band of gold . . . Holding the lantern high in her left hand she ran her right thumb along the head and then – *ouch!* So sharp was the tip that it drew blood. The moment it did a feeling washed over her, a feeling of such intense love for the sleeping Eros, such heat, passion and desire, such complete and eternal devotion, that she could not refrain from moving to kiss the curls on the nape of his neck.

Alas! As she did so, hot oil from the lantern dripped onto his right shoulder. He awoke with a yelp of pain which, when he saw Psyche standing over him, grew into a great roar of disappointment and despair. His wings opened and began to beat the air. As he rose Psyche launched herself forward and clung to his right leg, but his strength was too great and he shook her off without a word and flew away into the night.

The moment he left, everything fell apart. The walls of the palace rippled, faded and dissolved into the night air. A despairing Psyche watched the gold columns around her shiver into a dark colonnade of trees and the jewelled mosaic tiles beneath her feet churn into a mess of mud and gravel. Before long, palace, precious metals, precious stones – all had vanished. The sweet singing of the handmaidens turned into the howling of wolves and the screeching of owls, and the warm, mysterious perfumes whipped into chill and unrelenting winds.

Alone

A frightened, unhappy girl stood in a cold and desolate wood. She slipped down the trunk of a tree until she sat on the hard roots. The only thought in her mind was to end her life.

She was awoken by a beetle scuttling over her lips. She sat up with a shiver and unpeeled a damp leaf from her brow. She had not dreamed the horrors of the night before. She really was alone in a wood. Perhaps everything before was a dream and this had always been the reality? Or she had awoken inside another episode of a wider dream? It was hardly worth the bother of trying to puzzle it all out. Dream or reality, everything was intolerable to her.

'Don't do it, pretty girl.'

Shocked, Psyche looked up to see the god Pan standing before her. The humorous frown, the thick curling hair from which two horns sprouted, the wide hairy flanks tapering down to goats' feet – it could be no other figure, mortal or immortal.

'No, no,' said Pan, stamping the muddy ground with his hoofs. 'I can read it in your face and it is not to be. I won't allow it.'

'You won't allow what?' said Psyche.

'I won't allow you to dash yourself onto the rocks from off a high cliff. I won't allow you to court the deadly attentions of a wild animal. I won't allow you to pick belladonna and drink its poisonous juices. I won't allow any of that.'

'But I can't live!' cried Psyche. 'If you knew my story you would understand and you would help me die.'

'You should ask yourself what brought you here,' said Pan. 'If it's love, then you must pray to Aphrodite and Eros for guidance and relief. If your own wickedness caused your downfall then you must live to repent. If it was caused by others then you must live to revenge.'

Revenge! Psyche suddenly understood what needed to be done. She rose to her feet. 'Thank you, Pan,' she said. 'You've shown me the way.'

Pan bared his teeth in a grin and bowed. His lips blew a flourish of farewell across the top of the set of pipes in his hand.

Four days later Psyche knocked on the gates of the grand mansion of her brother-in-law Sato, the husband of Calanthe. A servant ushered her into her sister's receiving room.

'Psyche! Darling! Did all go as planned? You look a little –'

'Never mind me, dear sister. I will tell you what happened. I followed your instructions to the letter, shone a lamp over the sleeping form of my husband and who should he be but the great god Eros. Eros himself!'

'Eros!' Calanthe clutched at her amber necklace.

'Oh sister, imagine my heartbreak and disappointment when he told me that he had only taken me to his palace as a means of securing *you*.'

'Me?'

'That was his dark plan. "Fetch me your beautiful sister Calanthe," he said to me. "She of the green eyes and russet hair."'

'More auburn than russet –'

'"Fetch her. Tell her to go to the high rock. Launch herself onto Zephyrus, who will pick her up and bring her to me. Tell the beautiful Calanthe all this, Psyche, I beg." This is his message which I have faithfully relayed.'

You can imagine with what speed Calanthe prepared herself. She left a scrawled message for her husband explaining that they were not husband and wife after all, that their marriage had been a calamitous mistake, that the officiant who wed them had been drunk, incapable and unqualified, that she had never loved him anyway and that she was now a free woman, so there.

At the high basalt rock she heard the rustle of a breeze and, with a moan of ecstatic joy, launched herself onto what she thought was Zephyrus.

But the spirit of the West Wind was nowhere near. With a scream of frustration, rage, disappointment and fear, Calanthe tumbled down the hillside, bouncing from sharp rock to sharp rock until her whole body was turned inside out and she landed at the bottom as dead as a stone.

The identical fate befell her sister Zona, to whom Psyche told the same story.

The Tasks of Aphrodite

With her revenge meted out, Psyche had the rest of her life to consider. Every waking moment was filled with the love and longing she felt for Eros and with the pangs of misery that stabbed her, knowing she was doomed never to see him again.

Eros, meanwhile, lay in a secret chamber, racked by the agony of the wound on his shoulder. You and I could endure with ease the slight nuisance of a lamp-oil burn, but for Eros, immortal though he was, this was a hurt inflicted by the one he loved. Such wounds take a very long time to heal, if indeed they ever do.

With Eros indisposed the world began to suffer. Youths and maidens stopped falling in love. There were no marriages. The people began to murmur and grumble. Unhappy prayers were raised to Aphrodite. When she heard them, and learned that Eros was hiding away and neglecting his duties, she became vexed. The news that a mortal girl had stolen her son's heart and caused him such harm turned her vexation to anger. But when she discovered that it was the very same mortal girl that she had once commanded Eros to humiliate, she grew livid. How could her plan to make Psyche fall in love with a pig have backfired so terribly? Well, this time she would personally and conclusively ensure the girl's downfall.

Through enchantments that she did not know were being worked upon her, Psyche found herself knocking one day on a great palace door. Terrible creatures pulled her in by the hair and cast her into a dungeon. Aphrodite herself visited her, bringing sacks of wheat, barley, millet, poppyseed, chickpeas, lentils and beans, which she emptied onto the stone floor and stirred together.

'If you want your freedom,' she said, 'separate out all the different grains and seeds and sort them into their own heaps. Finish this task before next sunrise and I will free you.'

With a laugh that – unbecomingly for a goddess of love and beauty – fell somewhere between a cackle and a screech, Aphrodite left, slamming the cell door behind her.

Psyche fell sobbing to the floor. It would be impossible to separate those seeds, even if she had a month to do it.

Just then an ant, making its away across the flagstones, was engulfed by a hot, salt tear falling from Psyche's cheek.

'Watch out!' he cried angrily. 'It may be a little tear to you, but it's a deluge to me.'

'I'm so sorry,' said Psyche. 'I'm afraid I didn't see you. My misery got the better of me.'

'What misery can be so great that it causes you to go about half drowning honest ants?'

Psyche explained her plight and the ant, who was of an obliging and forgiving nature, offered to help. With a cry inaudible to human ears he summoned his great family of brother and sisters, and together they set about sorting the seeds.

With the tears drying on her cheeks Psyche watched in amazement as ten thousand cheerful ants shuttled and scuttled back and forth, sifting and separating the seeds with military precision. Well before rosy-fingered Eos had cast open the gates of dawn, the job was done and seven neat and perfect piles awaited Aphrodite's inspection.

The frustrated fury of the goddess was something to behold. Another impossible chore was instantly devised.

'You see the grove yonder, on the other side of the river?' said Aphrodite, yanking Psyche by the hair and forcing her to look out of the window. 'There are sheep there, grazing and wandering unguarded. Special sheep with fleeces of gold. Go there at once and bring me back a tuft of their wool.'

Psyche made her way out to the grove willingly enough, but with no intention of carrying out this second task. She resolved to use her freedom to escape not just the prison of Aphrodite's hateful curse but the prison of hateful life itself. She would throw herself into the river and drown.

But as she stood on the bank, breathing hard and summoning up the courage to dive in, one of the reeds nodded – although there wasn't a breath of breeze – and whispered to her.

'Psyche, sweet Psyche. Harrowed by great trials as you are, do not pollute my clean waters with your death. There is a way through your troubles. The sheep here are wild and violent, guarded by the most ferocious ram, whose horns could tear you open like a ripe fruit. You see them grazing there under that plane tree on the further bank? To approach them now would mean a swift and painful death. But if you lie down to sleep, by evening they will have moved to new pastures and you will be able to swim across to the tree where you will find tangles of golden wool clinging to its lower branches.'

That night an enraged and baffled Aphrodite cast the golden wool aside and insisted that Psyche descend to the underworld to beg a sample of beauty cream from Persephone. Since she had thought of little else but death since Eros had left her, the poor girl consented willingly and followed Aphrodite's directions to Hades, where she fully intended to stay and see out a miserable, lonely and loveless eternity.

The Union of Love and Soul

One day a garrulous swallow told Eros about the tasks which Psyche had been set by his jealous and intemperate mother. Trying to ignore the still agonizing pain of his wound, he rose up and with a mighty effort opened his wings. He flew straight to Olympus, where he demanded an immediate audience with Zeus.

Eros told his story to an enraptured audience of fascinated Olympians. His mother had always hated Psyche. Aphrodite's dignity and honour as an Olympian had been threatened by the girl's beauty and the willingness of a handful of foolish humans to venerate the mortal maiden ahead of the immortal goddess. And so she had sent Eros to cause Psyche to fall in love with a pig. He put his case well.

Zeus sent Hermes down to the underworld to fetch Psyche and an eagle to summon Aphrodite. When they were present before the heavenly company, Zeus spoke.

'This has been an extraordinary and undignified

entanglement. Aphrodite, beloved one. Your position is not threatened; it never can be. Look down at the earth and see how your name is everywhere sanctified and praised. Eros, you have too long been a foolish, impudent and irresponsible boy. That you love and are loved will be the making of you and may save the world from the worst excesses of your mischievous and misdirected arrows. Psyche, come and drink from my cup. This is ambrosia, and now that you have tasted it you are immortal. Here, witnessed by us all, you will for ever be yoked with Eros. Embrace your daughter-in-law, Aphrodite, and let us all be merry.'

All was laughter and delight at the wedding of Eros and Psyche. Apollo sang and played on his lyre, Pan joined in with his syrinx. Hera danced with Zeus, Aphrodite danced with Ares and Eros danced with Psyche. And they dance together still to this very day.*

---

* In due time Psyche gave birth to their child: a daughter, HEDONE, who was to be the spirit of pleasure and sensual delight. The Romans called her VOLUPTAS. Hedonism and voluptuousness, unsurprisingly, are hers.

THE TOYS OF ZEUS

PART TWO

MORTALS

Io

The humans of the Mediterranean world at this time were mostly ruled over by kings. How these autocrats established dominion over their peoples varied. Some were descended from immortals, gods even. Others, as is the human way, seized power through force of arms or political intrigue.

INACHUS was one of the very earliest rulers in Greece. He was the first King of Argos in the Peloponnese peninsula, then a bustling new town and now one of the oldest continuously inhabited cities in the world. Inachus was later semi-deified and turned into a river, but during his life as a human his consort MELIA bore him two daughters, IO and MYCENE.*

Mycene was satisfactorily married off to a nobleman called ARESTOR, but Io's fate was to be the first mortal girl to attract the predatory attentions of Zeus. Inachus had chosen Hera, the Queen of Heaven, as the patron deity of Argos and his daughter Io had been brought up as a priestess in the most important shrine to Hera in the Grecian world. For Zeus to dally with any female would be enough to cause his wife indignation, but any attempt to defile one of her own priestesses would stretch her anger to its limits. Yet he desired the lovely Io very much. How to have her without Hera finding out.

Zeus stroked his beard, thought hard and came up with what he believed was a masterstroke. He transformed Io into

---

* She gave her name to the city of Mycenae.

a cow, a beautiful plump young heifer with shivering flanks and large, gentle eyes.* If he hid her in a field Hera would never spot her and he could visit her whenever he liked. Or so he imagined. When lust descends, discretion, common sense and wisdom fly off and what may seem cunning concealment to one in the grip of passion looks like transparently clumsy idiocy to everyone else.

It is easier to hide a hundred mountains from a jealous wife than one mistress. Hera, to whom cows were sacred, and who possessed therefore a keen, expert eye for the species, noticed the animal and suspected its true identity straight away.

'What a delightful heifer,' Hera remarked casually to Zeus at breakfast on Olympus one morning. 'Such a perfect shape. Such long lashes and appealing eyes.'

'What, that old thing?' said Zeus, looking down with a feigned air of boredom to where Hera was pointing.

'That's one of your fields, darling, so she must be one of yours.'

'Possibly,' said Zeus, 'very possibly. One has thousands of cows browsing around. Can't be expected to keep tabs on all of them.'

'I should very much like that particular heifer,' said Hera, 'as a birthday present.'

'Er . . . really? That one? I'm sure I could find you a much fatter and fitter animal.'

'No,' said Hera – and those who knew her would have recognized the glint in her eye and the steel in her voice. 'That is the one I should like.'

'Certainly, certainly,' said Zeus affecting a yawn. 'She's yours. There's a jar of ambrosia at your elbow . . . chuck it down my end, would you?'

---

* A heifer is to a cow as a filly is to a mare.

Hera knew her husband all too well. Once his libidinous propensities were aroused there would be no taming them. She had Io moved to a small gated paddock and sent her servant ARGUS, Inachus's grandson, to watch over her.

Argus, son of Mycene and Arestor, was a loyal follower of Hera's like all the Argives at that time,* but he also possessed a very special gift which made him a perfect guardian of his aunt Io. He had a hundred eyes. His nickname was PANOPTES, the 'all-seeing'.† Obedient as ever to Hera's will, he stationed himself in the field, fixed fifty eyes on Io and let the other fifty range independently around and up and down, on the lookout for marauders.

Zeus saw this and paced about in a fury. His blood was up. He crashed his fist into his palm. He would have Io. It had become a matter of principle to defeat Hera in this silent and unacknowledged war. He knew the limits of his own cunning, however, so he called upon the wiliest and most amoral rogue on Olympus to aid him.

Hermes understood right away what needed to be done. Ever happy to oblige Zeus and sow mischief he hurried to Io's paddock.

'Hello, Argus. Let me keep you company for a while,' he said, unlatching the gate and slipping in. 'Nice heifer you've got there.'

Argus swivelled a dozen eyes towards Hermes, who sat down on the grass, took out a set of pipes and started to play. For two hours he played and he sang. The music, the

---

* 'Argive' meant 'citizen of Argos', but in later times was often used to mean any Greek – especially as distinct from a Trojan.

† There are those who like to suggest that the idea of Argus having a hundred eyes arose from a fanciful way of expressing his extreme watchfulness. It might just as well have been playfully said and then seriously believed, they maintain, that he had eyes in the back of his head. We repudiate such dull, unromantic propositions with the contempt they deserve. Argus had a hundred eyes. Fact.

afternoon heat, the scent of poppies, lavender and wild thyme, the soft lapping and purling of a nearby stream – slowly Argus's eyes started to close, one by one.

As the very hundredth eye at last winked shut Hermes lowered his pipes, stole forward and stabbed Argus in the heart. All the gods were capable of great cruelty – Hermes could be as vicious as any of them.

With Argus dead, Zeus opened the gate into the field and set Io free. But before he had a chance to change her back into human form Hera, who had seen what had happened, sent down a gadfly which stung Io so painfully and persistently that she bucked and screamed and galloped away, far from Zeus's reach.

Sorrowing at the death of her beloved servant, Hera took Argus's hundred bright eyes and fixed them onto the tail of a very dull, dowdy old fowl, transforming it into what we know today as the peacock – which is how the now proud, colourful and haughty bird came for ever to be associated with the goddess.*

Io, meanwhile, charged on along the northern shore of the Aegean Sea, swimming over at the place where Europe becomes Asia, the spot we still call in her honour the cow-crossing, or in Greek, the Bosporus.† On and on she careered, thrashing, tossing and squealing in her agony until she reached the Caucasus. There the gadfly seemed to relent for a while, enough for her to see the figure of Prometheus, racked in pain upon the mountainside.

'Sit down and catch your breath awhile, Io,' said the Titan. 'Be of good cheer. Things will get better.'

'They could hardly be worse,' wailed Io. 'I'm a cow. I'm being attacked by the largest and most spiteful gadfly the

* Painters and sculptors often depicted Hera on a chariot drawn by peacocks, and there is, of course, the Sean O'Casey play *Juno and the Paycock*.
† Strange that 'Oxford' and 'Bosporus' mean exactly the same thing.

world has ever seen. And Hera will destroy me. It's only a question of whether I am stung to death or go mad and drown myself in the sea.'

'I know it seems dark for you now,' said Prometheus, 'but I see into the future sometimes and I do know this. You will return to human shape. You will found a great dynasty in the land where Nilus crawls. And from your line will spring the greatest of all the heroes.* So chin up and be cheerful, eh?'

It was hard for Io, in all her tribulation, to ignore these words from one who – even as she looked on in horror – was being ripped open and gorged upon by a pair of evil-looking vultures. What were her minor inconveniences when set against his perpetual agony?

As things turned out, Io did return to human shape. She met up with Zeus in Egypt and bore him a son EPAPHUS, who will play an important part of the story of Phaeton, which is just coming up. *Supposedly* Zeus impregnated Io just by gently laying a hand on her – Epaphus means 'touch'. Io also had a daughter by Zeus, called KEROESSA, whose son BYZAS went on to found the great city of Byzantium. Whether Keroessa was conceived by touch or the more traditional method of generation we do not know.

Io may have been a cow, but she was a very influential and important one.

The Semen-Soaked Scarf

A rather touching story tells of how Athena, without sacrificing her chastity, had a role in the conception and birth of one of the founders of the city state of Athens.

---

* The very hero who would one day unchain Prometheus and set him free.

Lame Hephaestus, ever since splitting Zeus's head and thereby helping bring Athena into the world, had developed a strong passion for the goddess. One day, unable to control his lust, he tracked her down to some corner of high Olympus and tried to force himself on her. Alas, in his excitement he succeeded only in spilling his seed on her thigh. Athena, in silent disgust, removed her headband and used it to wipe up the mess before throwing it down the mountain.

The sodden fillet landed on the ground far below. Hephaestus's divine semen seeped into the earth and Gaia was made pregnant. From her was born a boy, ERECHTHEUS. Looking down from heaven Athena saw this and determined that this child should be immortal. She descended from Olympus, put the baby in a wicker basket, closed it up and placed it in the care of three mortal sisters, HERSE, AGLAUROS and PANDROSOS. On no account, Athena told them, must the basket ever be opened. But Aglauros and Herse could not resist peeping inside. They saw a wriggling baby boy bound up in the coils of a writhing snake. All snakes were sacred to Athena and this one was a part of the enchantment which the goddess was using to endow the infant Erechtheus with immortality. The shocking sight sent the two women instantly insane and they threw themselves off the topmost point of the hill now called the Acropolis, or 'high citadel'. Erechtheus grew up to be (or to father, the stories disagree) ERECHTHONIUS, the legendary founder of Athens.*

If you visit the Acropolis in Athens today you can still see, just to the north of the Parthenon, the beautiful temple called the Erechtheum. Its famous porch of caryatid

---

* The name 'Erechthonius' is sometimes used of both Erechtheus and various of his descendants. His chthonic birth out of Gaia can be seen in both names.

columns in the form of draped maidens is one of the great architectural treasures of the world. Shrines were erected not far away to poor Aglauros and Herse too, which is only fitting.*

---

* As for Pandrosos, the obedient sister who resisted looking into the basket, a temple was raised to her near that of Minerva, and a festival instituted in her honour called *Pandrosia*.

PHAETON

The Son of the Sun

Erechtheus had Athena as a proxy parent, Gaia as a mother and Hephaestus as a father. Three immortal parents could be regarded as overdoing it (and as boastfulness about their founder on the part of Athenians), but it was not uncommon for mortals to claim one such progenitor. The story of the brave but foolhardy PHAETON,* like the myth of Persephone, explains how certain changes to the geography of the world came about, as well as offering a very literal example of a favourite finger-wagging lesson of Greek myth – how pride comes before a fall.

Phaeton had divine parentage, but was brought up by his stepfather MEROPS, a disappointingly mortal man. Whenever Merops was away Phaeton's mother CLYMENE, who may or may not have been immortal,† would delight the boy

---

* Phaeton (like Apollo's alternative name 'Phoebus') means 'shining one'. Sometimes rendered as *Phaethon*, *Phaëton* or *Phathon*, it is usually pronounced to rhyme with 'Satan' or 'Nathan', though you can, if you prefer, rhyme it with 'Titan' or 'Python'.

† A daughter of Oceanus and Tethys, the Oceanid Clymene might be regarded as one of the most influential mothers in all Greek myth. From her couplings with the Titan Iapetus she was, on the one side, the mother of Atlas and Menoetius (two of the Titans who furiously opposed the gods during the Titanomachy and were duly punished) and, on the other, of Epimetheus and Prometheus. These offspring alone establish Clymene's importance as a great matriarch of the early world. Some, though, say that the Oceanid Clymene and the Clymene who was Phaeton's mother were not the same woman at all, and that actually the mother of Atlas and the other Titans should be called ASIA, so as not to muddle her with the mortal Clymene, mother of Phaeton. It all gets very confusing and is best left to academics and those with time on their hands.

with stories of his divine father, the glorious sun god Phoebus Apollo.*

When Phaeton was old enough he went to school alongside other mortal boys, some of whom were fully human and
others of whom, like him, could claim divine ancestry on
one side or another. One such was Epaphus, the son of Zeus
and Io. With such illustrious parents Epaphus felt entitled to
lord it over his schoolmates. Phaeton, who was a proud and
passionate youth, hated being bossed around by Epaphus
and was constantly irritated by the other's arrogance and air
of superiority.

Epaphus was always so maddeningly blasé about his
pedigree. He would say things like: 'Yes, next weekend dad –
Zeus, don't you know – is inviting me up to Olympus for
supper. He said he might let me sit on his throne, maybe
take a sip or two of nectar. Had it before, of course. There'll
just be a few of us. Uncle Ares, my half-sister Athena, a few
nymphs perhaps to round up the numbers. Should be a
laugh.'

Phaeton would always return home in a fury after enduring this oh-so-casual name-dropping. 'How come,' he would
complain to his mother, 'Epaphus gets to see his father every
weekend when I have never even *met* mine?'

Clymene would hug her son tightly and try to explain.
'Apollo is so busy, darling. Every day he has to drive his chariot of the sun across the sky. And when that duty is done he
has shrines at Delos and Delphi and goodness knows where
else to attend. Prophecies, music, archery . . . he is quite the
busiest of all the gods. But I'm sure he'll come and visit us
soon. When you were born he left this for you – I was going

* Even the nature of Phaeton's father is debated. In some versions of the story his father is the
sun Titan, Helios. I shall go along with Ovid and attribute the fatherhood of Phaeton to the
god Apollo.

to wait to give it to you when you were a little older, but you might as well have it now . . .'

Clymene went to a cupboard and took out an exquisite golden flute which she handed to him. The boy at once brought it to his mouth and blew, producing a breathy and far from musical hiss.

'What is it supposed to do?'

'Do? What do you mean, darling?'

'Zeus gave Epaphus a magic leather whip which makes dogs obey his every command. What does this do?'

'It's a flute, my love. It makes music. Beautiful, charming music.'

'How?'

'Well, you learn how to shape the notes and then you . . . well, you play it.'

'Where's the magic in that?'

'Have you never heard flute music? It's the most magical sound there is. It does take rather a lot of practice though.'

Phaeton threw the instrument down in disgust and stormed off to his bedroom, where he sulked for the rest of the day and night.

A week or so later, on the last day of term before the long summer holidays, he found himself being approached by the exasperatingly condescending Epaphus.

'Hi there, Phaeton,' he drawled. 'Wondered if you wanted to join me at the family villa on the North African coast next week? Small enough house party. Just dad, maybe Hermes, Demeter and a few fauns. We sail tomorrow. Could be a laugh. What do you say?'

'Oh, what a shame,' cried Phaeton. 'My father, Phoebus Apollo you know, has invited me to . . . to drive the sun-chariot across the sky next week. Can't let him down.'

'Excuse me?'

'Yes, didn't I mention it? He's always going on at me to help take the load off his shoulders, do a bit of the old sun-driving for him.'

'You're seriously telling me . . . *Bullshit*. Guys, you've got to come and listen to this!' Epaphus called the other boys over to where he and Phaeton stood facing each other. 'Tell them,' he demanded.

Phaeton was caught in the lie now. Pride, fury and frustration drove him on. He was damned if he was going to back down and let this insufferable snob win the day.

'It's really nothing,' he said. 'Just that my dad Apollo is insisting I learn to drive the horses of the sun. No big deal.'

The other boys, led by a sneering Epaphus, hooted their disbelief and derision. 'We all know your father is that boring old fool Merops!' one of them shouted.

'He's just my stepfather!' cried Phaeton. 'Apollo is my real father. He is! You'll see. Just you wait and see. It'll take me a while to get to his palace, but one day soon – look up at the sky. I'll wave down at you. That'll be me driving the day along. You'll see!'

And off he ran home, jeers, catcalls and the mocking laughter of his schoolfellows ringing in his ears. One of the boys, his friend and lover CYGNUS,* chased after him.

'Oh Phaeton,' cried Cygnus, 'what have you said? It can't be true. You've complained to me so many times that you've never even met your real father. Go back and tell them you were joking.'

'Leave me alone, Cygnus,' said Phaeton, pushing him away. 'I'm going to the Palace of the Sun. It's the only way to silence that pig Epaphus. By the time you see me again everyone will respect me at last and know me for who I really am.'

---

* Or Cycnus.

'But I know who you are,' said the unhappy Cygnus. 'You are Phaeton and I love you.'

Father and Sun

Nor was there anything Clymene could say to make Phaeton change his mind either. She watched in an agony of distress as he gathered up his few belongings.

'Look up and you'll see me,' he said, kissing her farewell. 'I'll wave as I ride by.'

The Palace of the Sun lay, of course, due east; in fact as far east as India. How Phaeton got there isn't agreed upon. I've read that magical sun hawks told Apollo of the boy's slow struggle from mainland Greece across Mesopotamia and the land we would now call Iran, and that the god instructed these splendid birds to bear him up and fly him the rest of the way.

However Phaeton got there, he arrived at night and immediately was summoned to the throne room of the palace, where Apollo sat robed in purple in the glimmer that gleamed from the gold, silver and jewels which decorated the chamber. The throne he sat on, that alone was studded with more than ten thousand rubies and emeralds. The youth fell to his knees, quite overpowered by the magnificence of the palace, the dazzle of the gemstones and above all by the radiant glory of his father the god.

'So, you are Clymene's boy, are you? Stand up, let's have a look at you. Yes, I can see that you might be the fruit of my loins. You have the cast of countenance, the colouring. I'm told you travelled a long way to be here. Why?'

The question was blunt and Phaeton found himself a little flustered. He managed to stammer out some words about Epaphus and 'the other boys' and was painfully aware that he sounded more like a spoiled child than the proud son of an Olympian.

'Yes, yes. Very mean, very disrespectful. And where do I come in?'

'All my life,' said Phaeton, burning with the pride and resentment that had smouldered inside him for so very long, 'all my life my mother has told me about great and glorious Apollo, the golden god, my shining perfect father. B-b-but you've never visited us! You've never invited us anywhere. You've never even acknowledged me.'

'Well, yes, I'm sorry about that. Remiss of me. I've been a terrible father, I wish I could make it up to you.' Apollo mouthed the words that absent fathers mouth everywhere and every day, but his mind was really on horses, music, drink . . . anything but this tedious, sulky and complaining child.

'If you could just grant me one wish. One wish, that's all.'

'Of course, of course. Name it.'

'Really? You mean it?'

'Of course.'

'You *swear* you'll grant it?'

'I swear,' said Apollo, amused by the boy's extreme earnestness. 'I swear by my lyre. I swear by the cold flowing waters of Styx herself. Name it, I say.'

'I want to drive your horses.'

'My horses?' said Apollo, not quite understanding. 'Drive them? What do you mean?'

'I want to steer the sun-chariot across the sky. Tomorrow.'

'Oh no,' said Apollo, a smile spreading across his face. 'No, no, no! Don't be silly. No one can do that.'

'You promised!'

'Phaeton, Phaeton. It's brave and splendid even to dream of doing such a thing. But no one, *no one* drives those animals but me.'

'You swore by Styx!'

'Zeus himself couldn't control them! They are the strongest, wildest, most headstrong and unmanageable stallions ever born. They answer to my touch and mine alone. No, no. You can't ask such a thing.'

'I *have* asked it. And you have *sworn*!'

'Phaeton!' The other eleven gods would have been astonished to hear such a pleading, desperate note in Apollo's voice. 'I *beg* of you! Anything else. Gold, food, power, knowledge, love . . . You name it, it's yours in perpetuity. But not this. Never this.'

'I have asked and you have sworn,' the stubborn youth replied.

Apollo bowed his golden head and cursed inwardly.

Oh, those gods and their quick tongues. Oh, those mortals and their foolish dreams. Will either ever learn?

'Right. Let's go and meet them then. But know this,' Apollo said as they neared the stables and the horsey smell grew stronger and sharper in Phaeton's nostrils. 'You can change your mind at any time. I won't think any the less of you. Frankly, I'll think a great deal the more of you.'

At the god's approach the four stallions, white with golden manes, stamped and shifted in their stalls.

'Hey, Pyrois! Whoa there, Phlegon! Hush now, Aeos! Quietly, Aethon!' Apollo called to each in turn. 'Alright, come forward, boy, let them get to know you.'

Phaeton had never seen such beautiful horses. Their eyes flashed gold and their hoofs struck sparks on the flagstones. He was filled with awe, but felt too a sudden stab of fear which he tried to play off as thrilled anticipation.

Lined up before the massive gates of dawn was a golden *quadriga*, the great chariot to which the four stallions would soon be harnessed. A quiet female figure in saffron robes hurried past. Phaeton caught from her a fragrance which he could not name but which made him dizzy with delight.

'That was Eos,' said Apollo. 'It will soon be time for her to open the gates.'

Phaeton knew all about Eos, the goddess of the dawn. She was called *rhododaktylos* – the 'rosy-fingered one' – and admired everywhere for her sweetness and soft beauty.

As he helped his father walk the stallions forward and into position at the head of the chariot, Phaeton suddenly felt himself pushed roughly aside.

'What is this mortal doing?'

A huge figure dressed in shining buff leather armour had taken the bridle of all four horses at once and was leading them forward.

'Ah, Helios, there you are,' said Apollo. 'This is Phaeton. My son Phaeton.'

'So?'

Phaeton knew that Helios was the brother of Eos and the moon goddess Selene and assisted Apollo in his daily duties with the chariot. Apollo seemed slightly awkward in the Titan's presence.

'Well, the thing is, Phaeton will be driving the chariot today.'

'Excuse me?'

'Well, he might as well learn now, don't you think?'

'You *are* joking?'

'I sort of promised.'

'Well, sort of *unpromise* then.'

'Helios, I can't. You know I can't.'

Helios stamped his feet and gave a roar that caused the horses to rear and whinny. 'You've never once let *me* drive, Apollo! Never. How many times have I asked and how many times have you told me I'm not ready? And now you let this . . . this shrimp take the reins?'

'Helios, you will do as you're told,' said Apollo. 'I have spoken and so I have . . . er, spoken.'

Apollo took the four leather traces from Helios and lifted Phaeton up and into the seat of the chariot. Helios gave a shout of laughter as he saw the youth slide back and forth.

'He rolls in it like a little pea!' he said with a surprisingly high-pitched giggle.

'He'll be fine. Now, Phaeton. These reins – they are your lines of communication with the horses. They know the way, they run this course every day, but you must show them that you are their master, you understand?'

Phaeton nodded eagerly.

Something of his nervous excitement and Helios's fury seemed to have been picked up by the horses, who bucked and snorted restlessly.

'The most important thing,' continued Apollo, 'is to fly neither too high nor too low. A middle course between the sky and the earth, yes?'

Again Phaeton nodded.

'Oh, I nearly forgot. Hold out your hands . . .' Apollo took a jar and poured oil from it into Phaeton's outstretched palms. 'Anoint yourself with that all over. It will protect you from the heat and light generated by the stallions as they gallop through the air. The earth below will be warmed and lit as you go, so keep a straight line westwards towards the Garden of the Hesperides. It's a twelve-hour drive. Be steady. Remember – the horses know. Call them by name, Aeos and Aethon, Pyrois and Phlegon.'

As Apollo said their names Phaeton saw their ears prick up.

'But it's not too late, boy. You've seen them, you've handled them, I'll give you gold sculptures of them cast by Hephaestus to take home. That should satisfy your school friends.'

Another high-pitched titter from Helios sent a flush to Phaeton's cheek.

'No,' he said stiffly. 'You gave a promise and so did I.'

Daybreak

As Phaeton spoke Eos came forward in a bright cloud of pearl and rose. She bowed smilingly to Apollo and Helios, looked a puzzled question at the blushing Phaeton in the chariot and took up her position at the gates of dawn.

To a traveller looking eastwards and upwards at the clouds in which the Palace of the Sun was hidden, the first sign that Eos was at work always came in the form of a flush of coral pink that suffused the sky. As she threw the gates wider, that soft pink hardened into a gleam of gold which grew ever brighter and fiercer.

To Phaeton, inside the palace, the effect was reversed: the doors opened to reveal the dark world beyond, illumined only by the silver gleam from Eos and Helios's sister, the moon goddess Selene, reaching the end of her nightly course. As Eos pushed the gates further open Phaeton saw pink and gold light radiate outwards, drowning the darkness of the night. As if that were a signal the four horses pricked their ears, shuddered and reared. Phaeton was jerked back and the chariot beneath him began to roll forward.

'Remember, boy,' shouted Apollo, 'don't panic. A firm hand. Don't snatch at the reins. Just let the horses know you're in control. Everything will be fine.'

'After all,' cried Helios as the chariot began to lift from the ground, 'what can possibly go wrong?' His squeals of falsetto laughter stung Phaeton like a lash.

Switching points of view again to the traveller looking

eastwards from the road below, the gold gleam is now a great ball of fire that is becoming harder and harder to observe without squinting. The short flush of dawn is over and the day has begun.

The Drive

Apollo's horses charged upwards, pawing the air. All was well. They knew what they were doing. They reached a certain height, levelled out and charged forward. This was easy.

Phaeton pulled himself upright, careful not to strain the traces, and looked around. He could see the curve that marked the separation of blue sky and star-filled darkness. He could see the effect of the light blazing out from the chariot. He was insulated, somehow magically safe from its heat and glare, but great clouds melted and fizzed into vapour as they approached. He looked down and saw the long shadows of mountains and trees contract as they flew forward. He saw the wrinkled sea send back a million scintillations of light, and he saw the sparkle of dew rising into a shimmering mist as they neared the coast of Africa. Somewhere, just west of Nilus, Epaphus would be holidaying on the beach. Oh, this was going to be the greatest triumph ever!

As the coastline swung more clearly into view Phaeton pulled at the reins, trying to nose down Aeos, the lead horse on his left hand side. Aeos had perhaps been thinking of other things, of golden straw or pretty mares, he had certainly not been imagining a tug to pull him off course. In a panic he shied and dived, pulling the other horses with him. The chariot bucked in the air and plummeted straight for the earth. In vain Phaeton tugged the reins, which had somehow become tangled in his hands. The green earth screamed towards him and he saw his certain death. He took one final desperate yank at the reins, and at the very last minute – either in response to that pull or as an instinctive move to save themselves – the four steeds swooped upwards and galloped blindly north. But not before Phaeton saw with terror and dismay that the terrible heat of the sun-chariot had set the earth on fire.

As they flew on, a raging curtain of flame swept across the land below, burning everything and everyone upon it to a crisp. The whole strip of Africa below the northern coast was laid waste. To this day most of the land is a great parched desert, which we call the Sahara, but which to the Greeks was the Land that Phaeton Scorched.

He was now terribly out of control. The horses knew for certain that the familiar firm hand of Apollo was not there to guide them. Was it wild joy at their freedom or panic at the lack of control that maddened the four? Having plunged down close enough to make the earth catch fire now they leapt up so far towards the purple curve that separated the sky from the stars that the world below grew cold and dark. The sea itself froze and the land turned to ice.

Thrashing, swaying, swooping and careering onwards, without any control or sense of direction, the chariot bounced and bucketed in the air like a leaf in a storm. Far below, the people of the earth looked up in wonder and alarm. Phaeton was screaming at the horses, begging them, threatening them, jerking at the reins . . . but all in vain.

The Fallout

On Olympus news of the devastation being wrought upon the surface of the earth reached the gods and, at last, the ears of Zeus himself.

'Look what's happening,' cried a distraught Demeter. 'The crops are being sun-burned or frost-bitten. It's a disaster.'

'The people are afraid,' said Athena. 'Please, father. Something must be done.'

With a sigh Zeus reached for a thunderbolt. He looked where the chariot of the sun was now plunging in a mad tumble towards Italy.

The thunderbolt, as all Zeus's thunderbolts did, hit its mark. Phaeton was blasted clear of the chariot and fell flaming to earth, where he dropped like a spent rocket into the waters of the River Eridanos with a hiss and a fizz.

The great sun-steeds were pacified by the absence of the panicky boy's yells and violent tugs at their traces and at last settled into their proper altitude and course, making their way instinctively to the land of the Hesperides in the far west.

Phoebus Apollo was not a good or affectionate father, but the death of his son hit him very hard. He vowed never again to drive the chariot of the sun, passing the duty on to the grateful and enthusiastic Helios, who for ever after became the sun's sole charioteer.*

Phaeton's affectionate friend Cygnus went to the River Eridanos, into whose waters poor dead Phaeton had plunged. He sat there on the bank mourning the loss of his lover with such a plaintive wail that a distraught Apollo struck him dumb and finally, out of pity and remorse for the youth's ceaseless but now silent and inconsolable suffering, transformed him into a beautiful swan. This species, the mute swan, became holy to Apollo. In remembrance of the death of the beloved Phaeton the bird is silent all its life until the very moment of its death, when it sings with terrible

---

* Sole indeed – SOL was Helios's Roman name. When you breathe in the gas named after him – helium – it makes you giggle with exactly the same mocking, high-pitched, hysterical squeak that Helios himself made when he jeered at Phaeton.

melancholy its strange and lovely goodbye, its swan song. In honour of Cygnus the young of all swans are called 'cygnets'.

And what of Epaphus? Did he look up and see Phaeton high above him steering the great chariot, or was he too busy eating dates and flirting with nymphs on board the ship sailing him and his friends to their holiday beach in North Africa? One would like to think that he did look up and that the glare of the chariot blinded him, a suitable punishment for his cruel taunts. In fact Epaphus went on to become a great patriarch. He married Nilus's daughter MEMPHIS, after whom he named the city that he had founded. They had a daughter, LIBYA, and his line, which included his great-grandson AEGYPTUS, went on to rule Egypt for generations.

Phaeton himself was eventually placed amongst the stars in the consolation constellation called Auriga, the Charioteer.* The French named a very sporty, lightweight, dangerous racing carriage the *phaéton* in his honour. It was the preferred conveyance of hot-headed young men of the late eighteenth and early nineteenth centuries, who, unwittingly re-enacting the myth of Phaeton in their youthful impetuosity, very often overturned their carriages, to the fury of their long-suffering fathers.

The American classicist and teacher Edith Hamilton offered this as Phaeton's epitaph:

> Here Phaeton lies who in the sun-god's chariot fared.
> And though greatly he failed, more greatly he dared.

---

* The rather pleasing word for being placed amongst the stars, the classical equivalent of canonization perhaps, is 'catasterism'. A mostly lost ancient prose work called the *Catasterismi*, telling of the mythological origins of the constellations, is credited to one Pseudo-Eratosthenes of Alexandria.

CADMUS

The White Bull

Thanks to Phaeton desert wastes and icy polar regions now gave mankind extremes of temperature to cope with, on top of the cycle of seasons caused by Persephone's stay in the underworld. The lesson of Phaeton did not stop humankind from reaching ever higher, however. No lesson, no matter how grim, ever seems to deter us. All over Greece kingdoms continued to rise and fall. The Grecian world encompassed Asia Minor too in those days, that bulge of land east of Greece that encompasses what we now call Turkey, as well as Syria and the lands of the Levant (modern-day Lebanon). The influence of this part of the world on Greek culture and myth was immense, bringing great trade, alphabetic writing and eventually the founding of the first example of the *polis*, the city state that was to reach its greatest pitch with the establishment of Troy, Sparta and Athens. It is a story of Zeus, transformations, a dragon, snakes, a city and a marriage.

The King of the Levantine city of Tyre, AGENOR (a son of Poseidon and Libya), and his Queen TELEPHASSA (a daughter of Nilus and the cloud nymph NEPHELE) had five children: a daughter, Europa, and four sons, CADMUS (or sometimes, in the more Greek spelling, KADMOS), CILIX, PHOENIX and THASOS.

The children of Agenor were playing in a flower-filled

meadow one afternoon when Europa wandered off and became separated from her brothers. Her eye had been caught by a beautiful white bull grazing in the long grass. As she approached, the animal lifted its head to look at her. Something in its gaze fascinated her. She moved closer. The bull's breath was sweet and its nose soft and strokeable. She threaded garlands of flowers around its horns and ran her fingers through its thick, warmly inviting coat. Then, without quite knowing why, she lifted herself onto its back. She leaned forward and took a horn in each hand.

'Oh, you beautiful thing,' she breathed into its ear. 'So strong and wise and kind.'

With a toss of its huge head the animal started to trot forward. The trot soon became something close to a gallop. Europa laughed and urged him on.

Cadmus and his younger brothers had been competing against each other to see who could throw a rock the greatest distance (Cadmus always won – he was an especially gifted thrower of stones, discuses and javelins). They turned just in time to watch their sister being carried out of sight on the back of a bull. They ran after it as fast as they could, but the bull possessed unbelievable speed. It seemed to the brothers, impossible as it must be, that the animal's hoofs were no longer touching the ground.

Panicking they called out Europa's name and shouted to her to throw herself off, but she either didn't hear or didn't heed them. The bull rose higher and higher in the air until it had vanished from sight.

Cadmus returned home and broke the news to his parents King Agenor and Queen Telephassa. Loud was the lamentation and great the recrimination.

In the meantime, the white bull flew Europa further and further west from her home kingdom of Tyre, across the

Mediterranean in the direction of the isles of Greece. Delighted and entirely unafraid, Europa laughed as first the ground flashed beneath her and then the sea. Europa was entranced. The journey was so remarkable that the whole landmass to the west of her homeland has been called Europe in her honour ever since.

They didn't stop until they reached the island of Crete where the bull revealed himself to be . . .

. . . who else but Zeus?

Whether it was Hera's transformation of Io into a heifer that inspired him to take the shape of a bull we cannot know, but the trick seems to have worked, for Europa stayed happily on Crete for the rest of her life. She was to bear Zeus three sons, Minos, Rhadamanthus and Sarpedon – who went on after their deaths, you may recall, to become the Judges of the Underworld, weighing the lives of dead souls and allotting them their punishments and rewards accordingly.

The Quest for Europa

Back home in Tyre, Europa's unhappy parents sent Cadmus and his three brothers to find their sister, with firm instructions not even to think of returning home without her.

The Tyrians were already famous navigators and traders. Cadmus's brother Phoenix (not to be confused with the mythical bird) would in time succeed Agenor as ruler of the kingdom, which he renamed Phoenicia after himself. The Phoenicians' skill as merchants would bring them great wealth and prestige. They dealt in silks and spices from the far east, but it was the invention and propagation of the *alphabet* that gave them such an advantage over their neighbours and rivals. For the first time in human history any language could be written down according to its sound, which meant the Mediterranean coastline, including North Africa and the Middle East was able to communicate for the first time using symbols on papyrus, parchment, wax or pottery shards that could be spoken out loud.* The marks on the page or screen that you are interpreting as you read now derive from that Phoenician alphabet. And it was Cadmus who would take his people's marvellous invention to Greece in the course of his long search for Europa.

For years they travelled in vain. For some reason, perhaps an unseen divine influence, Crete seems to have been the one place they failed to search. The island that they alighted on for the longest time was Samothrace, far in the northern Aegean.

On Samothrace there lived a Pleiad called ELECTRA.† The Pleiades, or Seven Sisters, were (if you recall) daughters of Atlas and the Oceanid Pleione. By Zeus, this Electra had given birth to two sons, DARDANUS‡ and IASION, as well as a daughter, HARMONIA.§ Cadmus was immediately captivated

---

* Before this great Phoenician idea, writing took the form of visual symbols such as hieroglyphs and pictograms. Like our numbers, these bore no relation to their sound. The written '24', for example, gives no clue to pronunciation at all and you'd say the sign differently according to the practices of your language. The alphabetical (i.e. phonetical) characters in *twenty-four* or *vingt-quatre* or *vierundzwanzig* tell you just how to say them. That was the crucial breakthrough. The Phoenician alphabet was adapted by the Greeks into the writing system more or less in use there today. Its close Cyrillic relation spread from Bulgaria in the ninth century AD to the Balkans, Russia and many other areas of eastern Europe and Asia, while the Romans adapted the Greek *alpha* and *beta* into the alphabetic system you are interpreting so fluently at this minute. Herodotus, the 'Father of History', who lived in the fifth century BC, still called such writing 'Cadmean'.

† Not the tragic ELECTRA, daughter of AGAMEMNON and CLYTEMNESTRA, but another much earlier one. The name is interesting; it is the female form of *electron*, the Greek word for 'amber'. The Greeks noticed that if you rub amber vigorously with a cloth it magically attracts dust and fluff. They called this strange property 'amberiness', from which all our words 'electric', 'electricity', 'electron', 'electronic', and so on, ultimately derive.

‡ He gave his name to the Dardanelles, site of the ill-fated Gallipoli landings in the First World War.

§ Some sources claim that Ares and Aphrodite were Harmonia's parents. Her later ascent to the status of goddess of harmony (CONCORDIA to the Romans) certainly hints at a more divine pedigree. Given what Ares was about to do to her, you might think him a most unnatural father – so loyal to his water dragon, so cruel to his human daughter. Other mythographers,

by Harmonia's beauty and sweet, placid manner and took her with him on his quest. How willing she was at first is not certain, but the pair left Samothrace and headed for mainland Greece – ostensibly in search of Europa, but really, as far as Cadmus was concerned, in search of a greater purpose.

The Oracle Speaks

Cadmus is often called 'the First Hero'. If you care to do the arithmetic you will see that he was a fifth-generation being, of equally human and divine parentage. He could trace his line back to the very beginnings of life through his paternal grandfather Poseidon, whose father was Kronos, son of Ouranos. Through his grandmother Libya he was descended from Inachus, adding a quantity of royal human blood to course through his veins. He had the restlessness and wanderlust that marks the hero, as well as the required measures of courage, confidence and self-belief. Poseidon was fond of his grandson, as was natural, but it was Athena who looked upon him with the greatest favour, especially now that he had allied himself to Harmonia, who was one of Athena's most devoted followers.

Just as Cadmus's brother Thasos had settled a smaller nearby island, called Thasos, and Phoenix had given his name to the Phoenician kingdom, so the third of Cadmus's brothers, Cilix, now abandoned the quest for Europa,

notably Roberto Calasso, an Italian writer whose creative interpretations of myth are well worth reading, have elegantly compromised and suggested that Harmonia was indeed the daughter of Aphrodite and Ares, but was given to be suckled and adopted by Electra of Samothrace.

returning east to Asia Minor to establish his own kingdom, which he called Cilicia.*

With Harmonia by his side and a large retinue of loyal followers from Tyre in attendance upon them both, Cadmus headed for Delphi to consult the oracle. He knew in his bones, as all heroes do, that he was destined for greatness, but he did not know quite where his future lay; and he still needed guidance in the matter of his search for the lost Europa.

You already know enough about oracles to be unsurprised by the eccentricity of the Pythia's response.

'Cadmus, son of Agenor, son of Poseidon,' she chanted. 'Cast aside the quest for your sister and follow instead the heifer marked with the half moon. Follow the cow until it drops down exhausted. Where it falls, there must you build.'

'Build what?'

'Farewell, Cadmus, son of Agenor, son of Poseidon.'

'What cow? I see no cow.'

'Where the cow falls, there must Cadmus, son of Agenor, son of Poseidon, build.'

'Yes, but this cow . . .'

'The heifer with the half moon will help Harmonia and her hero, son of Agenor, son of Poseidon.'

'Look here . . .'

'Farewe-e-e-e-ll . . .'

Cadmus and Harmonia looked at each other, shrugged and quit Delphi with their retinue of loyal Tyrians. It was possible that a cow really would materialize magically before them, or perhaps some celestial messenger might appear to guide them to such an animal. In the meantime, they might as well look around.

---

* It forms the wedge of land that separates Turkey from Syria and is now called Çukurova.

Now, Delphi and its oracle, stadium and temples are situated in the area of Greece called Phocis. The King of Phocis, PELAGON, hearing that Harmonia and Cadmus – by now famous throughout the land because of his gift of the alphabet – were in the area, sent out messengers to invite them to stay as his guests of honour at the royal palace. It was an invitation the travel-strained pair and their hungry retinue were only too pleased to accept.

The Phocian Games

Three days of feasting and revelry in their honour had passed agreeably and uneventfully when Cadmus and Harmonia, taking an evening walk about the palace gardens between banquets, found their way stopped by Pelagon's father, AMPHIDAMAS.

'I had a dream,' said Amphidamas, coming close to the couple and breathing the fumes of honey-wine all over them, 'in which you, Cadmus, ran races, hurled javelins, threw discuses and won the greatest prize the world has ever seen. Now, my son Pelagon inaugurates the Phocian Games tomorrow. A little local meeting, but dreams are dreams and have a purpose. When does Morpheus ever lie? My advice is that you enter.' With a benevolent hiccup, he tottered away.

'Well now,' said Cadmus, putting an arm about Harmonia's waist and gazing wistfully up at the moon. 'Why not? The man has not yet been born who can throw a discus or a javelin as far as I can. And I believe I'm pretty swift around the track too.'

'My hero!' sighed Harmonia, burying her head on his chest. She did this not in worshipful admiration but to muffle her laughter – she found the men's vanity when it came to physical prowess endlessly amusing.

The competition against which Cadmus pitted himself next day consisted chiefly of puny local youths and pot-bellied palace guards. When he sent the discus right out of the palace grounds with his first throw, a servant had to be sent to fetch it and the crowd cheered. By the end of the afternoon Cadmus had won every event. Harmonia glared at the women and girls who blew him kisses and threw flowers at his feet.

Pelagon, who was not a rich monarch, sent his chamberlain in search of a suitable prize for his noble *victor ludorum*.

'People of Phocis,' cried the king, placing a hastily plaited crown of olive leaves on Cadmus's brow, 'behold your champion, our honoured guest Prince Cadmus of Tyre. And here comes a prize worthy of his great speed and strength and grace.'

A loud cheer went up, which fell into a puzzled silence as the palace chamberlain came through the crowd driving ahead of him a large cow. The silence bubbled into a titter and the titter burst into outright laughter. The cow chewed its cud, lifted its tail and sent out a liquid spatter of dung from its rear. The crowd hooted with derision.

Pelagon turned scarlet. His father Amphidamas said to Cadmus with a wink, 'Oh well. Morpheus can't be right all the time, hey?'

But Harmonia nudged Cadmus in great excitement. 'Look,' she breathed, 'look, Cadmus, *look*!'

Cadmus saw at once what had attracted her attention. On the cow's back was a mark in the shape of a half moon. There was no other way to describe it. A clear half moon!

Pelagon was murmuring something unconvincing in his ear about the animal's pedigree and high milk yield, but Cadmus interrupted him.

'Your majesty could not have found a more marvellous and welcome prize! I am overcome with delight and gratitude.'

'You are?' said a faintly stunned Pelagon.

The chamberlain was so astonished to hear this that he dropped the switch of willow with which he had been slapping the beast towards the winner's rostrum. It took perhaps thirty seconds for the heifer to become aware that the stinging smack was no longer there to force her on, so she turned and started to amble away.

'Indeed,' said Cadmus jumping from the rostrum and helping Harmonia down after him. 'It really is the perfect present. Just exactly what we wanted . . .'

The cow made its way through the crowd. Cadmus and Harmonia, their backs to the royal party, began to follow. Over his shoulder Cadmus called back to the king, stammering out thanks and incoherent courtesies.

'Your majesty will excuse us . . . such a wonderful stay . . . so grateful for your hospitality . . . excellent food, marvellous entertainment . . . most kind . . . er . . . farewell . . .'

'So grateful,' repeated Harmonia. 'We'll never forget it. Never. The loveliest heifer! Goodbye.'

'B-but! What? I mean . . . ?' said Pelagon, puzzled by this swift and sudden leave-taking. 'I thought you were staying another night?'

'No time. Come, men. With us!' cried Cadmus, summoning his retinue of Tyrian servants, men-at-arms, camp-followers and attendants. Buckling up their armour on the run, dropping food and kissing farewell to new acquaintances they caught up with Cadmus, Harmonia and the cow.

'Mad,' said Amphidamas, watching the plume of dust spiral upwards in the distance as Cadmus's ragtag army disappeared from view. 'Quite mad. Said so from the first.'

For three days and three nights Cadmus, Harmonia and their train of loyal Tyrians followed the heifer with the half-moon markings as it lumbered up and down hills, through meadows, over fields and across streams. They seemed to be travelling in a southeasterly direction towards the province of Boeotia.*

Harmonia believed that the heifer might turn out to be Europa herself. After all, in ravishing her Zeus had transformed himself into a bull, so why mightn't she have taken bovine form too? Cadmus, hypnotized by the rhythmic swaying of the cow's broad posterior, was more inclined to think that the whole thing was a cruel hoax sent to perplex him.

Quite suddenly, after descending a steep hill and arriving at the edge of a wide plain, the heifer sank heavily down and gave vent to an exhausted groan.

'Good lord,' said Cadmus.

'Just as the oracle prophesied!' cried Harmonia. 'What did the Pythia say? "Where the cow falls, there must you build." So.'

'*So?*' said Cadmus, irked. 'What do you mean, "So"? Build? Build what? Build how?'

'I'll tell you what,' said Harmonia. 'Let's sacrifice the cow to Pallas Athena. The poor thing's almost dead anyway. Athena will guide us.'

Cadmus agreed and elected to pitch a primitive kind of

---

* A central region of Greece, north of the Gulf of Corinth. Without giving too much away it is worth relating that it once bore the name 'Cadmeis' . . .

camp right there. So that he could properly purify the sacrifice he sent some of his men to fetch water from a nearby spring.

Cadmus slit the cow's throat and was just sprinkling its blood on a makeshift altar bedecked with wild flowers and burnt sage when one of the Tyrians returned in the most pitiable state of distress, bearing awful news. A dragon, in the grotesque form of a giant water serpent, guarded the spring. It had already killed four men, constricting them in its coils and biting off their heads with its enormous jaws. What could be done?

Heroes do not wring their hands and wonder, heroes act. Cadmus hurried to the spring, picking up a heavy boulder on the way. Hiding behind a tree he whistled to attract the dragon's attention, and then threw the boulder at the dragon's head, smashing its skull and killing it outright.

'So much for water snakes,' said Cadmus, looking down at the monster's blood and brains as they mixed with the waters of the spring.

A voice sounded out loud and clear. 'Son of Agenor, why do you stare at the snake you have slain? You too shall be a snake and endure the stares of strangers.'

Cadmus looked around but could see no one. The voice must have sounded inside him. He shook his head and returned to the camp, delighted alike by the cheers of his supporters and the admiring kisses of Harmonia, to whom he said nothing about the voice he had heard.

Far enough away to be able to do so without Cadmus hearing, one of his men was drawing in his breath through his teeth with the irritating relish of those who have bad news to impart. This man came from Boeotia and whispered to his companions with a wise shake of the head that *Drakon Ismenios*, the Ismenian Dragon, which Cadmus had just slain, was known to be sacred to Ares, the god of war. Indeed, he went on, some believed that the creature was actually a *son* of Ares!

'No good will come of this deed,' he said, tutting and clicking. 'You do not cross the god of battles with impunity. No, sir. Makes no difference who your grandfather is.'

It is worth recognizing here that one of the most burdensome challenges faced by the heroes and mortals of that time concerned their relationships with the different gods. Picking your way around the jealousies and animosities of the Olympians was a delicate business. Show too much loyalty and service to one and you risked provoking the enmity of another. If Poseidon and Athena favoured you, as they did Cadmus and Harmonia, for example, then the chances were that Hera, or Artemis, or Ares, or even Zeus himself would do everything possible to hinder and hamper you. And heaven help anyone foolish enough to kill one of their favourites. All the sacrifices and votive offerings in the world couldn't mollify an affronted god, a vengeful god, a god who had lost face in front of the others.

Cadmus, by slaying an Arean favourite, had certainly made an enemy of the most aggressive and remorseless of the gods.* But he knew none of this, for the muttering in the ranks of his retinue had not reached his ears. He blithely lit the incense and completed his sacrifice to Athena, feeling that things were still going very much his way. This feeling was reinforced by Athena's immediate and benign appearance. Pleased by the offering of the heifer, she glided down from the cloud of fragrant smoke that Cadmus had sent up and favoured her humble worshippers with a grave smile.

---

* Ovid calls the Ismenian Dragon *Anguis Martius*, the 'Snake of Mars'. It seems *(ap)ophis* (snake) and *drakon* (dragon) were pretty much undifferentiated in Greek myth, much as *Wurm* (worm) and *Drachen* (dragon) are interchangeable in Germanic legend.

'Rise, son of Agenor,' said the goddess, stepping forward and raising the supplicant Cadmus to his feet. 'Your sacrifice was agreeable to us. If you follow my instructions carefully all will be well. Plough the fertile plain. Plough it well. Then sow the furrows with teeth from the dragon you have slain.'

With these words she stepped back into the smoke and disappeared. If Cadmus had not the assurance from Harmonia and the others that they had heard just the same words from Athena too, he might have believed that he had dreamed it. But divine instructions are divine instructions, however odd. In fact the odder, Cadmus was becoming aware, the more likely to be divine.

First he carved a ploughshare from holm oak wood. Then, since no draught animals were available, he harnessed a willing team of his most loyal attendants. They would have laid down their lives for this charismatic Prince of Tyre, so pulling a plough was nothing to them.

It was late spring and the soil of the plain was free-moving enough to be pulled into shallow but straight and well-marked furrows without too terrible an effort from the straining Tyrians.

The field ploughed, Cadmus now set to dibbling the furrows an inch or two deep with the blunt end of a spear. Into each dibbled hole he dropped a dragon's tooth. As we all know, humans have thirty-two teeth. Water dragons have rows and rows of them, like sharks, each ready to advance when the row in front has been worn down with too much grinding of men's bones. Five hundred and twelve teeth Cadmus planted in all. When he had finished he stood back to survey the field.

A light wind blew across the plain, catching the crests of

the furrows and sending up powdery flurries of soil. Dust devils whipped and whirled around. A great hush descended.

Harmonia was the first to see the earth in one of the furrows shift. She pointed and all eyes followed. A gasp and a muffled cry went up from the watching crowd. The tip of a spear was pushing through, then a helmet appeared, followed by shoulders, a breastplate, leathern-greaved legs ... until a fully armed soldier rose up, wild and fierce, stamping his feet. Then another, and another, until the field was filled with fighting men, marching on the spot in furrowed lines. The clanging and banging of their armour, the clashing and bashing of their buckles, belts and boots, the clamour and smacking of the metal and leather of their cuirasses, greaves and shields, their rhythmic grunting and martial shouts all built into a great and horrid din that filled the onlookers with fear.

All but Cadmus, who stepped boldly forward and raised a hand.

'Spartoi!' he called out across the plain, giving them a name that means 'sown men'. 'My Spartoi! I am Prince Cadmus, your general. At ease.'

Perhaps because they were born of dragon's teeth pulled from the jaws of a creature sacred to the god of war, these soldiers were filled from the first with extraordinary aggression. In reply to Cadmus's command they simply clattered and rattled their shields and spears.

'Silence!' yelled Cadmus.

The warriors paid no attention. Their marching on the spot turned into a slow march forward. In exasperation Cadmus picked up a rock which, with his customary skill and strength, he hurled into their ranks. It struck one of the soldiers on the shoulder. The man looked at the soldier next to him and, taking him to be the aggressor, lunged at him with a mighty roar, sword drawn. Within moments blood-curdling battle-cries were heard all around the field as the soldiers fell upon each other.

'Stop! Stop! I command you to stop!' yelled Cadmus like a frantic parent on the touchline watching their son being squashed in a scrum. Stamping the ground in frustration he turned to Harmonia. 'What is the point of Athena taking all this trouble to force me to create a race of men, only for them to destroy each other? Look at this violence, this bloodlust. What does it mean?'

But even as he spoke, Harmonia was pointing to the centre of the fray. Five of Cadmus's Spartoi stood in a circle, the sole survivors. The rest lay dead, their blood soaking back into the soil from which they had come. Forward came the five, their swords pointing to the ground. They reached Cadmus and knelt down, heads bowed.

Great was the relief, great the rejoicing from the Tyrians. The day had been strange, as strange a day as mortals had known in all history. But some kind of order seemed to have emerged.

'What is the name of this place?' Cadmus asked. 'Does anyone here know?'

A voice spoke up, the voice of the man who had warned that the Ismenian Dragon was sacred to Ares. 'I'm from hereabouts,' he said. 'We call this "the plain of Thebes".'

'Then on this plain shall I build a great city. From now on we are not Tyrians, but Thebans' – a great cheer went up – 'and these five Spartoi shall be my Theban lords.'

The Marriage of Cadmus and Harmonia

The Five Founding Lords of Thebes were given the names ECHION, UDAEUS, CHTHONIUS, HYPERENOR and PELOR.*

---

* Chthonius had the name that defined them all as chthonic beings.

Under the supervision of Cadmus and his loyal army of Tyrian followers they slowly built up a citadel (the Cadmeia) from which grew a flourishing town. In time this town became the powerful city state of Thebes.* The strong wall that encircled it was pierced by seven great bronze gates, each dedicated to the glory of an Olympian god.

The wall was constructed by AMPHION and ZETHUS, twin sons of Zeus by ANTIOPE, the daughter of the local river god ASOPOS. Hermes had been a lover of Amphion and taught him to play the lyre. When it came to the construction of the great wall around the Cadmeia, Amphion sang to the accompaniment of the lyre and the heavy stones carried by Zethus were so enchanted by the music that they floated into place and the city walls were finished in no time. As a result Amphion and Zethus, as well as Cadmus, are credited as co-founders of Thebes.

The work completed, Cadmus and Harmonia turned to the matter of their marriage. Descended from Titans and gods, allied to and punished by Olympians, but very mortal and very human, the pair might nowadays be called an 'iconic power couple'. Today's press and social media, one suspects, would hardly be able to resist dubbing them 'Cadmonia'.

Their status as the foremost lovers of the known world meant their wedding feast was an honour never before accorded a mortal union, attended by the highest in the land and the highest from heaven. The gifts were stupendous. Aphrodite lent Harmonia her girdle, a magical item of lingerie that had the power to provoke the most dizzying and

---

* The *polis* or 'city state' was to become the defining unit of government in ancient Greece. Athens was the best known, but Sparta, Thebes, Rhodes, Samos and many others flourished around the Greek world, forming alliances, trading and fighting with each other. Despite Greek giving us the word 'democracy', the *polis* could also be ruled either by a king (*tyrannos* in Greek, so when we say 'tyrant' we don't always mean 'despot') or by the 'rule of the few', which in Greek is *oligarchy*. From *polis* come all those words like 'polite', 'politics' and 'police'.

rapturous desire.* It is said that Harmonia was bed-shy and that her love for Cadmus had yet to be consummated. This girdle, loaned for the duration of her honeymoon by the goddess of love and beauty (who may well have been Harmonia's natural mother), was therefore a gift of great value.

But no wedding gift outshone the necklace that Cadmus conferred upon his bride. It was the most beautiful piece of jewellery yet seen. Fashioned from the choicest chalcedony, jasper, emeralds, sapphires, jade, lapis, amethyst, silver and gold, it caused gasps of wonder amongst the guests when he clasped it about his beautiful wife's neck.† The whisper went round that it too had been given by Aphrodite.

The whisper added that it had been made by Hephaestus. The whisper went further and suggested that Hephaestus had been urged to make it by his wife Aphrodite because she in turn had been urged to do so by her lover Ares, who – if you remember – nursed a grievance against Cadmus for slaying the Ismenian Dragon. For the cruel and shocking truth about the necklace was that it was cursed. Deeply and irrevocably cursed. Miserable misfortune and tragic calamity would rain down upon the heads of whosoever wore or owned it.

This is all confusing and fascinating in equal measure. If Ares and Aphrodite were indeed Harmonia's true parents, why would they want to doom their own daughter? All to avenge a dead water snake? Besides, could sweet Harmony really be the child of Love and War? And, if so, why would the gentle issue of those two powerful and frightening forces be cursed by them with such unnatural cruelty?

---

* I'm damned if I can find a convincing definition of 'girdle'. Some think it's a belt, others a device more like a Playtex panelled support or corset – others yet have described it as a 'mythical Wonderbra'. Calasso calls it 'a soft deceiving sash'.

† 'A garland of golden light dangling almost to the ground' is Roberto Calasso's excellent description in his book *The Marriage of Cadmus and Harmony*.

The pairing of Cadmus and Harmony seems, like that of Eros and Psyche, to suggest a marriage of two leading and contradictory aspects of ourselves. Perhaps the eastern tradition of conquest, writing and trade represented by Cadmus – his name derives from the old Arabic and Hebrew root *qdm*, which means 'of the east' – can be seen here fusing with love and sensuality to create a new Greece endowed with both.

But in this story, as in so many others, what we really discern is the deceptive, ambiguous and giddy riddle of violence, passion, poetry and symbolism that lies at the heart of Greek myth and refuses to be solved. An algebra too unstable properly to be computed, it is human-shaped and god-shaped, not pure and mathematical. It is fun trying to interpret such symbols and narrative turns, but the substitutions don't quite work and the answers yielded are usually no clearer than those of an equivocating oracle.

So back to the story. The marriage was a great success. The girdle did its (literally) aphrodisiac work and the happy pair were blessed with their own issue: two sons, POLYDORUS and ILLYRIUS, and four daughters:– AGAVE, AUTONOË, INO and SEMELE.

Cadmus still had to pay for his killing of the dragon, however. Ares bound him to labour on his behalf for an Olympian year, which seems to have been eight human years.

After this, Cadmus returned to rule over the city he had built. But the curse of the necklace was to pollute any happiness or satisfaction he might have enjoyed as king.

Consigned to the Dust

After many years of peace and prosperity in Thebes, Cadmus and Harmonia's daughter Agave had married PENTHEUS, the son of Echion, one of the Five Founding Lords (the last five Spartoi standing, you will remember). Tiring of kingship, but like so many heroes after him unable to restrain the itchy feet of wanderlust, Cadmus said to Harmonia one day: 'Let us travel. Let us see more of the world. Pentheus is ready to take the throne in our absence.'

They saw much. Many towns and many cities. They went as an ordinary middle-aged couple, asking for no great welcome or banquets in their honour. Only a small party of attendants accompanied them. It was unfortunate, though, that Harmonia included the cursed necklace in her luggage.

After a great deal of travelling around Greece they determined on a visit to the kingdom up towards the western Adriatic, south of the Balkans and facing the east coast of Italy, that had been established by their youngest boy, Illyrius, and which was unsurprisingly called 'Illyria'.*

Once there, Cadmus suddenly fell weary and was filled with an insupportable dread. He called up to the skies.

'For the last thirty years I have known in my heart that in killing that cursed water snake I killed any chance of happiness for me or my wife. Ares is remorseless. He will not rest until I am as flat on the earth as a snake. If it will calm him and bring more peace to my troubled life then let me end my life sliding through the dust. Let it be so.'†

No sooner were those words out of his mouth than his unhappy prayer became an unhappy reality. His body began to shrink sideways and stretch lengthways, his skin to blister and form smooth scales, and his head to flatten into a

---

* Scene of Shakespeare's *Twelfth Night* and Jean-Paul Sartre's *Les Mains Sales*. The *Dalmatae* (a name ultimately deriving from an early Albanian word for 'sheep') were an Illyrian tribe to the northwest of the region who gave their name to this Dalmatian coast (and the dog).

† Being from Tyre, Cadmus probably used the word for 'let it be so' most commonly used throughout the Middle East: *Amen*.

diamond shape. The tongue that had shouted that dreadful wish to the heavens now flicked and darted out from between two fangs. The man who was once Cadmus, Prince of Tyre and King of Thebes, fell writhing to the ground, a common snake.

Harmonia let out a great howl of despair.

'Gods have pity!' she cried. 'Aphrodite, if you are my mother show love now and let me join upon the earth the one I love. The fruits of the world are dust to me. Ares, if you are my father show mercy. Zeus if, as some say, *you* are my father then, in the name of all creation, take pity, I beg you.'

It was, however, none of those three who heard her prayers, but merciful Athena who transformed her into a snake. Harmonia glided through the dust after her serpent-husband and they coiled about each other with love.

The pair lived out their days in the shadows of a temple sacred to Athena, only showing themselves when they needed to heat their blood in the noonday sun. When the end came, Zeus returned them to their human shapes in time to die. Their bodies were taken to be buried with great ceremony in Thebes, and Zeus sent two great serpents to guard their tombs for eternity.

We will leave Cadmus and Harmonia to their everlasting rest. They died quite unaware that their youngest daughter, Semele, had, in their absence, unleashed a force into the world that would change it for ever.

TWICE BORN

The Eagle Lands

After Cadmus and Harmonia departed on their travels, their son-in-law Pentheus reigned in Thebes.* He was not a strong king, but he was honest and did the best he could with the limited store of character and cunning on which he was able to call. While the city-state flourished well enough under him, he needed always to look over his shoulder to the children of Cadmus, his brothers- and sisters-in-law, whose greed and ambition posed a constant threat. Even his wife Agave seemed contemptuous of him and anxious for him to fail. His youngest sister-in-law, Semele, was the only one with whom he felt at all at ease, in truth because she was less worldly than her brothers Polydorus and Illyrius, and nothing like as ambitious for wealth and position as her sisters Agave, Autonoë and Ino. Semele was a beautiful, kindly and generous girl, content with her life as a priestess at the great temple of Zeus.

One day she sacrificed to Zeus a bull of especially impressive size and vigour. The offering complete, she took herself off to the River Asopos to wash the blood from her. It so happened that Zeus, pleased with the sacrifice and intending anyway to look in on Thebes to see how the city prospered, was flying over the river at the time in his favourite guise of

---

* Cadmus and Harmonia's sons Polydorus and Illyrius were too young to rule. In time Polydorus would go on to reign in Thebes, and Illyrius would rule over the kingdom that bore his name, Illyria, as we have already seen.

an eagle. The sight of Semele's naked body glistening in the water excited him hugely and he landed, turning himself quickly back into his proper form. I say 'proper form', for when the gods chose to reveal themselves to humans they presented themselves in a reduced, manageable guise that did not dazzle or overawe. Thus the figure that stood on the riverbank smiling at Semele appeared human. Large, stunningly handsome, powerfully built and possessed of an unusual radiance, but human all the same.

Crossing her arms over her breasts Semele called out, 'Who are you? How dare you sneak up upon a priestess of Zeus?'

'A priestess of Zeus, are you?'

'I am. If you mean any harm to me I will cry out to the King of the Gods and he will rush to my aid.'

'You don't say so?'

'You may be sure of it. Now leave.'

But the stranger came closer. 'I am well pleased with you, Semele,' he said.

Semele backed away. 'You know my name?'

'I know many things, loyal priestess. For I am the god you serve. I am the Sky Father, the King of Olympus. Zeus, the all-powerful.'

Semele, still half in the river, gasped and fell to her knees.

'Come now,' said Zeus, striding through the water towards her, 'let me look into your eyes.'

It was splashy, frenzied and wet, but it was real lovemaking. When it was over Semele smiled, blushed, laughed and then wept, leaning her head on Zeus's chest and sobbing without cease.

'Don't cry, dearest Semele,' said Zeus, running his fingers through her hair. 'You have pleased me.'

'I'm sorry, my lord. But I love you and I know all too well that you can never love a mortal.'

Zeus gazed down at her. The eruption of lust he had felt was all over, but he was surprised to feel the stirrings of something deeper, glowing like embers in his heart. A god who operated in vertical moments with no real thought for consequences along the line, he really did experience just then a great wellspring of love for the beautiful Semele, and he told her so.

'Semele, I do love you! I love you sincerely. Believe me now when I swear by the waters of this river that I will always look after you, care for you, protect you, honour you.' He cupped her face in his hands and bent forward to bestow a tender kiss on her soft, receptive lips. 'Now, farewell, my sweet. Once every new moon I will come.'

Dressed in her gown, her hair still damp and her whole being warm and bright with love and happiness, Semele walked back across the fields towards the temple. Looking up, a hand shading her eyes, she saw an eagle sweep and soar through the sky, seemingly into the sun itself, until the dazzle of it made her eyes water and she was forced to look away.

The Eagle's Wife

Zeus meant well.

Those three words so often presaged disaster for some poor demigod, nymph or mortal. The King of the Gods did love Semele and he really meant to do his best by her. In the fervour of his new infatuation he managed conveniently to forget the torments Io had endured, maddened by the gadfly sent by his vengeful wife.

Alas, Hera may no longer have had Argus of the hundred eyes to gather intelligence for her, but she had thousands of eyes in other places. Whether it was one of the jealous sisters,

Agave, Autonoë or Ino, who spied on Semele and whispered to Hera the story of the love-making in the river, or whether it was one of the Queen of Heaven's own priestesses, is not known. But find out Hera did.

So it was that, one afternoon, Semele, returning with romantic sentiment to the place of her regular amorous encounters with Zeus, encountered a stooping old woman leaning on a stick.

'My, what a pretty girl,' croaked the old woman, slightly overdoing the cracked and cackling voice of a miserable crone.

'Why thank you,' said the unsuspicious Semele with a friendly smile.

'Walk with me,' said the hag, pulling Semele towards her with her cane. 'Let me lean upon you.'

Semele was polite and considerate by nature in a culture where the elderly were in any case accorded the greatest attention and respect, so she accompanied the old woman and endured her roughness without complaint.

'My name is Beroë,' said the old woman.

'And I am Semele.'

'What a pretty name! And here is Asopos,' Beroë indicated the clear waters of the river.

'Yes,' assented Semele, 'that is the river's name.'

'I heard tell,' here the old woman's voice lowered into a harsh whisper, 'that a priestess of Zeus was seduced here. Right here in the reeds.'

Semele went silent, but the flush that spread instantly up her neck to her cheeks betrayed her as completely as any spoken words.

'Oh, my dear!' screeched the crone. 'It was you! And now that I look, I can see your belly. You are with child!'

'I . . . I am . . .' said Semele with a becoming mixture of diffidence and pride. 'But . . . if you can keep a secret . . . ?'

'Oh, these old lips never tell tales. You may tell me anything you wish, my dear.'

'Well, the fact is that the father of this child is – none other than Zeus himself.'

'No!' said Beroë. 'You don't say so? Really?'

Semele gave a very affirmative nod of the head. She did not like the old woman's sceptical tone. 'Truly. The King of the Gods himself.'

'Zeus? The great god Zeus? Well, well. I wonder . . . No, I mustn't say.'

'Say what, lady?'

'You seem such a sweet innocent. So trusting. But, my dear, how can you *know* that it was Zeus? Isn't that exactly what some wicked seducer might say just to win you?'

'Oh no, it was Zeus. I know it was Zeus.'

'Bear with an old woman and describe him to me, my child.'

'Well, he was tall. He had a beard. Strong. Kindly . . .'

'Oh no, I'm sorry to say so, but that is hardly the description of a *god*.'

'But it *was* Zeus, it was! He turned himself into an eagle. I saw it with my very own eyes.'

'That's a trick that can be taught. Fauns and demigods can do it. Even some mortal men.'

'It was Zeus. I *felt* it.'

'Hm . . .' Beroë sounded doubtful. 'I have lived amongst the gods. My mother is Tethys and my father Oceanus. I raised and nursed the young gods after they were reborn from Kronos's stomach. It's true. I know their ways and their natures and I tell you this, my daughter. When a god manifests himself or herself as they truly are it is like a great explosion. A wondrous thing of force and fire. Unforgettable. Unmistakable.'

'And that's just what I felt!'

'What you felt was no more than the ecstasy of mortal love-making. Depend upon it. Tell me now, will this lover of yours come to you again?'

'Oh, yes indeed. He visits me faithfully every change of the moon.'

'If I were you,' said the old woman, 'I would make him promise to reveal himself to you *as he really is*. If he is Zeus you will know it. Otherwise I fear you have been made a fool of, and you are far too lovely and trusting and sweet-natured for that to be allowed. Now, leave me to contemplate the view. Shush, shush, go away.'

And so Semele left the crone, growing more and more hotly indignant all the while. She could not help it, but this warty and wrinkled old creature had got under her skin. So typical of old age to try to take away any pleasure that youth might feel. Her own sisters, Autonoë, Ino and Agave, had disbelieved her when she told them proudly of how she loved Zeus and Zeus loved her. They had shrieked with incredulous mocking laughter and called her a gullible fool. And now this Beroë doubted her story too.

Yet maybe, just *maybe* there was something in what her sisters and the old witch said. Gods surely had more to them than warm flesh and solid muscle, appealing as those were? 'Well,' Semele said to herself, 'two more nights and there'll be a new moon in the sky, and then I can prove that nasty interfering old hag wrong.'

Had Semele chanced to turn and look back towards the river, she might have witnessed the extraordinary sight of that nasty interfering old hag, now youthful, beautiful, magisterial and imperious, rising up to the clouds in a purple and gold chariot drawn by a dozen peacocks. And had she the gift of second sight, Semele might have been granted a

235

vision of the actual BEROË, innocent old nurse of the gods, living out her life miles away in respectable retirement on the coast of Phoenicia.*

The Manifestation†

It was with some impatience that, on the night of the new moon, Semele paced up and down by the banks of River Asopos, awaiting her lover. He arrived at last, this time as a stallion – black, glossy and fine, galloping through the fields towards her as the sun set in the west behind him, seeming to set his mane on fire. Oh, how she loved him!

He let her stroke his flanks and palm his hot nostrils before he transformed himself into the shape she knew and loved so well. Hugging and holding him hard, she began to cry.

'My darling girl,' said Zeus, his finger running down to her belly, where it traced the outline of their child, 'not weeping again? What am I doing wrong?'

'You really are the god Zeus?'

'I am.'

'Will you promise to grant any wish?'

'Oh, must you really?' said Zeus with a sigh.

'It's nothing – not power or wisdom or jewels, or anything like that. And I don't want you to destroy anyone. It's a small thing, really it is.'

'Then,' said Zeus, chucking her affectionately under the chin, 'I will grant your wish.'

'You promise?'

---

* The real Beroë, an Oceanid who had indeed nursed the young gods, gave her name to the city of Beirut.

† Another word for the appearance and revelation of a god to a mortal is 'theophany'.

'I promise. I promise by this river – no, I've already sworn one thing by it. I shall promise you by the great Stygian stream herself.'* Raising his hand with mock solemnity, he intoned, 'Beloved Semele, I swear by sacred Styx that I will grant your next wish.'

'Then,' said Semele with a deep breath, 'show yourself to me.'

'How's that?'

'I want to see you as you really are. Not as a man, but as a god, in your true divinity.'

The smile froze on Zeus's face. 'No!' he cried. 'Anything but that! Do not wish such a thing. No, no, no!'

It was the tone of voice that gods often used when they realized they had been trapped into a rash promise. Apollo cried out in the same way, you will remember, when Phaeton called upon him to honour his oath. Suspicion flared up in Semele.

'You promised, you swore by Styx! You swore, you swore an oath!'

'But my darling girl, you don't know what you're asking.'

'You *swore*!' Semele actually stamped her foot.

The god looked up at the sky and groaned. 'I did. I pledged my word and my word is sacred.'

As he spoke Zeus began to gather himself into the form of a great thundercloud. From the centre of this dark mass flashed the brightest light imaginable. Semele looked on, her face breaking into a broad and ecstatic smile of joy. Only a god could change like this. Only Zeus himself could grow and grow with such dazzling fire and golden greatness.

But the brightness was becoming so fierce, so terrible in

---

* It was common, as you may remember from Apollo's promise to Phaeton, for gods to swear by this dark and hateful river.

the ferocity of its glare, that she threw up an arm to shade her eyes. Yet still the brilliance intensified. With a crack so loud that her ears burst and filled with blood, the radiance exploded in bolts of lightning that instantly struck the girl blind. Deaf and sightless she staggered backwards, but too late to avoid the blazing force of a thunderbolt so powerful that it split her body open, killing her at once.

Above him, around him, inside him, Zeus heard the triumphant laughter of his wife. Of course. He might have known. Somehow Hera had tricked this poor girl into forcing the awful promise from him. Well, she would not get their child. With a peal of thunder Zeus returned to flesh and blood and plucked the foetus from Semele's belly. It was too young to breathe the air, so Zeus took a knife and sliced open his thigh and tucked the embryo inside. Holding it tight within this makeshift womb Zeus knelt down to sew the child safely into his warm flesh.*

The Newest God

Three months later Zeus and Hermes travelled to Nysus on the north coast of Africa, an area that lies, it is generally believed, somewhere between Libya and Egypt. There Hermes cut open the stitching on Zeus's thigh and delivered him of a son, DIONYSUS.† The infant was suckled by the rain nymphs of Nysus;‡ and, once weaned, was tutored by potbellied Silenus, who was to become his closest companion and follower – a kind of Falstaff to the young god's

---

* An astonishing story. As Ovid himself says of it: 'If man can believe this . . .'

† The name probably couples 'god' (*Dio*, meaning Zeus) with the Nysus, the birthplace.

‡ A grateful Zeus rewarded them by adding them to the heavens as the Hyades, a spiral constellation whose rising and setting the Greeks believed presaged rain.

Prince Hal. Silenus had his own train of followers too, the *sileni* – satyr-like creatures for ever associated with antic riot, rout and revelry.

It was as a youth that Dionysus made the discovery with which he will always be associated. He found out how to make wine from grapes. It is possible that CHIRON the centaur taught him the trick; but another, more charming story relates it to the young god's passionate love for a youth called AMPELOS.* Dionysus was so besotted that he arranged all kinds of sporting contests between himself and Ampelos, always letting the youth win. This seems to have caused the boy to become rather spoiled, or at least reckless and foolhardy. Riding a wild bull one day he made the error of boasting that he rode his horned steer more skilfully than the goddess Selene rode her horned moon. Choosing a punishment straight from Hera's vicious playbook, Selene sent a gadfly to sting the bull, which caused the maddened animal to throw and gore Ampelos.

Dionysus rushed to the dying youth's mangled side, but he could not save him.† Instead he caused the dead and twisted body to transform magically into a winding, writhing climbing plant, while the drops of blood solidified and swelled into luscious berries whose skin shone with the bloom and lustre

---

* Books 10, 11 and 12 of the sprawling forty-eight-book epic poem the *Dionysiaca*, written by the Greek poet Nonnus of Panopolis in the fifth century AD, details this relationship and its aftermath at great length.

† Nonnus interrupts the action here (a thing he does a lot: his poem is astonishingly dull, given its superb subject matter) by having Eros come to comfort Dionysus with tales of other great male lovers. He tells of KALAMOS and KARPOS (the latter being son of Zephyrus the West Wind and CHLORIS, nymph of greenery and new growth – as in 'chlorophyl' and 'chlorine'), two beautiful youths passionately in love with each other. During a swimming contest (athletics and hunting seem to be a theme with beautiful youths coming to a sticky end, as we shall see in the tales of HYACINTHUS, ACTAEON, CROCUS and ADONIS, amongst others), Karpos dies, and a desolated, grief-stricken Kalamos commits suicide. Kalamos is then changed into reeds and Karpos into fruit: they are the Greek words for 'reed' and 'fruit' to this day.

the god had so admired. His lover had become a vine (which is still called *ampelos* in Greece to this day). From it Dionysus produced the first vintage and drank the first draught of wine. This witchcraft, as it were, of turning the blood of Ampelos into wine became the god's gift to the world.

A combination of the intoxicating effects of his invention and the enmity of Hera – whose hatred of any bastard of Zeus's, divine or otherwise, was always implacable – sent Dionysus mad for a while. To escape her curses, he spent the next few years travelling far and wide, spreading viticulture and the techniques of winemaking around the world.* In Assyria he encountered the king and queen, STAPHYLOS and METHE, and their son BOTRYS. After a banquet in Dionysus's honour Staphylus died of the first fatal hangover. As compensation, and in their honour, Dionysus named bunches of grapes *staphylos*, alcoholic liquid and drunkenness *methe* and the grape itself *botrys*.

Science has taken these names and immortalized them in a way that splendidly exemplifies the continuing relationship between Greek myth and our language. When nineteenth-century biologists looked down their microscopes and saw a bacterium with a tail, from which clusters of grape-like nodules sprouted, they called it *Staphylococcus*. 'Methylated spirits' and 'methane' take their names from Methe. *Botrytis*, the 'noble rot' that benignly affects grapes on the vine, lending premium dessert wines their incomparable (and shatteringly expensive) bouquet, owes its name to Botrys.

Throughout his adventures, the new god was accompanied

---

* It is said that he gave the secrets of the vine to every known land except Britain and Ethiopia. It is sadly true that neither country has a great reputation for winemaking, although that is changing and these days English wines are making a name for themselves. Perhaps the same is true of Ethiopian vintages.

not just by Silenus and his retinue of satyrs, but by an intense band of women followers too – the MAENADS.*

Dionysus was soon established as the god of wine, revelry, delirious intoxication, uninhibited dissipation and 'the orgastic future'. The Romans called him by the name BACCHUS and worshipped him quite as devotedly as did the Greeks. He was to stand in a kind of polar opposition to Apollo – one representing the golden light of reason, harmonious music, lyric poetry and mathematics, the other embodying the darker energies of disorder, liberation, wild music, bloodlust, frenzy and unreason.

Of course the gods had living personalities and stories, and so they often strayed from such frozen symbolic identities. Apollo, as we shall see very soon, was himself capable of being bloody, crazed and cruel, while Dionysus could be more than just the embodiment of inebriation and debauchery. He was sometimes called 'the Liberator', a vegetal life-force whose licence could benevolently relieve and renew the world.†

Thirteen at Table

The vine leaf, the *thyrsus* – a staff topped with a pine cone – a chariot drawn by leopards or other exotic beasts, depraved attendants sporting roaring erections, jars flowing with

---

* The violent mysteries of these extreme worshippers were depicted in all their shocking savagery by the Athenian playwright Euripides in the fifth century BC in the *Bacchae*. In this bloody tragedy Dionysus returns to Thebes to wreak his revenge on those of his mother's sisters who refused to believe Semele's claim to be carrying Zeus's child. The god sends King Pentheus mad and causes his own bewitched aunts, Agave, Ino and Autonoë, to tear the poor man apart, limb from limb.

† Ovid, in his retellings of Dionysus' myths, commonly uses the name LIBER for him. It carries the sense of 'freedom' and of 'libertine' – as well as, unconnectedly, 'book'.

wine – the Dionysiac Idea added much to the world. The importance of this new god was such that he simply had to be welcomed into Olympus. But there was already a full complement of twelve gods in residence and thirteen was, even then, looked on as an unlucky number. The gods scratched their chins and wondered what could be done. They wanted Dionysus – the truth was they liked him and the festive energy he brought to every gathering. And more than anything they liked the idea of wine being added to nectar, instead of fermented honey and plain fruit juice.

'This comes at a perfect time,' said Hestia, rising to her feet. 'I feel more and more that I am needed down in the world to help people and their families and to be present in the temples that celebrate the virtues of hearth, home and hallway. Let young Bacchus take my place.'

There was an unconvincing murmur of protestation as Hestia stepped down, but she was insistent and the exchange was made to the delight of all the gods – save one. Hera regarded Dionysus as Zeus's grossest insult to her. Apollo, Artemis and Athena were shameful enough as illegitimate additions to the dodecatheon, but that a bastard *half-human* god should be admitted to heaven offended her to the core. She vowed always to abstain from Dionysus's poison drink and personally to shun the carousals with which he wrecked the peace and decorum of heaven.

When Aphrodite gave birth to a son by Dionysus, Hera cursed the baby, whose name was PRIAPUS, with ugliness and impotence and had it cast down from Olympus. Priapus became the god of male genitalia and phalluses; he was especially prized by the Romans as the minor deity of the major boner. But deflation and disappointment were his fate. He went about in a constant state of excitement which, on account of Hera's curse, always failed him when he tried to do anything about it. This chronic and embarrassing problem made it natural that he should be for ever associated with alcohol, his father's gift to the world that ever 'provokes the desire but takes away the performance'.

Nonetheless, whether Hera liked it or not, Dionysus the Twice Born, the only god to have a mortal human parent, rose to take his place now as a full member of the finally fixed Olympian Twelve.

THE BEAUTIFUL AND
THE DAMNED

ANGRY GODDESSES

Actaeon

The Cadmean house was one of the most important dynasties of the Greek world. First Cadmus, as founder of Thebes and bringer of the alphabet, and then his family were all central in the making of Greece. But, like many of the great houses, there was a curse attached to it. The killing of the water dragon allowed the city to be built, but it cast the curse of Ares over it too. The Fates seldom allowed glory and triumph without the accompaniment of suffering and sorrow.

Cadmus's daughter Autonoë had a son, Actaeon, by a minor god called ARISTAEUS, much venerated in Boeotia (he was sometimes referred to as 'the Apollo of the fields'). Like many of the later heroes, Actaeon was tutored and trained by the great and wise centaur Chiron. He grew up to become a much admired huntsman and leader, renowned for his fearlessness in the chase and the skill and tender strength with which he handled his beloved hounds.

One day, having lost the scent of an especially noble stag, Actaeon and his fellow huntsmen separated to pick up the trail. Stumbling through some bushes Actaeon happened on a pool where Artemis was bathing. As she was the goddess of his favourite pursuit, hunting, Actaeon should have known better than to stare dumbstruck at her nakedness. She was also the fierce queen of celibacy, chastity and virginity. But so beautiful was she, so much more lovely than any being Actaeon had ever beheld, that he stood rooted to the spot, his mouth open and his eyes – and not only his eyes – bulging.

It may have been a twig snapping beneath his foot, it may have been the sound of Actaeon's drool hitting the ground, but something made Artemis turn. She saw a young man standing there ogling, and her blood was fired. The thought of anyone spreading the word that they had seen her naked was so abhorrent to her that she called out.

'You, mortal man! Your staring is a profanity. I forbid you ever to speak. If you utter just one syllable your punishment will be terrible. Indicate to me that you understand.'

The unhappy youth nodded. Artemis disappeared from view and he was left alone to consider his fate.

Behind him a halloo started up as his fellow huntsmen announced that they were once more upon the scent. Instinctively Actaeon called out. The moment he did so Artemis's curse descended and he was changed into a stag.

Actaeon raised his head, now heavy with antlers, and galloped through the woods until he came to a pool of water. He looked down into the pool, and at the sight of himself he gave what should have been a groan but which came out as a mighty bellow. The bellow was answered by a great baying and yipping. Within seconds his own pack of hounds had streamed into the clearing. They had been trained by Actaeon himself to rip out a stag's throat and feast on its steaming blood for their reward.* As the yowling and snarling creatures leapt up at him snapping their jaws Actaeon raised his forelegs in the direction of Olympus, as if beseeching the

---

* If you want to impress your friends, you can learn the following list of the male and female hounds as given by Ovid in his version of the myth. If nothing else they might serve as useful names for online passwords.

gods for pity. They either did not hear or did not heed. In seconds he was torn to pieces. The hunter hunted!

Erysichthon

The goddess Demeter is associated with fruitful abundance and the generous bounty of nature, but if pushed beyond her usual forbearance she could be as vengeful as Artemis, as this tale of her ruthless punishment of ERYSICHTHON, King of Thessaly, clearly shows.

In need of timber for the construction of new apartments in his palace, the bold, fearless and impatient Erysichthon one day led a party of woodmen out to the forest, where they came upon a flourishing grove of oaks.

'Excellent,' he cried. 'Swing your axes, boys.'

But his men drew back muttering and shaking their heads.

Erysichthon turned to his foreman. 'What's the matter with them?'

'These trees are sacred to Demeter, sire.'

'Nonsense. She has more than she knows what to do with. Bring them down.'

More muttering.

Erysichthon snatched the foreman's whip, which its owner only ever really waved for show, and cracked it menacingly over the heads of the foresters.

'Chop those trees down, or feel its sting!' he cried.

With their king cracking the whip and urging them on,

Dogs: Melampus, Ichnobates, Pamphagos, Dorceus, Oribasos, Nebrophonos, Lailaps, Theron, Pterelas, Hylaeus, Ladon, Dromas, Tigris, Leucon, Asbolos, Lacon, Aello, Thoos, Harpalos, Melaneus, Labros, Arcas, Argiodus, Hylactor.
Bitches: Agre, Nape, Poemenis, Harpyia, Canache, Sticte, Alce, Lycisce, Lachne, Melanchaetes, Therodamas, Oresitrophos.

the men reluctantly chopped down the trees. But when they came to a giant oak that stood alone at the end of the grove they stopped again.

'Why, this is the tallest and broadest of them all!' said Erysichthon. 'That alone will provide the timber for the rafters and columns of my throne room and still leave enough over for a great bed for me.'

The foreman pointed a trembling finger at the oak's branches, which were hung with garlands.

The king was unimpressed. 'And?'

'My lord,' whispered the foreman, 'each wreath stands for a prayer that the goddess has answered.'

'If the prayers have already been answered she will have no need of flower arrangements. Cut it down.'

But seeing that the foreman and his team were too afraid to proceed, the impetuous Erysichthon snatched up an axe and set about it himself.

He was a strong man and, like most rulers, he loved to show off his will, skill and sinew. It was not long before the trunk creaked and the mighty oak began to sway. Did Erysichthon hear the plaintive cries of a hamadryad in the boughs? If he did he paid no heed but swung his axe again and again, until down crashed the tree – branches, votive wreaths, garlands, hamadryad and all.

As the oak died, so died its hamadryad. With her last breath she cursed Erysichthon for his crime.

Demeter heard of Erysichthon's sacrilege and sent word to Limos. Limos was one of the vile creatures that had flown from Pandora's jar. She was a demon of famine who might be regarded as Demeter's inverse, the goddess's necessary opposite in the mortal world. One the fecund and bountiful herald of the harvest, the other the mercilessly cruel harbinger of hunger and blight. Since the two existed in an irreconcilable matter–antimatter relationship, they could never meet in person, so Demeter sent a nymph of the mountains as her envoy, to urge Limos to deliver the hamadryad's curse on Erysichthon, a task the malevolent demon was only too happy to undertake.

Limos had, according to Ovid, rather let herself go. With sagging, withered breasts, an empty space for a stomach, exposed rotten bowels, sunken eyes, crusted lips, scaly skin, lank, scurfy hair and swollen pustular ankles, the figure and face of Famine presented a haunting and dreadful spectacle. She stole that night into Erysichthon's bedroom, took the sleeping king in her arms and breathed her foul breath into him. Her poison fumes seeped into his mouth, throat and lungs. Through his veins and into every cell of his body slid the terrible, insatiable worm of hunger.

Erysichthon awoke from strange dreams feeling very, *very* peckish. He surprised his kitchen staff with an enormous breakfast order. He consumed every morsel, yet still his appetite was unsated. All day he found that the more he ate the more ravenous he became. As days and then weeks passed, the pangs of hunger gnawed deeper and deeper. No matter how much he consumed he could never be satisfied, nor gain so much as an ounce of weight. Food inside him acted like fuel on a fire, causing the hunger to burn ever more fiercely. For this reason his people began referring to him behind his back as AETHON, which means 'burning'.

He was perhaps the first man ever to eat himself out of house and home. One by one all his treasure and possessions, and even his palace, were sold off to buy food. But still this wasn't enough, for nothing could appease his colossal appetite. At last, he was reduced to selling his daughter MESTRA to raise money to quieten the remorseless demands of his unassuageable appetite.

This was a more cunning and less barbarous act than perhaps it sounds: the beautiful Mestra had once been a lover of Poseidon's, who had rewarded her with the ability to alter her shape at will – a power in the especial gift of the god of the ever changing sea. Every week Erysichthon would offer his daughter to a rich suitor and accept the bride-money. Mestra would accompany her fiancé to his home, escape in the shape of one animal or another and return to Erysichthon, ready to be sold again to a fresh gullible suitor.

Even this arrangement proved insufficient to tamp down the dreadful flames of hunger, and in desperation one day he chewed off his left hand. The arm followed, then his shoulder, feet and hams. Before long, King Erysichthon of Thessaly had eaten himself all up. Demeter and the hamadryad were avenged.

THE DOCTOR AND
THE CROW

The Birth of Medicine

There was once an intensely attractive young princess called CORONIS, who came from the Thessalian kingdom of Phlegyantis. So great was her beauty that she caught the attention of the god Apollo, who took her as a lover. You might think that the companionship and love of the most beautiful of the gods would be enough for anyone, but Coronis – while pregnant with Apollo's child – fell for the charms of a mortal called ISCHYS and slept with him.

One of Apollo's white crows witnessed this act of betrayal and flew back to tell his master all about the insult to his honour. Enraged, Apollo asked his sister Artemis to take revenge. Only too willing, she attacked the palace at Phlegyantis with plague arrows – poisoned darts that spread a terrible disease throughout the compound. Many besides Coronis were infected. The crow saw all and returned to give Apollo a full report.

'She's dying, my lord, dying!'

'Did she say anything? Did she admit her guilt?'

'Oh yes, oh yes. "I deserve my fate," she said. "Tell the great god Apollo that I ask no forgiveness and beg no pity, beg no pity, only save the life of our child. Save the life of our child." Ha! Ha! Ha!'

With such malicious glee did the crow crow, that Apollo

lost his temper and turned it black. All crows, ravens and rooks ever since have been that colour.*

When Apollo, now filled with remorse, reached plague-stricken Phlegyantis he found Coronis lying dead on her funeral pyre, the flames licking all round her. With a cry of grief he leapt through the flames and from her womb cut out their child who was still living. Apollo raised Coronis to the stars as the constellation Corvus, the Crow.†

The rescued infant boy, whom Apollo named Asclepius, was put in the care of the centaur Chiron. Perhaps because he had been delivered by a surgical procedure (albeit a rather violent one), perhaps because while he had been in the womb infection had raged all around him, perhaps because his father was Apollo, god of medicine and mathematics – probably for all these reasons – Asclepius demonstrated early on some very remarkable talents in the field of medicine.

As the boy grew, it quickly became clear to Chiron that he allied an incisive, logical and curious mind with a natural gift for healing. Chiron, no mean naturalist, herbalist and reasoner himself, took enormous pleasure in training the boy in the medical arts. Besides giving him a thorough grounding in the anatomy of animals and humans, he taught him that knowledge is gained from observation and careful record-keeping rather than from spinning theories. He showed him how to gather medicinal plants, grind them, mix them, heat them, and work them into powders, potions and preparations that could be eaten, drunk or stirred into food. He instructed him how to staunch blood flow, concoct

---

* Although, on a BBC TV adaptation of the *Gormenghast* books, I worked with an albino crow called Jimmy White.

† *koronis* is a Greek word for 'crow' or 'rook'. Its original meaning is 'curved', whether in reference to the curves of the princess or of the bird's beak I cannot say.

fomented poultices, dress wounds and reset fractured bones. By the time he was fourteen he had saved a soldier's leg from being amputated, brought a fevered young girl back from the very brink of death, rescued a bear from a trap, saved the population of a village from an epidemic of dysentery and relieved the suffering of a bruised snake by the application of an ointment of his own devising. This last case proved to be invaluable, for the grateful serpent had licked Asclepius's ear in thanks, whispering as he did so many secrets of the arts of healing that were closed even to Chiron.

Athena, to whom snakes were sacred, bestowed her thanks too, in the form of a jar of Gorgon's blood. You might think this a poor gift. Far from it. Sometimes the law of opposites applies. A single drop of the silvery-gold ichor that keeps the gods immortal is fatal for humans to touch or taste. The blood of a creature as deadly and dangerous as a serpent-haired Gorgon, on the other hand, has the power to bring the dead back to life.

By the time he was twenty Asclepius had mastered all the arts of surgery and medicine. He embraced his teacher Chiron in a fond farewell and left to set up on his own as the world's first physician, apothecary and healer. His fame spread around the Mediterranean with great speed. The sick, lame and unhappy flocked to his surgery, outside which he hung a sign – a wooden staff with a snake twined round it, seen to this day on many ambulances, clinics and (often disreputable) medical websites.*

He married EPIONE, whose name means 'soothing' or

---

* Some use the staff of Asclepius (or Hippocratic staff) – a rough wooden stick, entwined with a single serpent. Others use the *caduceus* of Hermes – a more slender and elegant staff entwined by two serpents whose heads meet at the top and are surmounted by a pair of wings. There does not seem to be any professional or clinical significance in the choice; it is purely a matter of preference.

'relief from pain'. Together they had three sons and four daughters. Asclepius trained his girls as rigorously as Chiron had trained him.

The eldest, HYGIEIA, he taught the practices of cleanliness, diet and physical exercise that are today named 'hygiene' after her.

To PANACEA he revealed the arts of universal health, of medicinal preparation and the production of remedies and treatments that could heal anything – which is what her name means: 'cure all'.

ACESO he instructed in the healing process itself, including what we would now call immunology.

The youngest girl IASO specialized in recovery and recuperation.

The elder boys, MACHAON and PODALIRIUS, became prototypes of the army doctor. Their later service in the Trojan War was recorded by Homer.

The youngest son, TELESPHORUS, is usually depicted as being hooded and of very restricted growth. His field of study was rehabilitation and convalescence, the return of a patient to full health.

All might have gone well had Asclepius kept tightly sealed the jar that Athena presented to him. Tightly sealed. Whether it was the glory of being celebrated as a kind of saint and saviour or whether it was a genuine desire to beat death with his arts we cannot know, but Asclepius used the Gorgon's blood once to revive the corpse of a dead patient, then a second time, and soon he was using it as liberally and regularly as castor oil.

Hades began to grumble and fume. Unable to bear it any longer he went so far as to leave the underworld and stand angrily before the throne of his brother Zeus.

'This man is denying me souls. He pulls them back from Thanatos just as they are ready to cross over to us. Something must be done.'

'I agree,' said Hera. 'He is subverting the proper order of things. If a person is marked down for death it is quite unacceptable for a mortal to interfere. Your daughter did a very foolish thing in giving him Gorgon's blood.'

Zeus frowned. There was no denying the truth of what they said. He was disappointed in Athena. She had not betrayed him in so flagrant and unforgivable a manner as Prometheus, but there were points of similarity that troubled him. Mortals were mortal and that was that. Allowing them access to potions that gave them ascendancy over death was quite wrong.

The thunderbolt which struck Asclepius was wholly unexpected, as bolts from the blue always are. It killed him stone dead. All of Greece lamented the loss of their beloved and valued physician and healer, but Apollo did more than mourn the passing of his son. He raged. As soon as he heard the news he took himself off to the workshop of Hephaestus and with three swift arrows shot dead Brontes, Steropes and Arges, the Cyclopes whose eternal task and pleasure it was to manufacture the Sky Father's thunderbolts.

Such astounding rebelliousness was not to be brooked. Zeus was intolerant of any threat to his authority and always moved swiftly to put down the slightest hint of insurrection. Apollo was thrown from Olympus and commanded to serve the Thessalian king ADMETUS in a lowly position for a year and a day. Admetus had earned the approval of Zeus by his exceptionally warm hospitality and kindness to strangers – always a direct route to Zeus's heart.

Apollo had been punished when young, you will recall,

for slaying the serpent Python. His beauty, splendour and golden charm hid a stubborn will and a hot temper. He submitted to this punishment readily enough, however. Admetus was impossible to dislike and, serving as his cowherd, Apollo ensured that every cow under his care gave birth to twins.* Cattle and twins were special to him.

Asclepius, meanwhile, was raised to the heavens as the constellation Ophiuchus, the Serpent-Bearer.

Later traditions asserted that Zeus restored Asclepius to life and raised him up as a god. It is true that throughout the Mediterranean world he and his wife and daughters were worshipped as divine. Temples to him, known as *asclepia*, sprang up everywhere, bearing great similarities to modern spas and health clubs. Their officiating priests wore white and bathed, massaged and pampered the paying supplicants with preposterous oils, creams and patent mixtures, just as they do today. Ever sacred to Asclepius, snakes (the non-venomous kind) were encouraged to slither about the treatment rooms and clinics, a sight perhaps less common in our contemporary temples to health. The spirit and mind were as attended to then as they are now. 'Holistic' is, after all, a Greek-derived word. Dreams were told to priests on the morning after an overnight stay (known as an 'incubation') and Asclepius himself often manifested to patients. Especially, I believe, to those who paid the most.

The Asclepion of Epidaurus was as big a draw as the town's celebrated theatre is today. Those who visit it can still see records of the illnesses, treatments, diets and cures of the patients who flocked there.

---

* The poet and scholar Callimachus, who lived in the third century BC, suggested that Apollo and Admetus became enthusiastic lovers during this period of servitude.

CRIME AND PUNISHMENT

The regular appearance, interference and intercourse of the gods with human society, which would be so remarkable, thrilling and troubling to us if it happened today, was sometimes taken for granted by the more foolish and self-important mortals of the Silver Age. Some kings were so puffed up that they ignored the most elementary precepts of the gods and exhibited the most flagrant disrespect towards them. Such blasphemous acts of lese-majesty seldom went unpunished. Like parents admonishing children with gruesome moral fables, or like Dante or Hieronymus Bosch with their cautionary hellscapes, the ancient Greeks seemed to relish the details and delightful aptness of the often elaborate and excruciating tortures that Olympus and Hades reserved for those men and women whose transgressions most aggravated them.

Ixion

There was no graver sin in Zeus's eyes than the betrayal of *xenia*, the sacred duty of hosts towards guests, and guests towards hosts. Few mortals showed more contempt for its principles than Ixion, King of the Lapiths, an ancient tribe from Thessaly.

His first crime was one of simple greed. We are familiar with the idea of dowries, the practice of families of prospective brides paying to have their daughters taken off their hands. In the very earliest days things were done the other way around: prospective husbands paid the bride's family for the right to marry their daughter. Ixion wed the beautiful DIA but refused to pay her father, King DEIONEUS of Phocis, the agreed bride-price. In retaliation the affronted Deioneus sent a raiding party to take a herd of Ixion's best horses. Hiding his vexation beneath a wide smile Ixion invited Deioneus to dinner at his palace in Larissa. When he arrived Ixion pushed him into a fiery pit. This flagrant breach of the rules of hospitality was trumped by the even grosser sin of blood killing. The slaying of a family member was considered a taboo of the most heinous kind. With this action Ixion had committed one of the first blood murders; unless he was cleansed of his transgression, the Furies would pursue him until he went mad.

The princes, lords and neighbouring landowners of Thessaly had cause to dislike Ixion and none offered to perform the *catharsis*, the ritual process of purification that would redeem him. The King of the Gods, though, was in a surprisingly forgiving mood. The people of Thessaly had acted quickly to show their revulsion at Ixion's double crime of *xenia* abuse and kin-slaying. Zeus was minded to be merciful. He not only released Ixion from his torment but went so far as to invite him to a banquet on Olympus.

Such an honour was rare for mortals. The glamour and grandeur of an Olympian feast were beyond anything Ixion would have seen before. He was especially bowled over by the queenly beauty of Hera. Whether it was the intoxicating effects of the great occasion or the wine, nobody could afterwards decide – perhaps it was nothing more than congenital boorish idiocy – but far from behaving with the modest gratitude you might expect of any mortal invited to the immortal dinner table, Ixion committed the catastrophic error of trying to seduce the Queen of Heaven. He blew Hera kisses, winked at her, tried to nibble her ear, whispered lewd remarks and made concerted grabs at her breasts. He not only insulted the most dignified and proper of the Olympians but he once more transgressed the laws of *xenia*. Failing in the duties as a guest was considered as heinous as failing in the duties of a host.

After Ixion had staggered down from Olympus, slapping backs and belching out thanks, an offended Hera told Zeus of the outrage upon her honour. Zeus was equally incensed. He decided to lay a trap for Ixion. The Cloud Gatherer gathered a cloud and sculpted it into an anatomically exact and fully working likeness of Hera. He blew on it, animating it into life and sent it down to a meadow outside Larissa, where he had seen Ixion sprawled asleep on the grass, snoring off the effects of the banquet.

When Ixion awoke to find Hera beside him, he rolled over and coupled with her there and then. At the sight of this unspeakable blasphemy Zeus sent down a thunderbolt and a fiery wheel. The thunderbolt blasted Ixion into the air and pinned him to the wheel, which Zeus sent spinning across the heavens. In time the firmament was deemed too good for him and Ixion, bound to his wheel of fire, was sent down to Tartarus, where he revolves, spread-eagled and roasting in agony to this very day.

The Hera-Cloud was given the name NEPHELE. Her union with Ixion produced a son, CENTAUROS, an ugly and misshapen boy who grew into a lonely and unhappy man who took his pleasure, not with humans, but with the wild mares of Mount Pelion, where he liked to roam. The untameable and savage progeny of this unnatural union between man and horse were named, after him, 'centaurs'.*

Consequences

Many of the Greek myths lead to cascades of consequences. As we have already seen, leading figures in one story will go on to marry and found dynasties from whom are born yet more legendary heroes. And there are plenty of subsidiary myths that spin off from the Wheel of Ixion.

While on the subject of Mount Pelion, for example, it is worth mentioning the story of IPHIMEDIA, who was so in love with Poseidon that she would regularly sit by the shore, scooping up seawater and pouring it over her breasts and into her lap. Poseidon was touched by this show of adoration and swept out of the ocean in an embracing wave to conjoin with her. Twin sons were born, OTUS and EPHIALTES. They were true giants in our modern sense: as boys they grew by the breadth of a human hand every month. It was clear that when they reached manhood they would be the largest beings alive.

As you will recall, the jealous and ambitious Poseidon had always kept in mind the possibility that one day his younger brother Zeus might slip up and be toppled from his throne. The sea god put in the heads of his fast-growing boys the idea of challenging heaven by creating their own mountain

---

* Only one such equine–human hybrid had been seen on earth before: the great Chiron, tutor to Asclepius, Achilles and many others. Chiron's birth could be traced back to the time of Kronos, son of Ouranos and Gaia, father of Zeus and Hera. During a lull in the Titanomachy, Kronos fell for PHYLIRA, an Oceanid of great beauty. She repelled his advances until, tiring of her bashfulness, he transformed himself into a great black stallion and took her against her will. Chiron was the offspring of this union and – despite pre-dating Centauros by many hundreds of years – he is referred to as a centaur by convention.

from which to rule the world. Their plan was to pull up Mount Ossa and heap it on Olympus. On top of Ossa they would pile Mount Pelion. But before the twins had grown to the full height and strength necessary to achieve this, word reached Zeus of the possibility of their rebellion and Apollo was sent to fell them with arrows. Their punishment in the underworld was to be bound to pillars with writhing snakes.

Just to run the thread of the narrative right through to one of its conclusions (and as a further example of how one story could lead on to other, even more significant and far-reaching, myths), you should know that Nephele, the cloud image of Hera, went on to marry a Boeotian king called ATHAMAS,* by whom she bore two sons, PHRIXUS and HELLE. Nephele had cause to save the life of Phrixus – an Isaac to his father's Abraham – when Athamas tied his son to the ground and made to sacrifice him. Just as the Hebrew god revealed a ram in a thicket to Abraham and saved Isaac's life, so Nephele sent a golden ram to rescue her son Phrixus. The golden fleece of that ram gave rise to the great quest of Jason and his Argonauts. All on account of a drunken degenerate king who had the temerity to make eyes at Hera.

The Wheel of Ixion became a popular subject for artists and sculptors and the phrase 'a wheel of fire' is sometimes used to describe an agonizing burden, punishment or duty.† The expression 'to pile Pelion on Ossa' is seen too, meaning to add difficulty to difficulty.

---

* Athamas was a brother of Sisyphus, the reason for whose infamy we shall soon see.
† Shakespeare's King Lear cries out:

> Thou art a soul in bliss, but I am bound
> Upon a wheel of fire, that mine own tears
> Do scald like molten lead.

260

Tantalus

Perhaps the best-known torment the gods ever devised is that which was dreamed up for the wicked King Tantalus. The consequences of his crimes had ramifications that rang down through the years. The curse upon his house was not lifted until the very end of the mythic age.

Tantalus ruled the kingdom of Lydia in western Asia Minor, the region later known as the Turkish province of Anatolia. Mineral deposits from nearby Mount Sipylus had yielded him enormous riches, from which he established a prosperous city that he immodestly called Tantalis. He married DIONE (one of the Hyades, or rain nymphs, who had suckled the infant Dionysus) and by her had a son, PELOPS, and a daughter, NIOBE.*

Either there was a kink in Tantalus's personality or his power and wealth had fooled him into believing himself equal to the gods. Like Ixion before him he made the mistake of abusing Zeus's hospitality, in his case by returning from a banquet on Olympus with stolen ambrosia and nectar in his pockets. He also committed the unpardonable solecism of telling tales about the private lives and mannerisms of the gods, amusing his courtiers and friends with insolent mimicry and gossip.

But then he committed a blood murder, one even worse than Ixion's crime of casting his father-in-law into a pit of burning coals. Hearing that the Olympians were furious at his mockery and the theft of their nectar and ambrosia, he made a great show of repentance and begged that they accept his own hospitality in recompense for his misconduct.

---

* There was another son, BROTEAS, who liked to hunt and whose life seems to have been uneventful compared to that of his siblings. He is said to have carved a figure of Cybele, the Anatolian mother goddess, into the rock of Mount Sipylus. Parts of it are still visible to the tourist today.

Now, all of this took place around the time Demeter was searching for her abducted daughter Persephone. In her grief she had allowed all growing things to wither and die. The world was barren and infertile and no one knew how long this would last. The prospect of a feast came as a welcome excitement. Knowing of the opulent and ostentatious lifestyle of King Tantalus, the gods were greatly looking forward to the legendary pleasures of his table.* They were in for a shock.

As the Pelasgian king Lycaon had done before him, Tantalus served up his own son to the gods. The young Pelops was killed, jointed, roasted, slathered in a rich sauce and set before them. They sensed instantly that something was wrong and declined to eat. But Demeter, whose mind was wholly on her lost daughter, distractedly picked at and ate the boy's left shoulder.

When Zeus understood what had happened, he summoned one of the three Fates, Clotho, the spinner. She collected the body parts, stirred them in a great cauldron and put them back together. Demeter, awakened to her dreadful lapse, commissioned Hephaestus to carve a shoulder from ivory to replace the one she had consumed. Clotho attached the prosthetic, which fitted perfectly. Zeus breathed into the boy's body and Pelops stirred back into life.

Pelops's great beauty attracted Poseidon, and for a while they became lovers. Yet darker forces were at work with the youth, and his later life and deeds called down a curse upon him and all his house.† Compounded with the curse earned

---

* The Olympians may have subsisted on ambrosia and nectar, but they took great delight in the variety offered by mortal diets too.

† Named by historical convention the house of Atreus, after one his sons. The fall of the house of Pelops and Atreus involves the destinies of many heroes and warriors right down to the Trojan war and its aftermath. Agamemnon, Clytemnestra and Orestes were all descended from Pelops and said to have inherited his and Tantalus's curse. Pelops's name lives on, of course, in the Peloponnese, the great peninsula to the south west of the Grecian mainland.

by the abominable crime of Tantalus, this curse was to pursue his descendants down to the last of their line, ORESTES.

Tantalus himself was despatched straight to Tartarus and punished in a manner befitting one who dared tempt the gods into feasting on the flesh of the victim of a blood crime. He was placed in a pool of water up to his waist. Above his head waved the bough of a tree from which hung luscious and appetizing fruits. Hunger and thirst raged within him, but every time he stretched up to take a bite, the branch would swing out of his reach. Every time he stooped to drink, the waters of the pool would shrink back to deny him. He could not move away, for above him, threatening to crush him if he dared try to escape, hovered a great stone of the hard glaucus element that would one day be called 'tantalum'.*

There Tantalus stands to this day, agonizingly close to satisfaction, but always denied it, enacting the tortured frustration that bears his name – *tantalized*, but never satisfied, until the end of time.†

---

* Tantalum is one of those refractory metals that is essential these days in the manufacture of many of our electronic devices.

† A *tantalus* is a small cabinet containing two or three drinks decanters, usually of brandy, whisky or rum. The drinks are on display but the cabinet is locked, and thus tantalizingly out of the reach of the children of the household.

SISYPHUS

Brotherly Love

The eternal punishment Sisyphus endures in Hades has also entered language and lore, but there is much more to his story than the famous stone he is doomed endlessly and fruitlessly to push uphill. Sisyphus was a wicked, greedy, duplicitous and often cruel man, but who cannot find something appealing – heroic even – in the unquenchable zest and fist-shaking defiance with which he lived (in fact *out*-lived) his life? Few mortals dared to try the patience of the gods in so reckless a fashion. His foolhardy contempt and refusal to apologize or conform put one in mind of a Grecian Don Giovanni.

Deucalion and Pyrrha, the survivors of the Great Flood, had had a son named HELLEN, after whom the Greeks to this day call themselves Hellenes. Hellen's son AEOLUS had four sons – Sisyphus, SALMONEUS, Athamas and CRETHEUS. Sisyphus and Salmoneus hated each other with as visceral and implacable a hatred as the human world had yet witnessed. Rivals in their parents' affections, rivals in everything, from the cradle neither could bear to see the other succeed. The two princes outgrew their father's realm of Aeolia, as Thessaly was called in those days, and moved south and west to found their own kingdoms. Salmoneus ruled over Elis and Sisyphus established Ephyra, later called Corinth. From these fastnesses, they glared at each other across the Peloponnese, their bitter enmity growing with each passing year.

Sisyphus hated Salmoneus so much it robbed him of his sleep. He wanted him dead, dead, dead. The desire was so agonizing he stabbed himself repeatedly in the thigh with a dagger to relieve himself of it. But there was nothing he could do. The Furies would avenge themselves terribly if he dared murder a brother. Fratricide was amongst the worst of the blood crimes. Eventually he decided to consult the oracle at Delphi.

'Sons of Sisyphus and Tyro rise to slay Salmoneus,' intoned the Pythia.

This was sweet music to Sisyphus's ears. TYRO was his niece, daughter of his hated brother Salmoneus. All Sisyphus had to do was marry and get sons from her. Sons who would 'rise to slay Salmoneus'. Uncles could marry nieces without raising any eyebrows in those days and so he set about beguiling and seducing Tyro with horses, jewels, poems and oceans of personal charm, for Sisyphus was nothing if not captivating when he chose to be. In due course his wooing won her, they wed and she bore him two bouncing boys.

One day some years later, Sisyphus was out fishing with his friend MELOPS. Sunning themselves on the banks of the River Sythas, they fell into conversation. At exactly the same time, Tyro set out from the palace with a maid, the two boys – now aged five and three – and a hamper of food and wine, with the idea of surprising Sisyphus with a family picnic.

Back on the riverbank, Melops and Sisyphus talked lazily about horses, women, sport and war. Tyro's group made their way across the fields.

'Tell me, sire,' said Melops, 'it has always surprised me that despite your bitter feud with King Salmoneus, you chose to marry his daughter. For all that I can tell, you still dislike him as much as ever.'

'Dislike him? I abominate, loathe, despise and abhor him,' said Sisyphus with a loud laugh. A laugh that allowed the approaching Tyro to draw a bead on his exact position. As her party drew nearer she could now hear every word her husband spoke.

'I only married that bitch Tyro because I hate Salmoneus so much,' he was saying. 'You see, the oracle at Delphi told me that if I had sons by her they would grow up to kill him. So when he dies by the hand of his own grandchildren I will be rid of my vile pig of a brother without fear of the pursuit of the Erinyes.'

'That is . . .' Melops tried to find the word.

'Brilliant? Cunning? Ingenious?'

Tyro checked her sons, who were about to run to the spot from which they could hear their father's voice. Turning them round she pushed them at speed towards a bend in the river, the maid following behind.

Tyro had swallowed Sisyphus's charm whole, but she loved her father Salmoneus with a loyalty that overrode any other consideration. The idea of allowing her sons to grow up to kill their grandfather was out of the question. She knew how to defy the oracle's prophecy.

'Come child,' she said to the eldest, 'look down at the stream. Can you see any little fishes?'

The small boy knelt on the riverbank and looked down. Tyro put a hand to his neck and pushed him under. When he had stopped struggling she did the same to the youngest.

'Now,' she said quite calmly to the traumatized maid, 'this is what you will do . . .'

Sisyphus and Melops caught plenty of fish that afternoon. Just as the light was fading and they had started to pack up for the day, Tyro's maidservant appeared before them, bobbing a nervous curtsey.

'Beg pardon, majesty, but the Queen asks that you might greet the princes. They are by the riverbank, awaiting your majesty. Just behind the willow tree, sire.'

Sisyphus went to the place indicated to find his two sons lying stretched out on the grass, pale and lifeless.

The maid ran for her life and was never heard of again. Tyro, by the time the enraged Sisyphus had reached the palace with drawn sword, was safely on her way to her father's kingdom of Elis. On her arrival home Salmoneus married her to his brother Cretheus, with whom she was deeply unhappy.

Salmoneus himself, quite as proud and vainglorious as his hated brother, had set himself up in Elis as a kind of god. Claiming to equal Zeus's power to summon storms, he'd ordered the construction of a brass bridge over which he liked to ride his chariot at breakneck speed, trailing kettles, cauldrons and iron pots to mimic the sound of thunder. Flaming torches would be thrown skywards at the same time to imitate lightning. Such blasphemous impertinence caught the eye of Zeus, who ended the farrago with a real thunderbolt. The king, his chariot, brass bridge, cooking utensils and all were blasted to atoms and the shade of Salmoneus cast down to eternal damnation in the darkest depths of Tartarus.

Sisyphean Tasks

Sisyphus held a great feast to celebrate the death of his preposterous thunder-making brother. The morning after, he was awoken by a deputation of aggrieved lords, landowners and tenant farmers. After he had rubbed the sleep from his eyes and cleared his headache with a goblet of unwatered wine he consented to hear what might be the matter.

'Majesty, someone is stealing our cattle! Each one of us can report a loss. Your own royal herds are depleted too. You are a wise and clever king. Surely you can find out who is responsible?'

Sisyphus dismissed them with a promise to investigate. He had a very good idea that the thief was his neighbour AUTOLYCUS, but how to prove it? Sisyphus was guileful and smart, but Autolycus was a son of Hermes himself, the prince of robbers and rascals, the god who as an infant had rustled Apollo's cattle. From Hermes, Autolycus had inherited not only this propensity to take cows that didn't belong to him, but also powers of enchantment that made it very difficult to catch him in the act.* Besides, the cattle that Sisyphus and his neighbours had lost were brown and white and generously horned, while those of Autolycus were black and white and entirely hornless. It was baffling, but Sisyphus was sure that spells taught by Hermes were behind it and that Autolycus was secretly colour-changing stolen cows.

'Very well,' he said to himself, 'we shall see which proves the more powerful, the cheap magic of a trickster god's bastard or the native wit and intelligence of Sisyphus, founder of Corinth, the cleverest king in the world.'

He commanded that all his and his neighbours' cattle should have the words 'AUTOLYCUS STOLE ME' carved into their hoofs in tiny lettering. Over the next seven nights, as expected, the local herds continued regularly to be depleted. On the eighth day Sisyphus and the leading landowners paid Autolycus a visit.

'Greetings, my friends!' their neighbour cried with a cheery wave. 'To what do I owe the honour of this visit?'

---

* The rascally entertainer, pickpocket, tinker and 'snapper-up of unconsidered trifles' in Shakespeare's *The Winter's Tale* is called Autolycus.

'We have come to inspect your cattle,' said Sisyphus.

'By all means. Are you thinking of breeding black and whites yourself? My pedigree herd is unique in the region, they tell me.'

'Oh, it's unique alright,' returned Sisyphus. 'Whoever saw hoofs like this?' He lifted the foreleg of one of the cows.

Autolycus leaned forward, read the words carved into the hoof and gave a cheerful shrug. 'Ah,' he said. 'Fun while it lasted.'

'Take them all,' commanded Sisyphus. As the landowners led the animals away, Sisyphus looked towards Autolycus's house. 'I think I'll help myself to *all* your cows,' he said. 'Every last heifer.' By which he meant AMPHITHEA, Autolycus's wife.

Sisyphus was not a good man.*

The Eagle

The achievement of outsmarting the progeny of the trickster god went to Sisyphus's head. He began to believe that he really was the cleverest and most resourceful man in the world. He set himself up as a kind of royal problem-solver, pronouncing on all manner of issues brought to him and charging enormous sums for his rulings. But there is a difference between guile and good sense, cunning and judgement, quick-wittedness and wisdom.

Do you recall the Asopos? It was in the waters of this Boeotian river that the Theban priestess Semele had washed, attracting the attentions of Zeus and bringing about the birth

---

* This violation of Amphithea gave rise to the rumour that Sisyphus was the true father of Autolycus's daughter ANTICLEA. Anticlea begat LAERTES and Laertes begat the great hero ODYSSEUS aka Ulysses, who was known above all for his wiliness and resource.

of Dionysus. Unhappily the god of that river had a daughter, AEGINA, who was beautiful enough to catch Zeus's eye. In the form of an eagle the god swooped down and seized the girl, taking her to an island off the coast of Attica. The distraught river god searched everywhere for her, asking everyone he met if they had seen any sign of his beloved daughter.

'A young girl, dressed in goatskin, you say?' responded Sisyphus when his turn came to be pressed for information. 'Why, yes, I saw just such a maiden snatched up by an eagle not long ago. She had been bathing in the river when he dived out of the sun . . . It was the most –'

'Where did he take her? Did you see?'

'Are those bracelets real gold? I must say they are very fine.'

'Take them, they are yours. Only for pity's sake tell me what happened to Aegina.'

'I was high on a hill so I saw the whole thing. The eagle took her to – that ring of yours, an emerald, is it? Why thank you, now let me see . . . Yes, they flew across the sea and landed there, on that island. Come to the window. You can just make it out on the horizon, see? Oenone, they call the island, I believe. That's where you'll find them. Oh, are you leaving?'

Asopos chartered a boat and made his way to the island. He hadn't made it halfway over before Zeus saw him coming and sent a thunderbolt across his bows. Its blast swept Asopos and his boat in a great tidal bore up his own estuary and into his river.*

But Sisyphus! Zeus had had his eye on that villain for some time. It had not gone unnoticed to the god of *xenia* that

---

* Asopos had charge of at least two rivers. There was the one in Boeotia that watered Thebes, and this one, which ran through Corinth.

Sisyphus had a history of abusing the guests that travelled in his lands. Taxing them, plundering their treasures, making free with their women, shamelessly transgressing every canon of the sacred laws of hospitality. And now he presumed to interfere in matters that were none of his business, to meddle in the affairs of his betters, to tell tales on the King of the Gods himself. It was time to take measures. An example must be set that would serve as a warning to others. Death and damnation to him.

Despite Sisyphus's royal blood, his life had been too wicked, too shameless, Zeus ruled, to merit the dignity of his being conducted to the underworld by Hermes. Instead Thanatos, Death himself, was sent to shackle and escort him.

Cheating Death

Inasmuch as so gloomy a spirit was capable of so cheerful an emotion, Thanatos always enjoyed that moment when he manifested himself in front of those marked down for death.

Appearing before them, and visible to no one else, his gaunt form cloaked in black, wisps of hellish gasses streaming from him, he would stretch out his arm to his victims with a cruelly deliberate slowness. The moment he touched their flesh with the tip of his bony finger there would come a piteous whimper from the soul within them. Thanatos took great delight in watching his victim's skin go pale and the eyes flutter and film over as life was extinguished. Above all he loved the sound of the soul's last shuddering sigh as it emerged from its mortal carcass and submitted itself to his manacles, ready to be led away.

Sisyphus, like most wily, ambitious schemers, was a light sleeper. His mind was always turning, and the slightest noise could jerk him awake. Thus it was that even the silent whisper of Death gliding into his bedchamber caused him to sit up.

'Who the hell are you?'

'Who the hell indeed? *The Hell* is just who I am. Mwahahaha!' Thanatos unloosed the sinister, ghoulish laugh that so often sent dying mortals screaming mad.

'Stop groaning. What's the matter with you? Have you got toothache? Indigestion? And don't talk in riddles. What is your name?'

'My name . . .' Thanatos paused for effect. 'My name . . .'

'I haven't got all night.'

'My name is . . .'

'Have you even got a name?'

'Thanatos.'

'Oh, so you're Death, are you? Hm.' Sisyphus seemed unimpressed. 'I thought you'd be taller.'

'Sisyphus, son of Aeolus,' Thanatos intoned in quelling accents, 'King of Corinth, Lord of . . .'

'Yes, yes, I know who *I* am. You're the one who seems to have trouble remembering his name. Sit down, why don't you? Take the weight off your feet.'

'My weight is not on my feet. I am hovering.'

Sisyphus looked down at the floor. 'Oh yes, so you are. And you've come for me have you?'

Not confident that any words of his would be received with the respect and awe they deserved, Thanatos showed Sisyphus his manacles and shook them threateningly in his face.

'So you've brought shackles along. Iron?'

'Steel. Unbreakable steel. Fetters forged in the fires of

1. The wedding of Hera and Zeus

2. Hephaestus – god of fire, of blacksmiths, artisans, sculptors and metalworkers – at work in his forge.

3. Ares, god of war.

4. Ares sleeps peacefully while Aphrodite watches, awake and alert.

6. Pallas Athena, goddess of war.

5. Equipped with armour, shield, spear and plumed helmet, Athena rises out of the head of her father, Zeus.

7. For the messenger of the gods, Hephaestus fashioned what would become Hermes' signature footwear, the *talaria* – a pair of winged sandals.

8. Apollo, entranced by Hermes' gift to the god of music.

9. Artemis, goddess of the chase and the chaste, of hounds and hinds, queen of archers and huntresses.

10. Prometheus brings fire to mankind.

11. Zeus called to Prometheus: 'You will lie chained to this rock for ever. Each day these eagles will come to tear out your liver, just as you tore out my heart. Since you are immortal it will grow back every night. This torture will never end.'

12. The instant that human spirits departed their bodies, they were led to where the River Styx (Hate) met the River Acheron (Woe). There the grim and silent Charon held out his hand to receive his payment for ferrying the souls across the Styx.

13. The Golden Age of gods and mankind came to an end when Pandora opened the *pithos*, releasing Illness, Violence, Deceit, Misery and Want into the world.

14. For six months Persephone was Queen of the Underworld. For the other six months, she returned to her mother Demeter as the Kore of fertility, flowers and frolic.

15. Eros and Psyche . . . Cupid and Anima . . . Love and Soul.

16. Phaeton had begged his father Apollo to allow him to drive the chariot of the sun across the sky.

17. Silenus, the pot-bellied tutor of Dionysus, accompanied by the *sileni* – satyr-like creatures for ever associated with antic riot, rout and revelry.

18. To punish Marsyas for his *hubris* in daring to test an Olympian, Apollo peeled the skin from the satyr's living body.

19. Arachne, so proud of her weaving, challenged an Olympian to a contest.

Hephaestus by Steropes the Cyclops. Enchanted by my lord Hades. Whomsoever they bind cannot be unbound save by the god himself.'

'Impressive,' Sisyphus conceded. 'But in my experience nothing is unbreakable. Besides, there isn't even a lock or catch.'

'The hasp and spring are too cunningly contrived to be seen by mortal eyes.'

'So you say. I don't believe for a second that they work. I bet you can't close them round even your skinny arm. Go on, try.'

Such open ridicule of his prized manacles could not be borne. 'Foolish man!' cried Thanatos. 'Such intricate devices are beyond the understanding of a mortal. See here! Round my back once and pass in front. Easy. Bring my wrists together, then close up the bracelets. And if you would be good enough to press just here, to engage the clasp, there's an invisible panel and . . . behold!'

'Yes, I see,' said Sisyphus thoughtfully. 'I *do* see. I was wrong, quite wrong. What superb workmanship.'

'Oh.'

Thanatos tried to wave the manacles, but his whole upper body was now constrained and immobile. 'Er . . . help?'

Sisyphus sprang from his bed and opened the door of a large wardrobe at the end of the room. It was the simplest thing in the world to send the hovering, tightly bound Thanatos across the room. With one push he had glided in and bumped his nose on the back of the closet.

Turning the key on him Sisyphus called out cheerily. 'The lock to this wardrobe may be cheap and manmade, but I can assure you that it works as well as any fetters forged in the fires of Hephaestus.'

Muffled despairing cries came, begging to be let out, but

with a hearty 'Mwahahaha' Sisyphus skipped away, deaf to Death's entreaties.

Life without Death

The first few days of Thanatos's imprisonment passed without incident. Neither Zeus nor Hermes nor even Hades himself thought to verify that Sisyphus had been checked in to the infernal regions as arranged. But when a whole week passed without the arrival of any new dead souls, the spirits and demons of the underworld began to murmur. Another week went by and not a single departed shade had been admitted for processing, save one venerable priestess of Artemis, whose blameless life merited the honour of a personal escort to Elysium by Hermes, the Psychopomp. This sudden stemming of the flow of souls quite perplexed the denizens of Hades, until someone remarked that they hadn't seen Thanatos in days. Search parties were sent out, but Death could not be found. Such a thing had never happened before. Without Thanatos the whole system collapsed.

In Olympus opinion was divided. Dionysus found the whole situation hilarious and drank a toast to the end of lethal cirrhosis of the liver. Apollo, Artemis and Poseidon were more or less neutral on the subject. Demeter feared that Persephone's authority as Queen of the Underworld was being flouted. The seasons over which mother and daughter had dominion required that life be constantly ended and begun again, and only the presence of death could achieve this. The impropriety of such a scandal made Hera quite indignant, which made Zeus restive in turn. The usually merry and irrepressible Hermes was anxious too, for the smooth running of the underworld was partly his responsibility.

But it was Ares who found the situation most intolerable. He was outraged. He looked down and saw battles being fought in the human realm with their customary ferocity, yet *no one was dying*. Warriors were being run through with javelins, trampled by horses, gutted by chariot wheels and beheaded by swords but they would not die. It made a mockery of combat. If soldiers and civilians did not die, why then – war had no point. It settled nothing. It achieved nothing. Neither side in a battle could ever win.

Lesser deities were as divided over the issue as the Olympians. The Keres continued to drink the blood of those felled in battle and could not care less what happened to their souls. Two of the Horai, Diké and Eunomia, agreed with Demeter that the absence of death upset the natural order of things. Their sister Eirene, the goddess of peace, could barely contain her delight. If the absence of Death meant the absence of war then surely her time had come?

Ares nagged his parents Hera and Zeus with such incessant clamour that at last they could bear it no longer. They declared that Thanatos must be found. Hera demanded to know when he had last been seen.

'Surely, Hermes,' said Zeus, 'it wasn't so long ago that you sent him to fetch the soul of that black-hearted villain Sisyphus?'

'Damn!' Hermes slapped his thigh in annoyance. 'Of course! *Sisyphus*. We sent Thanatos to chain him up and escort him to Hades. Wait here.'

The wings at Hermes' heels fluttered, flickered and hummed and he was gone.

He returned in the blink of an eye. 'Sisyphus never reached the underworld. Thanatos was sent to Corinth to fetch him half a moon ago and neither has been seen since.'

'Corinth!' roared Ares. 'What are we waiting for?'

The locked wardrobe in the bedchamber was soon found and wrenched open, revealing a humiliated Thanatos sitting tearfully in the corner under some cloaks. Hermes took him to the infernal regions where Hades waved his hand to release the enchanted manacles.

'We will speak about this later, Thanatos,' he said. 'For the moment a logjam of souls awaits you.'

'First let me fetch that villain Sisyphus, sire,' pleaded Thanatos. 'He won't be able to trick me twice.'

Hermes arched an eyebrow, but Hades looked across to Persephone, sitting in her throne next to his. She nodded. Thanatos was her favourite amongst all the servants of the underworld.

'Just make sure you don't foul it up,' grunted Hades, dismissing him with a wave of the hand.

Burial Rites

We have established that Sisyphus was no fool. He did not imagine for a second that Thanatos would stay locked in his closet for eternity. Sooner or later Death would be released and set upon his trail once more.

In the town villa in which he had made temporary lodging, Sisyphus addressed his wife. After his niece Tyro drowned his sons and left him he had married again. His new young queen was as kindly and obedient as Tyro had been wilful and contrary.

'My dear,' he said, drawing her to him, 'I feel that soon I shall die. When I have breathed my last and my soul has fled what will you do?'

'I will do what must be done, my lord. I will wash and anoint you. I will place an *obolus* on your tongue so that you might pay the ferryman. We will stand guard seven days and seven nights over your catafalque. Burnt offerings will be made to please the King and Queen of the Underworld. And in this way your journey to the Meadows of Asphodel shall be a blessed one.'

'You mean well, but that is exactly what you must *not* do,' said Sisyphus. 'The moment I am dead I want you to strip me naked and have me thrown into the street.'

'My lord!'

'I am quite serious. *Deadly* serious. This is my desire, my entreaty, my command. No matter what anyone else says, you will send up *no* prayers, make *no* sacrifices, perform *no* obsequies. Treat my remains as you would those of a dog. Promise me that.'

'But –'

Sisyphus took her by the shoulders and looked deep into her eyes to reinforce the earnestness of his commands. 'As you love me and are bound to me, as you hope never to be haunted by my angry shade, promise to do *exactly* as I have said. Swear it on your soul.'

'I – I swear it.'

'It is good. Now, let us drink. A toast – "To life!"'

His timing, as ever, was impeccable, for that very evening Sisyphus was awoken by the whisper of Death at his bedside.

'Your time is come, Sisyphus of Corinth.'

'Ah, Thanatos. I've been expecting you.'

'Do not hope to trick me.'

'Me? Trick you?' Sisyphus stood and bowed in meek submission, putting up his wrists for shackling. 'Nothing could be further from my mind.'

The manacles were attached and the pair glided down to the mouth of the underworld. Thanatos left Sisyphus at the near bank of the Styx and departed, anxious to make headway with the great backlog of souls that were awaiting collection.

Charon the ferryman sculled his boat across and Sisyphus stepped aboard. As he poled the boat off the bank, Charon stretched out his palm.

'Nothing doing,' said Sisyphus, patting his pockets.

Without a word Charon pushed him overboard into the blackness of the Styx. It was cold, abominably cold, but Sisyphus managed to get across. The waters burned and blistered his skin almost beyond endurance, but once he was on the other side he knew that he presented just such a piteous sight as he had intended.

Shades flitted past him, averting their eyes.

'Which way to the throne room?' he asked of one. Following their directions he found himself in the presence of Persephone.

'Dread queen,' Sisyphus inclined his head. 'I beg an audience with Hades.'

'My husband is in Tartarus today. I speak for him. Who are you and how can you dare stand before me in this condition?'

Sisyphus was naked, an ear was torn off and one of his eyes hung down from its socket. His spectral body was covered in bite marks, welts, bruises, gashes and open sores, testimony to its physical counterpart's rough treatment on the streets of Corinth above. His wife had obeyed his instructions.

'Madam,' he bowed low before Persephone, 'no one feels the impropriety of this as keenly as I. My wife, my spiteful, wicked, monstrous, blasphemous wife — it is she who has brought me to this pitiable state. Even as I lay dying I heard her say to her women, "We will not waste gold on burial rites. The gods of the underworld are nothing to us. Throw his body outside for the dogs to eat. Spend the money he set aside for his funeral on a great feast. The heifers he kept for sacrificing to Hades and Persephone shall be roasted for our pleasure." She laughed and clapped her hands and those, dread queen, were the last sounds I heard in the world.'

Persephone was outraged. 'She *dared*? She *dared*? She shall be punished.'

'Aye, majesty. But how?'

'Flayed alive . . .'

'Yes. Not bad. But I say permit me, wouldn't it, be funny –' Sisyphus smiled as an idea struck him, '– wouldn't it be funny if you returned me to the upper world alive? Imagine her shock!'

'Hm . . .'

'And I would make sure that every day she paid for her insolence and disrespect. No gold or feasting, nothing but harsh treatment, insults and servitude. I can't *wait* to see her face when I appear in front of her, alive and well and whole . . . and perhaps . . . perhaps even more youthful and vital and handsome than ever? She is only twenty-six, but imagine her torment if I outlived her! I would use her as my slave. Every day would be *torture* to her.'

Persephone smiled at the thought and clapped her hands. 'Let it be so.' The years spent in the underworld had given Persephone a regal pride and rigid belief in the proper running of the infernal kingdom.

And thus it was that Sisyphus was led out to the upper world where he and his delighted queen lived happily ever after.

His death, when it finally did come, was another matter.

Rolling the Rock

Zeus, Ares, Hermes and Hades had not been pleased when they found out how Sisyphus had evaded death for a second time. Persephone had made her decision, however, and the ruling of one immortal could not be undone by another.

When, after nearly fifty more years of serene and prosperous living, Sisyphus's wife's mortal span came at last to its end, the contract between Persephone and Sisyphus expired with her. Thanatos paid him a third and final visit.

This time Sisyphus gave Charon the fee and crossed the Styx in good order. Hermes awaited him on the further bank.

'Well, well, well. King Sisyphus of Corinth. Liar, fraud, rogue and trickster. A man after my own heart. No mortal has managed to cheat death once – you contrived to do it twice. Clever you.'

Sisyphus bowed.

'Such an achievement deserves a chance at immortality. Follow me.'

Hermes led Sisyphus down innumerable passageways and galleries to a vast underground chamber. A great ramp sloped up from the floor to the ceiling. A boulder stood at the bottom, lit by a shaft of light.

'The upper world,' said Hermes indicating the source of the light.

Sisyphus saw that the slope led up to a square inlet high in the roof through which a beam of daylight shone. As Hermes pointed the inlet closed up and the shaft of light disappeared.

'Now, all you have to do is roll that boulder up the slope. When you reach the top, that hole will slide open. You will be able to climb out and live for ever as the immortal King Sisyphus. Thanatos will never visit you again.'

'That's it?'

'That's it,' said Hermes. 'Of course, if you don't like the idea I can take you to Elysium, where you will spend a blissful eternity in the company of other souls of the virtuous departed. But if you choose the stone you must keep trying until you have succeeded and won your freedom and immortality. Make your choice. An idyllic afterlife down here or a shot at immortality above.'

Sisyphus examined the boulder. It was bulky, but not colossally so. The slope was steep, but not precipitously. Forty-five degrees of gradient, but no more. So. An eternity skipping though the fields of Elysium with the dull and well behaved or eternity up above in the real world of fun, filth, frolic and frenzy?

'No tricks?'

'No tricks, no pressure,' said Hermes, putting his hand on Sisyphus's shoulder and flashing his most dazzling smile. 'Your choice.'

You know the rest. Sisyphus put his shoulder to the boulder and began to push it up the slope. Halfway there and he was confident that life eternal was assured. Three-quarters done and he was tired, but not blown. Four-fifths and . . . damn, this was hard work. Five-sixths, pain. Six-sevenths, *agony*. Seven-eighths . . . He was within an inch of the top now, within a fingernail's length, just one more supreme effort and . . . *Noooooooo*! The stone slipped, bounced over Sisyphus and rolled down to the bottom. 'Well, not bad for a first effort,' Sisyphus thought to himself. 'If I take my time, if I conserve my strength, I can get there. I know I can. I'll discover a technique. Maybe I'll go up backwards, taking the weight on my back. I can do this . . .'

Sisyphus is still there in the halls of Tartarus, pushing that boulder up the hill and getting almost to the top before it rolls back down and he has to start once again. He will be there until the end of time. He still believes he can do it. Just one last supreme effort and he will be free.

Painters, poets and philosophers have seen many things in the myth of Sisyphus. They have seen an image of the absurdity of human life, the futility of effort, the remorseless cruelty of fate, the unconquerable power of gravity. But they have seen too something of mankind's courage, resilience, fortitude, endurance and self-belief. They see something heroic in our refusal to submit.

HUBRIS

To the Greeks *hubris* was a special kind of pride. It often led mortals to defy the gods, bringing about inevitable punishment of one kind or another. It is a common, if not essential, flaw in the makeup of the heroes of Greek tragedy and of many other leading characters in Greek myth. Sometimes the failing is not ours but the gods', who are too jealous, petty and vain to accept that mortals can equal or surpass them.

All Tears

You may remember that Pelops was not the only child of Tantalus and Dione. They also had a daughter, Niobe. Despite the terrible fate that befell her father and the bleak adventures of her brother, she was a proud, confident woman. She had met and married Amphion, the son of Zeus and Antiope. He was a former lover of Hermes, you may recall, one of the twins who had constructed the walls of Thebes, enchanting the stones with his singing and strumming of the lyre.* Between them Niobe and Amphion had seven daughters and seven sons, the Niobids.

Swollen with dangerous levels of conceit and self-regard, Niobe liked to tell all who would listen how important she was and just how royal and divine her bloodlines were.

---

* Once he had married Niobe and taken her to Thebes, the city he helped found, Amphion added three strings to that lyre's original four, so that, in honour of her birthplace in Asia Minor, he could play music in what is still called the Lydian mode.

'On my mother's side I claim descent from Tethys and Oceanus – they're first-generation Titans, you know. On my father's side, well there's TMOLUS, of course, the most high-born of all the Lydian mountain deities. My dear husband Amphion is a son of Zeus, and of Antiope, the daughter of King NYCTEUS, one of the original Theban Spartoi who sprang from the dragon's teeth. So my darling sons and daughters really can boast the most distinguished lineage, one feels justified in saying, of any family in the world. Not that I ever allow them to boast, of course. The well bred are never puffed up.'

Such foolishness might have been no more than faintly sad were it not that Niobe even presumed to compare herself to the Titaness Leto, mother of gods. On the very day that the people of Thebes gathered annually to sing Leto's praises and tell the story of Artemis and Apollo's miraculous birth on Delos – on that very day, sacred to the Titaness and her dignity – Niobe unburdened herself of her haughtiest broadside.

'I mean, I'd be the first to admit that Leto's dear twins Artemis and Apollo are charming and fully divine, of course they are. But only *two* children? One girl and one boy? Good heavens, how she can even call herself a mother I fail to understand. And who's to say that of my seven sons and seven daughters there won't be some, if not *all*, who will ascend to divine and immortal rank?* Given their birth I think it rather more likely than not, don't you? In my view, celebrations of such a lazy, vulgar and unproductive mother

_____

* At this time, as in the subsequent Age of Heroes, there was always the possibility of humans attaining immortal rank. It was to happen to HERAKLES. In later civilizations Roman emperors could be deified, Roman Catholics sanctified and film actors catasterized in the Hollywood Walk of Fame.

as Leto are in extremely poor taste. Next year I shall make sure the festival is cancelled altogether.'

When word reached Leto that this jumped-up Theban was insulting her in such a fashion, and daring to set herself up over her, she burst into tears in front of her sympathetic twins.

'That terrible, boastful, conceited woman,' she choked. 'She called me lazy for having only two children . . . She said I was unproductive . . . and she called me vulgar. She said she would prevent the people of Thebes from celebrating my f-f-festal day . . .'

Artemis put an arm round her while Apollo paced up and down, slamming the ball of his fist into his palm.

'She has fourteen children,' wailed Leto, 'so I suppose, compared to her, I am inadequate . . .'

'Enough!' said Artemis. 'Come, brother. She has made our mother weep. It is time this woman knew the meaning of tears.'

Artemis and Apollo went straight to Thebes, where they hunted down every one of Amphion's and Niobe's fourteen children. Artemis shot the seven daughters dead with her silver arrows; Apollo shot the seven sons dead with his golden ones. When Amphion was brought news of the slaughter he took his own life by falling on his sword. Niobe's grief was also insupportable. She fled to her childhood home and found refuge on the slopes of Mount Sipylus. No matter how snobbish, reckless, proud and absurd she had been, such wretched and inconsolable unhappiness was terrible to behold. The gods themselves could not bear to hear her unceasing lamentations, and so turned her to stone. But not even solid rock had the power to hold back such tears as these. Niobe's weeping pushed her tears through the stone and sent them cascading in waterfalls down the mountainside.

Even today, visitors to Sipylus, now called Mount Spil, can see the rock formation in which the outlines of a female face can still be discerned. In Turkish this is known as *Ağlayan Kaya* or 'Weeping Rock'.* It looks down on the city of Manisa, the modern name for Tantalis. The waters that gush from this rock will flow for ever in their grief.

Apollo and Marsyas: Puffed Cheeks

Mortal humans were not the only beings capable of exhibiting excessive pride. The goddess Athena's injured self-regard led, indirectly, to the downfall of a conceited creature called MARSYAS.

It all began when Athena proudly invented a new musical instrument which she named the *aulos*. It was a double-reeded pipe of what we would call the woodwind family, not unlike the modern oboe or cor anglais.† There was one problem with this splendid instrument: whenever Athena played it – gorgeous as the music that emerged undoubtedly was – it elicited from her fellow Olympians nothing but roars of laughter. There was no way for Athena to get a good sound from it without blowing so hard that her cheeks bulged. To see this goddess, the very personification of dignity, going all pink and swelling up like a bullfrog was more than her disrespectful family could take without howling out loud. Wise as Athena was, and free (for the most part) of affectation and conceit, she was not *entirely* without vanity and

---

* The rock is limestone, but the element niobium, very similar in composition and characteristics to tantalum, is named after the queen of tears.

† It is a pleasing coincidence that one of the chief uses of palladium, the element named in Pallas Athena's honour, is in the manufacture of woodwind instruments. Or *is it* a coincidence? Hm . . . ?

could not bear to be mocked. After three attempts to win the gods over with the mellifluous sounds of her new instrument, she cursed it and cast it down from Olympus.

The *aulos* fell to earth in Asia Minor, in the kingdom of Phrygia, near the source of the Maeander river (whose winding course lends its name to all mazy, wandering streams), where it was picked up by a satyr called Marsyas. As a follower of Dionysus, Marsyas was gifted with curiosity as well as many more disreputable traits. He dusted the *aulos* off and blew into it. A small *peep* was the only result. He laughed and scratched at the tickling buzz in his lips. He puffed and blew hard again until a long, loud musical note was produced. This was fun. He went on his way, blowing and blowing until he could, after a surprisingly short time, play a real tune.

Within a month or two his fame had spread around all of Asia Minor and Greece. He became celebrated as 'Marsyas the Musical', whose skill on the *aulos* could make trees dance and stones sing.

He revelled in the fame and adulation that his musicianship brought. Like all satyrs he required little more than wine, women and song to make him happy, and his mastery of the third ensured a ready supply of the other two.

One evening, the fire crackling, Maenads at his feet gazing up adoringly at him, he called drunkenly to the heavens.

'Hey there, Apollo! You, god of the lyre! You think you're so musical, but I bet if there was a compishon . . . a compention . . . a condition . . . What's the word?'

'Competition?' suggested a drowsy Maenad.

'One of them, yes. If there was . . . what she said . . . I'd win. Easy. Hands down. Anyone can strum a lyre. Boring. But my pipes. My pipes beat your strings any day. So there.'

The Maenads laughed, Marsyas laughed too, belched and fell into a contented sleep.

The Competition

The next day Marsyas set off with his many followers to Lake Aulocrene. They had arranged to meet other satyrs there for a great feast at which Marsyas would play wild, corybantic dances of his own composition. He would pluck some reeds from the shores of the lake (whose very name testified to their abundance – *aulos* means 'reed' and *krene* is 'fountain' or 'spring') and cut himself a new mouthpiece for his *aulos*. Piping and dancing he led his followers in a merry trail of music until he turned a corner to find his way blocked by a dazzling and disturbing spectacle.

In the meadow a stage had been erected on which sat the nine Muses in a broad semicircle. At the centre of the stage, lyre in hand, stood Apollo, a grim smile playing on his beautiful lips.

Marsyas skidded to a halt, the assorted satyrs, fauns and Maenads behind bumping into him and each other in a concertina of confusion.

'Well, Marsyas,' said Apollo. 'Are you ready to put your brave words to the test?'

'Words? What words?' Marsyas had forgotten his drunken boast of the night before.

'"If there was a competition between me and Apollo," you said, "I would beat him hands down." Now is your chance to find out if that is true. The Muses themselves have travelled from Parnassus to hear us and judge. Their word is final.'

'B-b-but . . . I . . .' Marsyas's mouth was suddenly very dry and his legs suddenly very wobbly.

'Are you or are you not a finer musician than I?'

Marsyas heard behind him a murmur of doubt from his followers and the flames of his pride flared up again.

'In a fair contest,' he declared with a burst of bravado, 'I can certainly outplay you.'

Apollo's smile widened. 'Excellent. Join me up on the stage here. I shall start. Here is a little air. See if you can reply to it.'

Marsyas took up a position next to Apollo, who bent to tune his lyre. When this was done he gently strummed and delicately plucked. The most beautiful melody emerged – subtle, sweet and seductive. It came in four phrases, and as the last one sounded, Marsyas's followers broke into appreciative applause.

Immediately Marsyas put the *aulos* to his mouth and repeated the phrases. But he gave each a little tweak and modulation – a shower of grace notes here, a riffle of accidentals there. A gasp of admiration from his followers and even a nod from Calliope herself encouraged him to end with a flourish.

Apollo replied at once with a variation on the phrases in double time. The complexity of his picking and strumming was marvellous to the ear, but Marsyas responded with even greater speed, the melody bubbling and singing from his pipes with a magical splendour that provoked yet more applause from the audience.

Now Apollo did something extraordinary. He turned his lyre upside down and played the phrases backwards – they still held up as a tune, but now they were imbued with a mystery and a strangeness that enthralled all who heard. When he finished Apollo nodded to Marsyas.

Marsyas had an excellent ear and he started to play the inverted tunes just as Apollo had, but the god interrupted him with a sneer. 'No, no, satyr! You must turn your instrument upside down as I did mine.'

'But that's . . . that's not fair!' Marsyas protested.

'How about this then?' Apollo played on his lyre and sang, 'Marsyas can blow down the infernal thing. But while he does it, can he sing?'

Infuriated, Marsyas played for all he was worth. His face purple with the effort and his cheeks swollen so that it looked as if they must rupture, hundreds of notes exploded in a volley of quarter notes, eighth notes, sixteenth notes – filling the air with a music that the world had never heard before. But Apollo's divine voice, the chords and arpeggios that flew from the golden strings of his lyre – how could Marsyas's pipes compete with such a sound?

Panting with exhaustion, sobbing with frustration, Marsyas cried aloud, 'Not fair! My voice and breath sing into my *aulos* just as much as your voice sings out into the air. Of course I cannot turn the instrument upside down, but any unbiased judge can tell that my skill is the greater.'

Judgement

With a final *glissando* of triumph Apollo turned to the jury of Muses. 'Sweet sisters, it is not for me to say, it is of course for you to decide. To whom do you award the palm of victory?'

Marsyas was out of control now. Humiliation and a burning sense of injustice drove him to turn on the judges. 'They can't be impartial, they are your aunts or your step-sisters or some such incestuous thing. They are family. They will never dare to . . .'

'Hush, Marsyas!' pleaded a Maenad.

'Don't listen to him, great god Apollo!' urged another.

'He's hysterical.'

'He's good and honourable.'

'He means well.'

It did not take the Muses long to confer and to announce the results.

'We unanimously declare,' said Euterpe, 'that Apollo is the winner.'

Apollo bowed and smiled sweetly. But what he did next might make you for ever think less of this golden and beautiful god, the melodious Apollo of reason, charm and harmony.

He took Marsyas and flayed the skin off him. There is no nice way of saying it. To punish Marsyas for his *hubris* in daring to challenge an Olympian he peeled the skin from the living body of the screaming satyr and hung it on a pine tree as a lesson and warning to all.*

The 'Flaying of Marsyas' became a favourite subject for painters, poets and sculptors. For some his tale echoes the fate of Prometheus: a symbol of the artist-creator's struggle to match the gods, or of the gods' refusal to accept that mortal artists can outdo the divine.†

---

* Now, if you really cannot stomach the idea of such cruelty from an otherwise so admirable god, you might prefer another reading of the story. The Hungarian philologist and mythographer Károly Kerényi, one of the great pioneers of the study of Greek myth, pointed out that satyrs customarily dressed themselves in pelts of animal skin. He maintains that what Apollo actually did was confiscate the hide from Marsyas so that he had to go naked. That was all. The punishment was no greater than that. This is an amiable and convincing interpretation but not one that generations of artists ever believed.

† One version of the myth maintains it was a capricious and sulky Apollo who challenged the gifted Marsyas, not the other way around, making the fable more about divine jealousy than mortal *hubris*.

ARACHNE

The Weaver

In a small cottage outside a little town called Hypaepae in the kingdom of Lydia* there dwelt a merchant and craftsman called IDMON. He worked in the nearby Ionian city of Colophon as a trader in dyes, specializing in the highly prized colour Phocaean purple. His wife had died giving birth to a girl, ARACHNE. Idmon was as proud of Arachne as ever father was of daughter. For since her early childhood she had shown the most extraordinary skill as a weaver.

Spinning and weaving were naturally of great importance in those days. Next to the growing of food few things were as crucial to human welfare as the reliable manufacture of textiles for clothing and furnishing. And 'manufacture' is quite the right word. It literally means 'making by hand' – and all such work was done by hand then. Fleece or flax was spun into threads and loaded onto looms to be woven into woollen or linen cloth. It was so much the province of skilled women that the very gender itself was given names in some cultures and languages that reflected the practice. In English we still talk of the 'distaff side' of a family, meaning the female line. The distaff was the spindle around which the wool or flax was wound preparatory to spinning. And those who spun were called 'spinsters', a name

---

* Lydia is a common setting for many of the myths. The Greeks colonized the area they called Ionia, which included Lydia, and which today we would recognize as the Anatolian region of Turkey.

which once applied without negative connotation to any unmarried woman.

But as with almost all human practices, there are those who have the mysterious ability to raise the everyday and ordinary to the level of art.

From the very first Arachne's skill at the loom was the talk and pride of all Ionia. The speed and accuracy of her work were astonishing; the assurance and dexterity with which she selected one coloured thread after another, almost without looking, stunned the admirers who often crowded into Idmon's cottage to watch her at work. But it was the pictures, patterns and intricate designs that emerged from under the blur of her shuttle that caused onlookers to burst into spontaneous applause and declare her without equal. The forests, palaces, seascapes and mountain views she created were so real that you felt you could jump into them. It wasn't only the mortal citizens of Colophon and Hypaepae that came to see her at her loom: local naiads from the River Pactolus and oreads from nearby Mount Tmolus crowded into the cottage and shook their heads in wonder too.

All were agreed that Arachne was the kind of phenomenon that might come only once in five centuries of history. To be so technically skilled was cause for admiration enough, but to be endowed with such taste – she never overdid the use of purples or other costly and showy dyes, for example – that was the miracle.

Such praise as she daily received would have gone to anyone's head. Arachne was not a spoiled or conceited child – in fact when not at the loom she came across as practical and prosaic rather than flighty or temperamental. She understood that she had been given a gift and was not one to claim personal credit for it. But she did value her talent and believed

293

that in rating it at its proper worth she was simply being honest.

'Yes,' she murmured, gazing down at her work one fateful afternoon, 'I truly think if Pallas Athena herself were to sit down and spin with me she would find herself unable to match my skill. After all, I do this every day and she only weaves once in a while, for amusement. It's no wonder I am so far her superior.'

With so many nymphs present in the front room of Idmon's cottage you can be sure that news soon got back to Athena of Arachne's ill-chosen words.

The Weave-Off

A week or so later, the usual crowd gathered round her, Arachne sat at the loom completing a tapestry that represented the founding of Thebes. Gasps and moans of appreciation greeted her depiction of the dragon-tooth warriors rising from the earth, but the oohs and aahs of her admirers were interrupted by a loud knocking on the cottage door.

It was opened to reveal a bent and wrinkled old woman. 'I do hope I've come to the right place,' she wheezed, dragging in a great sack. 'I'm told a wonderful weaver lives here. Ariadne, is it?'

She was invited inside. 'Her name is Arachne,' they told her, pointing to the girl herself seated at her loom.

'Arachne. I see. May I look? My dear, these are your own? How superb.'

Arachne nodded complacently.

The old woman plucked at the weave. 'Hard to believe that a mortal could do such work. Surely Athena herself had a hand in this?'

'I hardly think,' Arachne said with a touch of impatience, 'that Athena could do anything half so fine. Now, please don't unpick it.'

'Oh, you think Athena inferior to you?'

'In the matter of weaving it's hardly a matter of opinion.'

'What would you say to her if she was here now, I wonder?'

'I would urge her to confess that I am the better weaver.'

'Then urge away, foolish mortal!'

With these words the wrinkles on the ancient face smoothed away, the dull, clouded eyes cleared to a shining grey and the bent old woman straightened herself into the magnificent form of Athena herself. The crowd of onlookers fell back in stunned surprise. The nymphs in particular shrank into the corners, ashamed and frightened to be seen wasting their time admiring the work of a mortal.

Arachne went very pale and her heart thudded within her, yet outwardly she managed to keep her composure. It was disconcerting to have those grey eyes fixed upon her but all their wisdom and steadiness of gaze could not alter the plain truth.

'Well,' said she with as much calmness in her voice as she could manage, 'I've no wish to offend, but it is, I think, undoubtedly true that as an artist of the loom I have no rival, on earth *or* on Olympus.'

'Really?' Athena arched an eyebrow. 'Let's discover then. Would you like to go first?'

'No, please . . .' Arachne vacated her seat and pointed to the loom. 'After you.'

Athena examined the frame. 'Yes, this will do,' she said. 'Phocaean purple, I see. Not bad, but I prefer Tyrian.' So saying she pulled from her sack a quantity of coloured wools. 'Now then . . .'

Within seconds she was at work. The boxwood shuttle flew back and forth and, magically, wonderful images began to appear. The crowd of people pressed forward. They saw that Athena was bringing to life nothing less than the story of the gods themselves. There was the gelding of Ouranos in all its gory detail; how sticky the blood looked. There the birth of Aphrodite; how fresh and damp the ocean spray. Here was a panel that showed Kronos swallowing Rhea's children, and here another of the infant Zeus being suckled by the she-goat Amalthea. Athena even wove into the tapestry the story of her own birth from Zeus's head. Next came a dazzling depiction of all twelve gods enthroned on Olympus. But she wasn't finished yet.

As if deliberately and publicly to humiliate Arachne for her presumption, Athena now created panels that showed the price paid by mortals for daring to set themselves up as equals or superiors to the gods. In the first she showed Queen RHODOPE and King HAEMUS of Thrace, who were changed into mountains for daring to compare their grandeur as a couple to that of Hera and Zeus. And in another panel Athena wove the image of GERANA, Queen of the Pygmies, who proclaimed her beauty and importance to be greater by far than that of the Queen of Heaven and had been transformed by an enraged Hera into a crane-bird. In that same corner she wove a picture of ANTIGONE, who had her hair turned into snakes for a similar act of impudence.*
Finally Athena adorned the border of her work with designs of olive – the tree holy to her – before standing to receive the acclamation that was her due.

---

* The gods later took pity on her and changed her into a stork. Storks ever after ate snakes, apparently. This was not the Theban ANTIGONE, daughter of OEDIPUS, but a Trojan girl of the same name.

Arachne was gracious enough to join in the applause. Her mind had worked as fast as Athena's shuttle and she knew just what she was going to create. A kind of madness had overcome her. Having found herself in the unlooked-for position of competing against an Olympian goddess, she now wanted to show the world not just that she was the better weaver, but that humans were better than gods in every way. It maddened her that Athena should present so grandiose a subject as the birth and establishment of the Olympian deities and then depict such clumsy fables of punished *hubris*. Well, two could play the game of parables. She would show her!

Arachne sat down, cracked her knuckles and began. The first form that came to life beneath her flying fingers was that of a bull. There was a young girl riding it. Another panel showed the bull rising in the air and crossing the sea. The girl looked back over the waves towards young men running in panic to the cliffside. Could it be? Was this scene the ravishing of Europa and were those boys Cadmus and his brothers?

A murmur rose from the onlookers who pressed round on all sides to get a closer look. The following series of images made it all too clear what Arachne was up to. Here was AS-TERIA, daughter of the Titans Phoebe and Coeus, despairingly turning herself into a quail to try and escape the rapacious attentions of Zeus in the shape of an eagle. Next to this Arachne wove a picture of Zeus as a swan insinuating himself around the body of TYNDAREUS's wife LEDA. Now he was a dancing satyr chasing the beautiful Antiope; next the lustful god appeared in one of his strangest metamorphoses – a shower of golden rain, in which unlikely manifestation he could be clearly seen impregnating the imprisoned DANAË, daughter of King ACRISIUS of Argos. Many of these ravishings and seductions were the subjects of mortal gossip. For Arachne to be bringing them to life in coloured silk was unpardonable. Further scenes of Zeus's depraved career followed – the hapless nymph Aegina and the lovely Persephone molested by him in the form of a speckled snake. The rumour that in this manner Zeus had once taken Persephone, his own daughter by Demeter, had been whispered before, but for Arachne to show it now was sacrilege.

Yet Zeus was not the only god whose tales of degeneracy she wrote in thread. Scenes of Poseidon now appeared, the sea god shown first as a bull, galloping after the frightened ARNE of Thessaly, then disguised as the mortal ENIPEUS so as to win the lovely Tyro, finally as a dolphin in his pursuit of the enchanting MELANTHO, daughter of Deucalion.

Apollo's depredations were the next to appear: Apollo the hawk, Apollo the lion, Apollo the shepherd, all despoiling maidens without pity or shame. And Dionysus too was portrayed, disguising himself as a large cluster of grapes to deceive the beautiful ERIGONE, and in a fit of temper, transforming ALCATHOË and the MINYADES* into bats for daring to prefer a contemplative life to one of frenzied revelry.

All these episodes and more were summoned by Arachne's art. They shared the common theme of the gods taking deceitful and often savage advantage of mortal women. Arachne completed her work by weaving around it a patterned edge of interlacing flowers and ivy leaves. When she was done she calmly pushed the shuttle to one side and stood up to stretch.

---

* Daughters of Minyas, a King of Boeotia. They were LEUCIPPE, ARSIPPE and ALCATHOE. A recently discovered species of European bat is named the *Myotis alcathoe* in her honour. The sisters' fate was often used as a warning to those who were tempted away from a life of Dionysian revelry – we are more likely to expect warnings in the other direction these days.

The Reward

The onlookers drew back horrified, fascinated and disturbed. The girl's audacity was breathtaking, but there could be no denying the supreme skill and artistry with which this bold but blasphemous work had been executed.

Athena came forward to examine every inch of the surface and could see no blemish or flaw. It was perfect. Perfect but sacrilegious and impermissible. In silence she ripped the web and tore up every scene. Finally, unable to master her rage, she snatched up the shuttle and hurled it at Arachne's head.

The pain of the shuttle striking her brow seemed to waken Arachne from her trance. What had she done? What madness had possessed her? She would never be allowed to weave again. She would be made to pay a terrible price for her insolence. The punishments that had been visited on the girls whose fates she had registered in her tapestry would be as nothing to those visited upon her.

She took a length of thick hemp from the floor. 'If I cannot weave I cannot live!' she cried and ran from the cottage before anyone could even think of stopping her.

The spectators pressed around the window and the open door and watched in frozen horror as Arachne ran across the grass, swung the rope over the branch of an apple tree and hanged herself. They turned as one to look at Athena.

A tear rolled down the goddess's cheek. 'Foolish, foolish girl,' she said.

The crowd of onlookers followed her in appalled silence as she made her way out of the cottage and towards the tree. Arachne was swinging at the end of the rope, her dead eyes bulging from her head.

'A talent like yours can never die,' Athena said. 'You shall spin and weave all your days, spin and weave, spin and weave . . .'

As she spoke Arachne started to shrivel and shrink. The rope she dangled from stretched itself into a thin filament of glistening silk up which she now pulled herself, a girl no longer but a creature destined always busily to spin and weave.

This is how the first spider – the first *arachnid* – came into being. It was not a punishment as some would have it, but a prize for winning a great competition, a reward for a great artist. The right to work and weave masterpieces in perpetuity.

MORE METAMORPHOSES

We have seen the gods transform men and women into animals out of pity, punishment or jealousy. But, just as they could be as proud and petty as humans, so the gods could be equally motivated by desire. Mortal flesh, as we have seen, was as appealing to them as immortal. Sometimes their urges were little more than primitive lust, but they could fall genuinely in love too. There are many stories of the gods chasing after and transforming the loveliest youths and young women into animals, new plants and flowers, and even rocks and streams.*

Nisus and Scylla

NISUS was a King of Megara, a city on the coast of Attica.† He had been granted invincibility in the form of a single lock of purple hair which kept him immune from any human harm. For some reason his kingdom was attacked by the forces of King Minos of Crete. One day Nisus's daughter, the

---

* Sometimes these myths can be regarded as *aetiological* – in other words, offering explanations for how things got to be the way they are. Arachne could be seen as a story that explains why the spider weaves, Melissa tells us why the bee makes honey, and so on. Sort of 'How the Elephant Got Its Trunk' fables. Certainly the names of flowers and animals that relate to many of these types of myth have come down to us in Latinate scientific nomenclature such as 'Daphne Laureola' for the spurge laurel, or the common or garden names, Narcissus, Hyacinth, etc.

† Attica is the area of Greece that includes Athens. 'Attic Greek' is the classical form of the language that comes down to us in the poetry, drama, oratory and philosophy of the great Athenian writers of the fifth and early fourth centuries BC. To many Greeks from outside Attica it was perhaps what England is to the other countries of the United Kingdom, the snooty dominant region that outsiders tactlessly and lazily think of when they say 'Greece'.

Princess SCYLLA,* caught sight of Minos on board one of his warships as it passed close to the walls of Megara and fell in love with him. So maddened by desire did she become that she decided to steal her father's lock of purple hair and give it to Minos on board his ship; in return he would repay her generosity with love. But once she had stolen the lock Nisus became as vulnerable as any mortal. And while she was still secretly making her way to Minos, her father was killed in a palace uprising.

Minos, far from being pleased by Scylla's act of disloyalty to her own father, was disgusted, and would have nothing to do with her. He kicked her off his ship, hoisted sail and left Megara, vowing never to return.

So overmastering was her passion that even now Scylla could not give up on the man she loved. She swam after Minos, calling pathetically. She mewed and cried so plaintively after him that she was turned into a gull. Such was the humour of the gods that at the same time her father Nisus was transformed into a sea-eagle.

In revenge he has relentlessly harried his daughter across the oceans ever since.

Callisto

Before he was turned into a wolf – as you may recall – during the early days of Pelasgian mankind, King Lycaon of Arcadia† had a beautiful daughter called CALLISTO, who was raised as a nymph dedicated to the virgin huntress Artemis.

---

* Not to be confused with SCYLLA the cruel sea monster that, with the whirlpool CHARYBDIS, formed such an impassable barrier to sailors in the Straits of Messina between Sicily and the Italian mainland.

† Who was turned by Zeus into a wolf you may recall, during the early days of Pelasgian mankind.

Zeus had long frothed with desire for this beautiful, unattainable girl and tricked her one day by transforming himself into the very image of Artemis herself. She readily fell into the arms of the great goddess she followed, only to find herself ravaged by Zeus.

Some time later, bathing naked in the river, she was seen by Artemis who, enraged by her follower's state of pregnancy, expelled poor Callisto from her circle. Alone and unhappy she wandered the world, before giving birth to a son, ARCAS. Hera, never one to show mercy to even the most innocent and guileless of her husband's lovers, punished Callisto further by transforming her into a bear.

Some years later Arcas, now a youth, was hunting in the forest when he came upon a great she-bear. He was just about to launch his javelin at her when Zeus intervened to prevent an inadvertent matricide and raised them up into the heavens as Ursa Major and Ursa Minor, the constellations of the Great Bear and the Little Bear. Hera, still angry, cursed these constellations so that they would never share the same waters which (I am told) explains their permanently opposing circumpolar positions.*

Procne and Philomela

King PANDION of Athens had two beautiful daughters, PROCNE and PHILOMELA. Procne, the elder, left Athens to marry King TEREUS of Thrace, by whom she had a son, ICTYS.

One year, her younger sister Philomela came to Thrace to stay with the family for the whole summer. The dark heart of

---

* In fact Callisto does double duty in the heavens as she lives on as one of Jupiter's moons.

Tereus, one of the darkest that ever beat, was fiercely disturbed by the beauty of his young sister-in-law and he dragged her to his chambers one night and raped her. Fearful that his wife and the world might discover the hateful crime, Tereus tore out Philomela's tongue. Knowing that she was unable to read and write, he felt safe that she could never communicate to anyone the abominable truth of what had taken place.

But over the next week or so Philomela wove a tapestry in which she depicted for her sister Procne all the details of her violation. The wronged and raging sisters planned a revenge that would match the monstrous evil of the crime. They knew how to hurt Tereus most. He was a violent and repulsive man given to wild rages and unspeakable depravities, but he had one weakness – his deep love for his boy Ictys. This unbounded affection Procne and Philomela knew well. Ictys was Procne's son too, but what maternal love she once felt had been quite overwhelmed by hatred and an unquenchable lust for revenge. Abandoning all pity, the sisters went to the child's bedchamber and murdered him in his sleep.

'Philomela will be leaving for Athens soon,' Procne told her husband the next morning. 'Why don't we hold a banquet tonight to bid her farewell and to honour the kindly hospitality you have offered her?'

Philomela whimpered and nodded her head vigorously.

'She seems to think it would be a good idea too.'

Tereus grunted his assent.

At the feast that night a succulent stew was served which the king greedily consumed. He soaked up all its juices with hunks of bread, but found he still had room for more. Just out of arm's reach lay a dish covered by a silver dome.

'What's under that?'

Philomela pushed the dish towards him with a smile.

Tereus lifted the dome and gave a shout of horror when he saw his dead son's head grimacing up at him. The sisters screeched with laughter and exultation. When he realized what had been done to him, and understood why the stew was so deliciously tender, Tereus gave a great roar and snatched down a spear from the wall. The two women ran from the room and cried out to the gods for aid. As King Tereus chased them out of the palace and down the street he found himself suddenly rising into the air. He was being transformed into a hoopoe bird, and his yells of pain and fury began to sound like forlorn whoops. At the same time, Procne was changed into a swallow and Philomela into a nightingale.

Although nightingales are famous for the melodious beauty of their song, it is only the male of the species that sings. The females, like tongueless Philomela, remain mute.* Many species of swallow are named after Procne to this day and the hoopoe bird still wears a kingly crown.

Ganymede and the Eagle

In the northwest corner of Asia Minor there lay a kingdom called Troad, or Troy, in honour of its ruler King TROS. Troy looked across the Aegean Sea westwards to mainland Greece; behind it lay the whole of what is now Turkey and the ancient lands to the east. To the north were the Dardanelles and Gallipoli and to the south the great island of Lesbos. The

---

* The Greeks thought the sound the hoopoe made was *pou? pou?* which means 'where? where?' – perhaps indicating the distraught Tereus calling for his son. Shakespeare called the nightingale 'Philomel' in Sonnet CII – 'As Philomel in summer's front doth sing' – but confusingly Philomela's name is most commonly seen in the scientific name for the song-thrush: *Turdus philomelos*.

principal city Ilium (which was to become known simply as the city of Troy) derived its name from ILOS, the eldest son of Tros and his queen CALLIRRHOË, a daughter of the local river god SCAMANDER. Of the royal couple's second boy, ASSARACUS, little is recorded, but it was their third son, GANYMEDE, who took the eye and indeed the breath of all who encountered him.

No more beautiful youth had ever lived and moved upon the earth than this Prince Ganymede. His hair was golden, his skin like warm honey, his lips a soft, sweet invitation to lose yourself in mad and magical kisses.

Girls and women of all ages had been known to scream and even to faint when he looked at them. Men who had never in all their lives considered the appeal of their own sex found their hearts hammering, the blood surging and pounding in their ears when they caught sight of him. Their mouths would go dry and they found themselves stammering foolish nonsense and saying anything to try to please him or attract his attention. When they got home they wrote and instantly tore up poems that rhymed 'thighs' with 'eyes', 'hips' with 'lips', 'youth' with 'truth', 'boy' with 'joy' and 'desire' with 'fire'.

Unlike many born with the awful privilege of beauty, Ganymede was not sulky, petulant or spoiled. His manners were charming and unaffected. When he smiled the smile was kind and his amber eyes were lit with a friendly warmth. Those who knew him best said that his inner beauty matched or even exceeded his outer.

Had he not been a prince it is likely that more fuss would have been made of his startling looks and his life would have been made impossible. But because he was the favoured son of a great ruler no one dared try to seduce him, and he lived a blameless life of horses, music, sport and friends. It was supposed that one day King Tros would pair him off with a

Grecian princess and he would grow into a handsome and virile man. Youth is a fleeting thing after all.

They had reckoned without the King of the Gods. Whether Zeus had heard rumours of this shining beacon of youthful beauty or whether he accidentally caught sight of him isn't known. What is a matter of record is that the god became simply maddened with desire. Despite the royal lineage of this important mortal, despite the scandal it would cause, despite the certain fury and jealous rage of Hera, Zeus turned himself into an eagle, swooped down, seized the boy in his talons and flew him up to Olympus.

It was a terrible thing to do, but surprisingly enough it turned out to be more than an act of wanton lust. It really did seem to have something to do with real love. Zeus adored the boy and wanted to be with him always. Their acts of physical love only reinforced his adoration. He gave him the gift of immortality and eternal youth and appointed him to be his cupbearer. From now until the end of time he would always be the Ganymede whose beauty of form and soul had so smitten the god. All the other gods, with the inevitable exception of Hera, welcomed the youth to heaven. It was impossible not to like him: his presence lit up Olympus.

Zeus despatched Hermes to King Tros with a gift of divine horses to recompense the family for their loss.

'Your son is a welcome and beloved addition to Olympus,' Hermes told him. 'He will never die and, unlike any mortal, his outward beauty will always match his inner which means that he will always be content. The Sky Father loves him completely.'

Well, the King and Queen of Troy had two other sons and they really were the finest gift horses in all the world, not to be looked in the mouth, and if their Ganymede were to be a permanent member of the immortal Olympian company and if Zeus really did love him . . .

But did the boy adore Zeus? That is so hard to know. The ancients believed he did. He is usually represented as smiling and happy. He became a symbol of that particular kind of same-sex love which was to become so central a part of Greek life. His name, it seems, was a kind of deliberate word play, deriving as it did from *ganumai* 'gladdening' and *medon* 'prince' and/or *medeon* 'genitals'. 'Ganymede', the gladdening prince with the gladdening genitals became twisted over time into the word 'catamite'.

Zeus and Ganymede stayed together as a happy couple for a very long time. Of course the god was as unfaithful to Ganymede as he was to his own wife, but they became almost a fixture nonetheless.

When the reign of the gods was coming to an end Zeus rewarded this beautiful youth, his devoted minion, lover and friend, by sending him up into the sky as a constellation in the most important part of the heavens, the Zodiac, where he shines still as Aquarius, the Cupbearer.

Dawn Lovers

A word about two immortal sisters. We have met in passing Eos, or AURORA as the Romans called her, and know that her task was to begin each day by flinging wide the gates that let first the god Apollo and then her brother Helios drive the sun-chariot through. Their sister Selene (LUNA to the Romans) drove the nocturnal equivalent, the moon-chariot, across the night sky. By Selene, Zeus had fathered two daughters, PANDIA (whom Athenians celebrated every full moon) and ERSA (sometimes HERSE), the divine personification of the dew.

Eos fell in love a number of times. A fine, heroic youth called CEPHALUS caught her eye and she abducted him. She gave no thought to the fact that he was already spoken for – married, in fact, to PROCRIS, a daughter of Erechtheus, first King of Athens (the issue of Hephaestus's spilled semen), and his queen, PRAXITHEA. Despite Eos's radiant beauty and the luxurious sun palace she installed him in, the kidnapped Cephalus found himself missing his wife Procris dreadfully. No matter what rosy arts of love the goddess of the dawn employed, she failed to arouse him. Disappointed and humiliated, she agreed to return him to his wife. All the time jealousy and injured pride were boiling inside her. How dare he prefer a human to a goddess? The idea that an ordinary woman could stimulate Cephalus while her divine being left him cold . . .

With mischievous insouciance she began to plant doubts in his mind.

'Aiee,' she sighed, sorrowfully shaking her head as they approached his home, 'it saddens me to think how the oh-so-pure Procris will have been behaving in your absence.'

'What can you mean?'

'Oh, the number of men she will have been entertaining. Doesn't bear thinking about.'

'How little you know her!' Cephalus returned with some heat, 'She is as faithful as she is lovely.'

'Ha!' said Eos. 'All it takes is honey and money.'

'What's that?'

'Honeyed words and silver coins turn the most virtuous to treachery.'

'How cynical you are.'

'I rise before first light and see what people do in the dark. That's not cynicism, it's realism.'

'But you don't know Procris,' Cephalus insisted. 'She's not like other people. She is faithful and true.'

'Pah! She'd leap into bed with anyone when your back's turned. I tell you what . . .' Eos stopped, as if an idea had suddenly struck her. 'If you were to make her acquaintance *in disguise*, yes? Show yourself willing, shower her with compliments, tell her you love her, offer her a few trinkets – I bet she'd be all over you.'

'Never!'

'Up to you, but . . .' Eos shrugged and then pointed to the verge along which they had been walking. 'Oh look – there's a heap of clothes and a helmet. Imagine if you had a beard too . . .'

Eos vanished and at that very moment Cephalus found that he was indeed bearded. The change of wardrobe that had inexplicably appeared by the roadside seemed to beckon to him.

Despite his protestations to the contrary, Eos's words had planted a seed of doubt. In putting on this absurd costume, Cephalus told himself that he was not yielding to this doubt, but rather setting out to show Eos that her cynicism was misplaced. He and Procris would call up to her that very morning as the sky turned pink, 'How wrong you were, goddess of the dawn!' they would cry, 'how little you understand a loving mortal heart.' Words to that effect. That would show her.

A short while later, Procris opened the door to a handsome bearded, helmeted, gowned stranger. She was looking a little haggard and drawn. The sudden and unexplained disappearance of her husband had hit her hard. Before she had time to enquire of her visitor, however, Cephalus shouldered his way into the house and dismissed the servants.

'You are a very beautiful woman,' he said in a thick Thracian accent.

Procris blushed. 'Sir, I must . . .'

'Come, let us seat ourselves on this couch.'

'Really, I cannot . . .'

'Come now, no one's looking.'

She knew that it was pushing the boundaries of hospitable *xenia* a little further than was called for, but Procris complied. The man was so forceful.

'What's a beauty like you doing all alone in such a big house?' Cephalus picked a fig from a copper bowl, took a lascivious bite from it and dangled the soft juicy half that remained in front of Procris.*

'Sir!'

As her mouth opened to remonstrate, Cephalus pushed in the squashy fig.

'A sight to enflame the gods themselves,' he said. 'Be mine!'

'I'm *married*!' she tried to say through the seeds and pulp.

'Marriage? What's that? I'm a rich man and will give you whatever jewels or ornaments you ask for, if only you will yield. You are so beautiful. And I love you.'

Procris paused. It may have been that she was trying to swallow the remains of the fig. It may have been that she was tempted by the offer of precious things. Perhaps she was touched by this sudden and intense declaration of love. The pause was long enough to cause Cephalus to rise in fury, cast off his disguise and reveal himself.

---

* The Greek for 'one who shows figs' is *sycophant* – it seems that *either* sellers of the fruit in the streets and marketplaces were known for their fawning, flattering attentions, *or* showing a fig was the equivalent of a phallic gesture (figs have always been considered an erotic fruit after all) *or* it may have been something to do with the way figs are harvested. Whatever the reason, fig-showing/sycophancy became a word associated in Athenian legal contexts with those who brought frivolous, malicious or unjustified private prosecutions. Their toadying manner caused the word 'sycophancy' to take on its common meaning today.

'So!' he thundered, 'This is what happens when you are alone! Dishonourable, deceitful woman!'

Procris stared in disbelief. 'Cephalus? Is that you?'

'Yes! Yes, it is your poor husband! *This* is how you behave when I am away. Go! Leave my sight, faithless Procris. Away with you!'

He lunged forward, shaking his fist, and the terrified Procris fled. Out of the house she ran, out into the woods, never stopping until she collapsed with exhaustion on the fringes of a grove sacred to Artemis.

The goddess discovered Procris lying there the next morning and coaxed from her the story of what had happened.

For a year and a day she stayed with the divine huntress and her retinue of fierce maidens, but at last she could bear it no longer.

'Artemis, you have looked after me, tutored me in the arts of the chase and shown me how men are always to be shunned. But I cannot lie to you: in my heart I love my husband Cephalus as much as ever I did. He wronged me, but the wrong he did came from his great love for me and I yearn to forgive him and lie in his arms, his wife once more.'

Artemis was sorry to see her go, but she was in a charitable mood. Not only did she let Procris return to her husband without first plucking her eyes out or feeding her to the pigs (actions that were by no means alien to her) but she bestowed upon her two remarkable gifts to present to Cephalus as a peace offering.

Lailaps and Alopex Teumesios

One of the gifts that Procris received was a remarkable dog called LAILAPS which had the power to catch anything, absolutely anything that it pursued. Set it to chase a deer, boar, bear, lion or even human being and it could never fail to bring its quarry down. The second gift, of equal value, was a javelin that would always hit its mark. Whosoever was possessed of both could rightly call themselves the greatest mortal hunter in the world. Little wonder that Cephalus was pleased to welcome his wife, laden with such gifts, back to hearth and home, bosom and bed.

The reputation of Cephalus now grew and grew – tales of his hunting skills were whispered in awe from kingdom to kingdom. News reached the ears of the Theban regent, CREON.* As so often in its benighted history, Thebes at this time was being laid low by a scourge, in this instance a ferocious fox, called locally the Cadmean Vixen and feared throughout the Greek World as ALOPEX TEUMESIOS, the Teumessian Fox, a marauder whose special gift was that it was divinely ordained never to be caught, no matter how many dogs, horses or men were on her trail or set in position to trap her. It was thought this vulpine terror was unleashed by Dionysus, still thirsting for revenge upon the city that had shunned and mocked his mother Semele.

An increasingly desperate Creon, having heard tell of the almost supernatural gifts of Cephalus and his wonderdog, Lailaps, sent word to Athens begging to borrow it. Cephalus was happy enough to lend Creon the marvellous hound, which was soon set on the fox's trail.

The ensuing debacle reveals a marvellous quality of the Greek mind: their fascination with paradox. What happens when an uncatchable fox is set upon by an inescapable

---

* Creon was that soul of pragmatism and good governance whose tragic family history was the subject of Sophocles Theban Cycle of plays, *Oedipus the King*, *Oedipus at Colonus* and *Antigone*. I played him when I was sixteen and received reviews. I'll say no more.

hound? This is akin to the problem of the irresistible force meeting an immovable object.

Round and round dashed the Cadmean Vixen, while hot on her tail flew Lailaps, from whom no prey could escape. They would still be caught in that logic loop now I suppose, if Zeus hadn't done something about it.

The King of the Gods looked down at the sight and pondered the strange self-contradicting problem that presented such an affront to all proper reason and sense, and so vexingly subverted the notions embodied in that splendid Greek word *nous*. Zeus's authority was underwritten by a deep law that said no god had the power to undo the divine enchantments of another. This meant that the dog and the vixen were fated to be locked in this impossible condition for ever, making a public mockery of the order of things. Zeus solved the conundrum by turning the fox and the dog to stone. In this way they stayed frozen in time, their perfect possibilities unachieved for eternity, their destinies for ever unreconciled. At length, even this locked state seemed to him to challenge common sense, so he catasterized them – removed them to the heavens – where they became the constellations of the Greater and Lesser Dogs, Canis Major and Canis Minor.

Cephalus and Procris, I am sorry to say, did not prosper long. Deprived of Lailaps, but still armed with the enchanted javelin that could never fail to find its target, Cephalus loved nothing better than rambling about the hills and valleys that surrounded Athens, taking what prey he happened on. One fiercely hot afternoon, after three hours of chasing and spearing, tired and drenched in sweat, he lay down to doze. The heat of the day, even in the shade of his favourite great oak, made him uncomfortable.

'Come Zephyrus,' he called up lazily to the West Wind,

'let me feel you on my skin. Embrace me, calm me, ease me, soothe me, play on me . . .'

By the greatest misfortune, Procris had come out to where Cephalus was, to surprise him with a dish of olives and some wine. Just as she drew near she heard her husband's last few words, 'let me feel you on my skin. Embrace me, ease me, soothe me, play on me . . .' After all that show of possessive rage he was now betraying her? Procris could not believe her ears! The dish and the wineskin fell from her nerveless fingers and she gave an involuntary gasp.

Cephalus sat up. What was that stumbling in the undergrowth? That snuffle! A pig, by heaven! He reached for his spear and threw it towards the bushes from which the noise had come. He had no need to be careful in his aim. The enchanted javelin would do all the work.

It did. Procris expired in his grieving arms.

A charmingly strange and unhappy tale.* It all came about, we should remind ourselves, merely because Eos had decided to abduct an appetizing mortal.

Endymion

Cephalus was not the only young man to catch the eye of one of these two goddesses. One night, as Eos's sister Selene sailed her silver chariot across the sky over western Asia Minor, she spotted far below ENDYMION, a young shepherd of great beauty lying naked and fast asleep on the hillside outside a cave on Mount Latmos. The sight of his lovely limbs all

---

* In Shakespeare's *A Midsummer Night's Dream* Bottom and his confused friends memorably mangle the names of these doomed lovers in their performance of 'Pyramus and Thisbe':

Pyramus (Bottom): Not Shafalus to Procrus was so true.
Thisbe (Flute): As Shafalus to Procrus, I to you.

silvered by her moonbeams and the enticingly seductive smile that played on his lips as he dreamed so filled Selene with desire that she cried out to Zeus, Endymion's father, to ensure that he would never change. She wanted to see him in exactly that attitude every night. Zeus granted the wish. Endymion stayed just where he was, locked in eternal slumber. Each new moon, the one day in the lunar month when her chariot could not be seen, Selene would come down and make love to the sleeping boy. This unconventional conjugal practice did not prevent her from bearing fifty daughters by him. I will let you picture the physical practicalities, postures and positions which allowed that.

An odd relationship, but one which worked and made Selene happy.*

---

* It forms the subject of John Keats's extended poem *Endymion*.

EOS AND TITHONUS

The love life of Selene's sister Eos continued to be tumultuous. Some time ago the goddess of the dawn had emerged from a dramatically disastrous affair with the god of war. When Aphrodite, Ares' jealous lover, found out about the liaison she ordained in her heart that Eos would never find joy in the one realm in which Aphrodite was sovereign – love.

Eos was a full-blooded Titaness with all the appetites of that race. Moreover, as bringer of the dawn, she believed in the hope, promise and opportunity heralded by each new day. And so, over the years, Eos stumbled with tragic optimism from relationship to relationship, each one doomed by Aphrodite's curse, of which she was blithely unaware.

The cougarish Eos was especially drawn to young mortal men: Just as she had abducted Cephalus, so she tried to do the same again to a youth called CLEITUS. This led to heartbreak, for he was mortal and died in what to her was the twinkling of an eye.

There must have been something in the air of Troy in those days. LAOMEDON, the nephew of Zeus's beloved cupbearer, Ganymede,* had a son called TITHONUS, who grew up to be quite his great-uncle's equal in beauty. Tithonus was perhaps a little slighter, slimmer and smaller in stature than Ganymede, but this made him no less desirable. He had a laughing sweetness that was entirely his own and made him

---

* Laomedon was the son of Ganymede's elder brother Ilos, the King of Troy.

enchanting and irresistible. You just wanted to put an arm round him and own him for ever.

One afternoon Eos saw this exquisite young man walking on the beach outside the walls of Ilium. All her numberless dalliances, abductions, crushes and flings, even the affair with Ares . . . all these, she now realized, had been but childish whims, meaningless infatuations. This was the real thing. This was *it*.

Love at First Sight

As Eos approached along the sand, Tithonus looked up and fell in love with her quite as instantly and entirely as she had fallen in love with him. They held hands straight away, without even having exchanged a word, and walked up and down on the shoreline as lovers do.

'What is your name?'

'Tithonus.'

'I am Eos, the dawn. Come away with me to the Palace of the Sun. Live with me and be my lover, my husband, my equal, my ruler, my subject, my all.'

'Eos, I will. I am yours for ever.'

They laughed and made love with the waves crashing around them. Eos's rosy fingers found ways to drive Tithonus quite mad with joy. For her own part she knew that *this time* she could make it work.

Her coral, pearl, agate, marble and jasper apartments within the Palace of the Sun became their home. Few couples had ever been happier. Their lives were complete. They shared everything. They read poetry to each other, went on long walks, listened to music, danced, rode horses, sat in companionable silence, laughed and made love. Every morning he watched with pride as she threw open the gates to let Helios and his chariot thunder through.

The Boon

A problem nagged at Eos, however. She knew that one day her beautiful beloved mortal youth must be taken from her, as Cleitus had been. The thought of his death caused her an inner despair that she could not quite conceal.

'What is it my love?' Tithonus asked one evening, surprising her fair countenance in a frown.

'You trust me, don't you, darling boy?'

'Always and entirely.'

'I am going away tomorrow afternoon. I shall return as soon as I can. Do not ask me where or why I go.'

Her destination was Olympus and an audience with Zeus.

'Immortal Sky Father, Lord of Olympus, Cloud-Gatherer, Storm-Bringer, King of all the . . .'

'Yes, yes, yes. What do you want?'

'I crave a boon, great Zeus.'

'Of course you crave a boon. None of my family visits me for any other reason. It's always boons. Boons, boons, boons and nothing but boons. What is it this time? Something to do with that Trojan boy, I suppose?'

A little flustered by this, Eos pressed on. 'Yes, dread lord. You know how it is when we consort with a mortal youth . . .' she allowed herself a look towards Ganymede, who was standing behind Zeus's throne, ever ready to refill his cup of nectar. At her glance Ganymede smiled and dropped his gaze, blushing prettily.

'Yes . . . *and?*' Zeus had started drumming his fingers on the arm of his throne. Never a good sign.

'One day Thanatos will come for my Prince Tithonus and that I can not bear. I ask that you grant him immortality.'

'Oh. Do you? Immortality, eh? That's all? Immortality. Hm. Yes, I don't see why not. Immunity from death. That really is all you want for him?'

'Why, yes, lord, that is all.'

What else could there be? Had she caught him in a good mood? Her heart began to leap with delight.

'Granted,' said Zeus clapping his hands. 'From this moment on, your Tithonus is immortal.'

Eos sprang from her prostrate position of supplication with a squeal of joy and rushed forward to kiss Zeus's hand. He seemed mightily pleased too and laughed and smiled as he accepted her thanks.

'No, no. Such a pleasure. I'm sure you'll be coming back to thank me soon enough.'

'Of course, if you would like me to?' It seemed an odd request.

'Oh, I'm sure you'll be along before we know it,' said Zeus, still unable to stop himself from grinning. He didn't know what had planted the imp of mischief in his mind. But we know it was the curse of Aphrodite doing its implacable work.

Eos hurried back to the Palace of the Sun where her adored spouse was waiting patiently for her return. When she told him the news he hugged her and hugged her and they danced around the palace making so much noise that Helios banged on the walls and grumbled that some people had to be up before dawn.

Be Careful What You Wish For

Eos bore Tithonus two sons: EMATHION, who was to rule Arabia, and MEMNON, who grew up to become one of the greatest and most feared warriors in all the ancient world.

One evening, Tithonus lay with his head in Eos's lap while she idly twisted his golden hair around her fingers. She was humming softly but broke off with a sudden hiss of surprise.

'What is it, my love?' murmured Tithonus.

'You trust me, don't you, darling one?'

'Always and entirely.'

'I am going away tomorrow afternoon. I shall return as soon as I can. Do not ask me where or why I going.'

'Haven't we had this conversation before?'

Her destination was Olympus and another audience with Zeus.

'Ha! I said you'd be back, didn't I? Didn't I, Ganymede? What were my very words to you, Eos?'

'You said, "I'm sure you'll be coming back to thank me soon enough."'

'So I did. What's this you're showing me?'

Eos's hand was outstretched towards Zeus. She was holding something between trembling rosy forefinger and trembling rosy thumb. It was a single filament of silver.

'Look!' she said in throbbing accents.

Zeus peered down. 'Looks like a hair.'

'It *is* a hair. It came from my Tithonus's head. It is *grey*.'

'And?'

'My lord! You *promised* me. You swore that you would grant Tithonus immortality.'

'And so I did.'

'Then how do you explain this?'

'Immortality was the boon you asked for and immortality was the boon I granted. You didn't say anything about *ageing*. You never requested eternal youth.'

'I . . . you . . . but . . .' Eos staggered backwards, appalled. This could not be!

'"Immortality" you said. Isn't that right, Ganymede?'

'Yes, my lord.'

'But I assumed . . . I mean, isn't it obvious what I meant?'

'Sorry, Eos,' said Zeus, rising. 'I can't be expected to interpret everyone's requests. He won't die. That's the thing. You'll always be together.'

Eos was left alone, her hair wiping the floor as she wept.

The Grasshopper

The faithful Tithonus and their two bouncing children welcomed Eos back on her return. She did everything she could to hide her woe, but Tithonus sensed something was distressing her. When the boys had been put down to sleep for the night he took her through to the balcony and poured her a cup of wine. They sat and watched the stars for a while before he spoke.

'Eos, my love, my life. I know what it is that you aren't telling me. I can see it for myself. The looking glass tells me every morning.'

'Oh Tithonus!' she buried her head against his chest and sobbed her heart out.

Time passed. Each morning Eos did her duty and opened the doors to a new day. The boys grew up and left home. The years succeeded each other with the remorseless inevitability that even gods cannot alter.

What scant hair that remained on Tithonus's head was now white. He had become most dreadfully wrinkled, shrunken and weak with extreme old age, yet he could not die. His voice, once so mellow and sweet to the ear had become a harsh, dry scrape of a sound. His skin and frame were so shrivelled that he could barely walk.

He followed the beautiful, ever young Eos around as faithfully and lovingly as ever. 'Please, pity me,' he would screech in his hoarse, piping tones. 'Kill me, crush me, let it all end, I beg.'

But she could no longer understand him. All she heard were husky cheeps and chirps. Inside, however, she guessed well enough what he was trying to say.

Eos may not have had the ability to grant immortality or eternal youth, but she was gifted with enough divine power to do something to end her beloved's misery. One evening, when she felt neither of them could take any more, she closed her eyes, concentrated hard and watched through hot tears as Tithonus's poor shrunken body made the very few changes necessary to turn him from a withered, old man into a grasshopper.*

In this new form Tithonus hopped from the cold marble floor onto the ledge of the balcony before leaping out into the night. She saw him in her sister Selene's cold moonlight, clinging to a long blade of grass that swayed in the night breeze. His back legs scraped out a sound that might have been a grateful chirrup of loving farewell. Her tears fell and somewhere, far away, Aphrodite laughed.†

---

* A cicada in some versions. I was always taught a grasshopper perhaps because they are commonly found in Britain. Books for British children probably thought a cicada would be a harder insect for us to visualize. Oddly Tithonus's name lives on biologically not as a cicada or grasshopper, but in a type of birdwing or swallowtail butterfly, *Ornithoptera tithonus*.

† A happy thought inspired the geologist Albert Oppel to name one of the late Jurassic ages the Tithonian as a bow to Eos, for it is the age that marks the *dawn* of the Cretaceous. Alfred, Lord Tennyson's 'Tithonus' is one of his most loved and anthologized poems. It takes the form of a dramatic monologue addressed to Eos, in which he begs her to deliver him from his senility.

. . . After many a summer dies the swan.
Me only cruel immortality
Consumes: I wither slowly in thine arms,
Here at the quiet limit of the world,
A white-hair'd shadow roaming like a dream . . .

It contains a famous line that might be considered one of the great themes of Greek myth:
The Gods themselves cannot recall their gifts.

THE BLOOM OF YOUTH

The story of Eos and Tithonus can be considered a kind of domestic tragedy. Greek myth offers us many more stories of love between gods and mortals that more often fit into the genre 'doomed romance', sometimes with an element of rom-com, farce or horror thrown in. In these love affairs the gods seem always to say it with flowers. The Greek for flower is *anthos* – so what follows is, quite literally, a romantic anthology.

Hyacinthus

Hyacinthus, a beautiful Spartan prince, had the misfortune to be loved by two divinities, Zephyrus, the West Wind, and golden Apollo. Hyacinthus himself much preferred the beautiful Apollo and repeatedly turned down the wind's playful but increasingly fierce advances.

One afternoon Apollo and Hyacinth were competing in athletic events and Zephyrus, in a fit of jealous rage, blew Apollo's discus off course, sending it skimming at speed straight towards Hyacinth. It struck him hard on the forehead, killing him stone dead.

In a flood of grief Apollo refused Hermes the right to transport the youth's soul to Hades, instead mixing the mortal blood that gushed from his adored one's brow with his own divine and fragrant tears. This heady juice dropped into the soil and from it bloomed the exquisite and sweet-smelling flower that bears Hyacinth's name to this day.

Crocus and Smilax

Crocus was a mortal youth who pined without success for the nymph SMILAX. Out of pity, the gods (we don't really know which one) turned him into the saffron flower that we call crocus, while she became a brambly vine, many species of which still flourish under the name *Smilax*.

According to another version of this myth, Crocus was the lover and companion of the god Hermes, who accidentally killed him with a discus and in his sorrow turned him into the crocus flower. This is so similar to the story of Apollo and Hyacinthus that you wonder if some bard somewhere got drunk or confused.

Aphrodite and Adonis

There was an early King of Cyprus called THEIAS who was renowned for his remarkable good looks. He and his wife CENCHREIS had a daughter SMYRNA, also known as MYRRHE or MYRRHA, who grew up harbouring secret incestuous love for her handsome father.

Now, Cyprus was sacred to Aphrodite, being the island on which she first set foot after her birth from the foam of the sea, and it was a spiteful Aphrodite who had breathed into Smyrna this unnatural desire for her own father. It seems that the goddess had of late been aggrieved by the inadequacy of King Theias's prayers and sacrifices to her.

He had displayed the temerity to open a new shrine dedicated to Dionysus, a cult which was proving popular amongst the islanders. Aphrodite regarded the neglect of her temples as the worst possible crime, far worse than incest. In the minds of mortals, though, even those of the notoriously laissez-faire and decadent Cyprus, incest was a taboo of the gravest kind. An anguished Smyrna attempted to smother her guilty feelings. But Aphrodite, who really seemed determined to sow mischief, bewitched Smyrna's maid HIPPOLYTE and brought the whole business to a disturbing crisis.

One evening, when Theias had got himself good and drunk, as he liked to do since his discovery of the vinous virtues of the god Dionysus, Hippolyte, under the spell of Aphrodite, led Smyrna to his chamber and into his bed. The king made greedy love to his daughter there, too intoxicated to question his good fortune. In the dark of night and the fog of wine he failed to recognize the fruit of his own loins; he only knew that a young, desirable, and passionately obliging girl had appeared to pleasure him like some kind of divine succubus.

After a week of these intense and joyful visitations Theias awoke one morning with a determination to know more about her. He put out word that he would reward with a mountain of gold anyone who could discover the identity of the mysterious stranger who had lately made his nights so wildly pleasurable.

Smyrna had been acting out her passion in a kind of mad dream of lust, but when she heard that all Cyprus was now trying to find out the secret of her nightly visits to Theias, she ran from the palace to hide in the woods. She wanted to die, but she could not forsake the child that she already felt growing inside her. Railing at the laws of man that made her love criminal, she begged heaven to take pity on her.* In answer to her prayer, the gods transformed Smyrna into a weeping myrrh tree.

After ten months the tree burst open and disgorged a mortal baby boy. Naiads anointed the child with the soft tears that wept from the myrrh – a balm which remains the source of the most important birth and coronation oils to this very day – and he was given the name Adonis.

Smyrna's baby grew up to be a youth of the most unparalleled physical attractiveness. Oh dear, I've written this too many times for you to believe me again. But it's true that all who looked upon him were smitten for ever and true also that his name lives on as a descriptor of paragons of male beauty. At the very least it's necessary for us to know that Adonis was lovely enough to attract, as no other mortal ever had, the one who had done so much to bring about his birth: the goddess of love and beauty herself, Aphrodite.

They became lovers. It had been a wild and tortuous path to this coupling: the goddess, in a spirit of malicious revenge, had caused a father to commit a forbidden act with his daughter which brought forth a child whom Aphrodite loved perhaps more completely than any other being. A lifetime of therapy could surely not clear up such a psychic mess as that.

They did everything together, Adonis and Aphrodite. She knew that the other gods hated the boy – Demeter and Artemis could not bear to see so many girls sickening with love for him, Hera stonily disapproved of the issue of so shamefully and flagrantly indecent an affront to the sacred institutions of marriage and family, while Ares was stormily jealous of his lover's intense infatuation. Aphrodite sensed all this and

---

* 'Human civilization has made spiteful laws, and what nature allows, the jealous laws forbid.' is her complaint, according to Ovid in his *Metamorphoses*.

determined to keep Adonis safe from the harm her resentful family might do him.

Because her precious mortal lover, like most Greek boys and men, showed a great passion for hunting, the protective Aphrodite told him that while he was free to chase prey of manageable size and limited ferocity – hares, rabbits, doves and pigeons, for example – he was absolutely forbidden from pursuing lions, bears, boars and the larger stags. But boys will be boys, and when the girls are away they cannot resist reverting to type and showing off. And so it came about that, one afternoon, Aphrodite's beloved found himself alone on the trail of a great boar (some say the boar was actually Ares himself in disguise). Adonis cornered the beast and was just pulling back his spear ready for the kill when it turned on him with a savage roar, tusks bristling. Adonis dropped his spear in fright as he leapt back, but he was a brave young man and managed to steady himself and plant his feet firmly enough to meet the boar's charge. As it rushed forward, Adonis spun his body round in a graceful turn like a dancer – the brute missed him and Adonis seized it by the neck as it passed. But the boar was cunning. It dropped its head to the ground, letting the boy think he had subdued it. Kneeling down Adonis pushed with one hand against the animal's head, feeling with his spare hand for the knife he kept in his belt. The boar sensed its chance and pulled its head up with a snarl, lifting and twisting its great tusks. They tore Adonis's stomach open and he fell, mortally wounded, to the ground.

Aphrodite arrived in time to see her lover bleeding to death and the boar – or was it Ares? – grunting in triumph as it galloped away deep into the forest. There was nothing the weeping goddess could do but hold Adonis and watch him choke out his last in her arms. From his blood and her tears sprang up bright red anemones named after the winds (*anemoi* in Greek) that so quickly blow away the petals of this exquisitely lovely flower, which is known to be as short-lived as youth and as fragile as beauty.*

---

* Shakespeare's long poem *Venus and Adonis* retells the myth, basing itself on the version Ovid tells in his *Metamorphoses*. In Shakespeare's rendition the death of Adonis causes Venus to curse love and decree that henceforward it should always be tinged with tragedy. As she prophesies in her grief:

> Sorrow on love hereafter shall attend . . .
> It shall be cause of war and dire events
> And set dissension 'twixt the son and sire . . .
>   They that love best their loves shall not enjoy.

A prophecy that seems to have come all too true.

ECHO AND NARCISSUS

Tiresias

The best known of all the stories that involve the transformation of a youth into a flower begins with a worried mother taking her son to see a prophet. As well as the soothsayers and Sibyls who spoke on behalf of the divine oracles, there existed certain select mortal beings whom the gods also privileged with the gift of prophecy. Arranging a consultation with one of these was not unlike making an appointment to see a doctor.

The two most celebrated seers of Greek myth were CASSANDRA and TIRESIAS. Cassandra was a Trojan prophetess whose curse was to be entirely accurate in her prognostications yet always just as entirely disbelieved. The Theban Tiresias underwent an equally stressed existence. Born male, he was turned female by Hera as a punishment for striking two mating snakes with a stick, something which annoyed her greatly at the time, for reasons best known to herself. After seven years of serving Hera as a priestess, Tiresias was returned to his original male form, only to be struck blind by Athena for looking on her naked while she bathed in the river.* That is one story that explains his blindness, but I prefer the variant that tells how he was brought up to

---

* Note the similarity of the offence to Actaeon's crime of spying on Artemis. The modesty of the gods while bathing was prodigious.

  T. S. Eliot makes memorable reference to Tiresias in 'The Fire Sermon' section of his poem *The Waste Land*:

Olympus to arbitrate in a wager between Zeus and Hera. They had been arguing over which gender enjoyed sex the most. Since Tiresias, having been both male and female, was in a unique position to answer this question, it was agreed that his judgement would be final.

Tiresias declared that in his experience sex was *nine times* more enjoyable for females than males. This enraged Hera, who had bet Zeus that men got the most pleasure from the act. Perhaps she was basing her opinion on the inexhaustible libido of her husband and her own more moderate sex drive. For his pains Hera rewarded Tiresias by striking him blind. One god can never reverse the effects of another, so the best Zeus could do for Tiresias was to award him the compensatory faculty of second sight, the gift of prophecy.*

Narcissus

There was once a naiad called LIRIOPE, who coupled with the river god CEPHISSUS and gave birth to a son, NARCISSUS, whose beauty was so remarkable that she worried for his future. Liriope had seen enough of life to know that extreme beauty was an awful privilege, a dangerous attribute that could lead to dire and even fatal consequences. When

---

I Tiresias, though blind, throbbing between two lives,
Old man with wrinkled female breasts, can see . . .
I Tiresias, old man with wrinkled dugs
Perceived the scene, and foretold the rest . . .
And I Tiresias have foresuffered all . . .

* The honour of being asked to adjudicate amongst the gods might seem great for a mortal, but as this story shows, and as the Trojan prince Paris was to discover, the results could be catastrophic.

Narcissus reached the age of fifteen and started to attract unwanted attentions, she decided to act.

'We are going to Thebes,' she told him, 'to see Tiresias and have your fortune told.'

And so mother and son walked for two weeks all the way to Thebes and joined the queue to see the prophet that formed every morning outside the temple of Hera.

'Although you are blind and cannot see my son,' she explained to Tiresias when their turn came at last, 'you may take my word for it that all who do see him are dazzled by his looks. No more beautiful mortal ever trod the earth.'

Narcissus blushed to his golden roots at this and shuffled his feet in an agony of embarrassment.

'I know enough of the gods,' continued Liriope, 'to fear that such beauty might be more curse than blessing. The world knows what happened to Ganymede, to Adonis, Tithonus, Hyacinth and all those other boys far less beautiful than my son. So I would have you tell me, great seer, if Narcissus will live a long and happy life. Is it his *moira* to reach a contented old age?* You who are blind see all that is invisible to the rest of us. Tell me, I beg, my beloved son's destiny.'

Tiresias put out his hands and traced the outlines of Narcissus's face.

'Fear not,' he said. 'So long as he fails to recognize himself, Narcissus will live a long and happy life.'

Liriope laughed aloud. 'So long as he fails to recognize himself!' Such a strange pronouncement could have no serious application. How can anyone recognize themselves?

---

* The Moirai, you will remember, were the Fates. The Greeks felt that for every individual there was a personal, singular *moira* that could be expressed as a mixture of necessity, doom, justice and fortune. Something between luck and *kismet*.

Echo

We leave Liriope joyfully thanking Tiresias at the temple of Hera in Thebes and travel a short distance over to the foothills of Mount Helicon, where the streams and meadows outside the township of Thespiae were filled with the comeliest nymphs in all Greece. So comely that they often received visitations from Zeus himself, whose weakness for a comely nymph we have already noted.

The oread ECHO was not the least comely of these, but she did have one personality trait which caused Zeus and other potential suitors to be wary of her – she was the most tremendous *talker*. A compound of village gossip, nosy neighbour and over-solicitous best friend, Echo found it impossible to hold her tongue. There was nothing malicious about her prattling, indeed she often went out of her way to speak up for her friends, to cover for them, praise them and paint them in the best light. There was an element of vanity here, for she had a lovely voice, pretty in both speech and song. Like many people gifted with a mellifluous tongue, she loved to exercise it. She was protected to some extent by the goddess Aphrodite who admired her singing, which was always in praise of love. In short, Echo was a romantic. Her detractors might call her sentimental and even slushy, mushy and gushy, but they could not deny her good intentions and fullness of heart.

Zeus enjoyed visiting Echo's sister oreads and cousin naiads in secret and Echo enjoyed being a confidante and best friend to them all. It rather thrilled her to think that her relations and companions were having liaisons with Zeus, the Cloud-Gatherer and King of the Gods himself. It was a secret she loved to hug to herself.

Hera had always been suspicious of Zeus's absences, but recently they had become prolonged. She heard from a chaffinch loyal to her that it was the lower slopes of Helicon that her husband had been visiting, so she decided one golden afternoon to make her way there and see if she could catch him in the act of betrayal. She had barely dismounted from her chariot when a mountain nymph skipped up to her, bubbling with inconsequential chatter. It was Echo in full voluble flow.

'Queen Hera!'

Hera drew up her eyebrows. 'Do I know you?'

'Oh, majesty!' cried Echo, falling to her knees. 'How lucky we are to see you here! What *honour* you do us! And in your chariot, too! Is it permitted to feed the peacocks? To have a god of Olympus *here*! I cannot remember the last time an Olympian deigned to take notice of us. It is such –'

'Surely my husband Zeus is a regular visitor to these woods and waters?'

Echo knew full well that Zeus was not far away on a riverbank doing improper things with a pretty river nymph. Her love of intrigue, drama and romance now drove her to protect the pair. With tumbling torrents of inconsequential babble gushing from her like water from a fountain, she guided the goddess's footsteps in the direction away from the river.

'There is a very fine ilex tree just in this clearing, majesty, which I was thinking of consecrating to you, with your permission . . . Excuse me – *Zeus*? Oh no, I've never seen him here.'

'Really?' Hera fixed Echo with a hard stare. 'I heard a rumour that he was here now. This very day.'

'No, no, my queen! No, no, *no*! In fact . . . a servant of the Muses came down from Helicon just half an hour ago to draw water from our stream and he mentioned specifically that today mighty Zeus is in Thespiae today, honouring his temple there.'

'Oh. I see. Well, I thank you.' Hera nodded curtly and uncomfortably, returned to her chariot and flew off into the clouds. It is mortifying to be witnessed trying to catch your husband out.

Echo skipped away, pleased to have been useful to her fellow nymph and to Zeus. In all fairness she would have been just as happy to have been protecting a mortal pair of lovers. It delighted her to ease the path of all lovers everywhere. She had never really felt love herself, except the love of helping others to love, which she felt was the highest love of all. So selfless was she that she never even bothered to tell Zeus or her sister of her useful act, which someone hoping for a reward would most certainly have done. She sang as she gathered flowers and felt that the life of a nymph was a good life.

Echolalia

The next day, back on Olympus, Hera sent for the chaffinch that had first whispered to her of Zeus's infidelity.

'You lied to me,' she shrieked. 'You made me look a fool!'

Hera grasped the bird by the beak so that he could hardly breathe and was about to punish him in some strange and dreadful way that would for ever have altered our conception of chaffinches, when his mate fluttered about her ears and hair bravely calling out. 'But dread queen, he told you true! I saw King Zeus there myself. Even as you were talking to that nymph Echo, he was lying with a naiad not half a mile away. If you don't believe me, the butterflies and herons can tell you. Ask the priestesses at the temple at Thespiae when he last visited them. He hasn't been there for three moons!'

Hera relaxed her grip and the bird, who had gone almost scarlet, breathed again, but male chaffinches still sport pink breasts to this very day.

Echo was paddling playfully in a stream when Hera and her peacock carriage descended once more. The nymph splashed and skipped her way up the riverbank to greet the goddess, a wide and welcoming grin splitting her perfectly dimpled features. The smile of welcome quickly turned to a rounded 'O' of fear when she saw the look of rage on Hera's face.

'So,' said the goddess, with icy calm. 'You say my husband has not been here. You say he was not here yesterday. You say he was in Thespiae sanctifying a temple.'

'That's – that's certainly my understanding,' stammered a frightened Echo.

'You foolish, gossiping, chattering, scheming *liar*! How dare you try to deceive the Queen of Heaven? Who do you think you are?'

'I – . . .' For once in her life Echo could think of nothing to say.

'Well may you stutter and stammer. You love the sound of your voice, don't you? Hear this . . .'

Hera drew herself up and raised her arms high. Her eyes seemed to shine with a purple light. Echo quailed before the grandeur of the sight and wished the ground could swallow her up.

'I command your wicked, lying powers of speech to be still. From this moment you will be mute unless spoken to. You will have no power to reply except to repeat the last thing that has been said to you. None can undo this curse. Only I can. Understand?'

'. . . . can understand!' cried Echo.

'That's what happens when you disobey the gods.'

' . . . obey the gods!'

'I do not forgive. No mercy.'

'. . . give no mercy!'

With a snort and sneer of triumph Hera whisked herself away, leaving the unhappy nymph shivering in fear and frustration. No matter how much she tried to speak, no words would come. Her throat seemed to catch and tighten every time. One of her sisters came upon her wordlessly retching and spluttering. 'Hello, Echo – what are you doing?'

'What are you doing?' said Echo.

'I asked first.'

'I asked first.'

'No *I* did.'

'No *I* did!'

'Well, if you're going to be like that, go to hell.'

'Go to hell!' Echo cried after her, wild with misery.

One by one all her friends and all her family shunned her. The curse inflicted upon one who had lived her life for gleeful gossip, who valued nothing above cheerful chatter and who had derived all her pleasure from prattling repartee was so terrible that Echo now wished for nothing more than to be left alone to welter in silent agony.

Echo and Narcissus

Into the painful solitude of Echo's private hell there crashed one day all the laughter, shouting and boisterous clamour of a hunt. The youths of Thespiae had chased a boar all the way into the wood, and one of the huntsmen had become separated. He was a youth of such transcendent beauty that Echo, whom the tender passion had passed over all her life, was instantly lovestruck.

The youth was Narcissus, now older and more dazzling than ever. He had never fallen victim to the tender passion either. He had become so used to girls and boys, men and women, fauns and satyrs, nymphs and dryads, oreads and centaurs, and all manner of beings, sentient and non-sentient, shrieking and sighing and fainting away in his presence that he thought the whole business of love absurd. It turned sensible people stupid. Narcissus hated being mooned and swooned over. It maddened him to see the unmistakable look of love leaping into the eyes of others. There was something so angry and ugly about that look. Something so hungry, lost and despairing, so brooding, haunted and unhappy.

To Narcissus love and desire were sicknesses. He had been taught that lesson in the worst way possible a year before, when a boy called AMEINIAS had declared his love to him. Narcissus had replied, as kindly as he could, that he did not return his love. But Ameinias would not accept 'no' for an answer and took to haunting Narcissus's every step. He joined him on his morning walk to school, tagging along and gazing at him like a lost and adoring puppy until Narcissus could stand it no longer and yelled at him to go away and never come near him again.

That night Narcissus had been awoken by a strange sound outside his bedroom. He looked out of his window and saw in the moonlight Ameinias hanging from a pear tree, a rope around his neck. He choked out a curse before he died.

'May you be as unlucky in love as I have been, beautiful Narcissus!'*

Since then Narcissus had got into the habit of keeping his head down, covering his body as much as possible and being short and gruff to strangers, never meeting them in the eye.

But now, as he looked about him, he saw that the rest of the hunting party had gone and that he was splendidly alone.

---

* Ameinias, according to some sources, became a sweet-smelling herb. Possibly dill. Perhaps cumin. Maybe anise.

He decided to take advantage of the cool waters of the stream and its inviting mossy banks. He slipped out of his clothes and plunged into the water.

As soon as she caught sight of that lissom and golden form, half sunlit, half dappled by the shade and all streaming with water, Echo caught her breath. And when, peeping through the leaves she saw the face, the beautiful, beautiful face of Narcissus, she could no longer control her senses. Were it not for Hera's curse she would have cried out there and then. Instead she gazed in silent wonder as the naked youth laid his clothes and bow and arrows on the grass and stretched himself out to sleep.

When love comes late it comes like a tornado. Poor Echo's whole being was swept up by her feelings for this impossibly beautiful youth. Nothing, not even the horror of Hera's curse, had ever caused her heart to hammer so violently inside her. The blood pounded and surged in her ears. It was as if she was swirling in the centre of a great cyclone. She simply *had* to take a closer look at this lovely youth. If she felt such tumultuous passions swirling inside her at the sight of *him*, then perhaps it was in the nature of things that he would feel the same at the sight of *her*? Surely that must be so? She crept forward, hardly daring to breathe. With each step she found herself more and more thrilled until she was quivering and trembling all over with excitement. The stories of love at first sight that she had heard sung all her life were true after all! This beautiful boy would be bound to return her love. Cosmos and creation would not make sense otherwise.

Of course, you and I know that Cosmos and creation make no sense at all and never have. Poor Echo was about to discover the truth of this.

Whether it was her pounding heart or the cry of a bird, something made the sleeping Narcissus open his eyes just as Echo drew near.

His eyes met hers.

Echo was a pretty nymph, lovely in fact. But it was only her eyes that Narcissus saw. That look again! That haggard, hungry, haunted look. Those needing, pleading eyes. Ugh!

'Who are you?' he said, turning away.

'Who are you?'

'Never you mind. That's my business.'

'That's my business!'

'No it isn't. You woke me.'

'You woke me!'

'I suppose like all the others you've fallen in love with me.'

'Love with me!'

'Love! I'm fed up with love.'

'Up with love!'

'It'll never happen. Never. Go away!'

'Never go away!'

'I don't care how much you wail at me. I hate the sight of you.'

'The sight of you!'

'Stop it, will you? Just don't!' cried Narcissus. 'Go away!'

'Don't go away!'

'You're driving me crazy.'

'Driving me crazy!'

'Go away before I do something so desperate . . .'

'So desperate!'

'Don't tempt me, now.'

'Tempt me now!'

Narcissus picked up his hunting sling and loaded it with a stone. 'Go. Just go. I'll hurt you if you don't. Understand?'

'You don't understand.'

The first stone missed her, but Echo turned and fled before Narcissus could reload and try again. As she ran he called out after her.

'And never come back!'

'Never come back,' she cried.

She ran from him and kept running until she fell weeping to the ground, her heart bursting with grief and shame.

The Boy in the Water

Narcissus watched her go. He shook his head angrily. Would he never be free of these silly wailing people and their whining, clutching madness? Love and beauty! Words, just words.

Hot and thirsty from all the stress and drama he knelt down to drink from the stream. He caught his breath in astonishment when in its waters, he saw the loveliest face he had ever laid eyes upon, the sweet and surprised face of a most beautiful young man. He had golden hair and soft red lips. Narcissus recognized with a thrill that the youth's beguiling and loving eyes had the hungry, needy look he had always found so repellent in others. But the very same expression on the gorgeous face of this mysterious stranger made Narcissus's chest swell and heart thump with joy. It must mean that the glorious creature in the river felt the same way as he did! Narcissus leaned down to kiss the lovely lips and the lovely lips came up to kiss his, but just as Narcissus lowered his face, the stranger's features broke into a thousand dancing, rippling pieces until he could see them no longer and Narcissus found he was kissing nothing but cold water.

'Stay still, lovely one,' he breathed, and the boy seemed to whisper the same to him.

Narcissus raised a hand. The boy raised his hand in reply. Narcissus wanted to stroke the boy's lovely cheek and the boy wanted to do the same. But the face fractured and dissolved the moment Narcissus got close.

Again and again each one tried.

Meanwhile, in the bushes behind them, Echo – fired and strengthened by her great love – had returned to try her luck again. Her heart skipped a beat when she heard him say:

'I love you!'

'I love you!' she called back.

'Stay with me!'

'Stay with me!'

'Never leave me!'

'Never leave me!'

But when she came closer Narcissus turned with a snarl and hissed at her –

'Go away! Leave us alone. Never come back! Never, never, never!'

'Never, never, never!' wailed Echo.

With a savage roar Narcissus picked up a stone and hurled it at her. Echo ran and tripped. Narcissus then grabbed his bow and would surely have shot her dead had she not scrambled to her feet and disappeared into the wood.

Narcissus looked anxiously back to the stream, frightened that perhaps the marvellous boy had gone. But there he was – a worried and flushed look on his face – but as beautiful and loving as ever and with a wonderful gleam in his deep blue eyes. Narcissus lay down again and brought his face closer to the water . . .

The Gods Take Pity

Echo ran and ran up the hillside, sobbing with grief and desolation. She hid in a cave high above the river by whose banks the lovely Narcissus lay.

Inside her head Echo framed the words of a prayer to her

favourite goddess, Aphrodite. In mute despair she begged to be relieved of the pain of love and the intolerable burden of her cursed existence.

Aphrodite answered the nymph's prayers as best she could. She freed the nymph of her body and most of her physical self. She did not have the power to lift Hera's curse, so the voice remained. The voice that had got Echo into all that trouble in the first place, the voice that was doomed to repeat and repeat. Nothing more was left of the once beautiful nymph, just the answering voice. You can hear Echo still, returning your last few words when you call out near caves, canyons, cliffs, hills, streets, squares, temples, monuments, ruins and empty rooms.

And Narcissus? Day after day he lay by the river, passionately and hopelessly in love with his own reflection, gazing at himself, filled with love for himself and longing for himself, with eyes only for himself, and consideration for no one and nothing but himself. He drooped down over the water, pining and pining until at last the gods turned him into the delicate and beautiful daffodil that bears his name and whose lovely head always bows down to look at itself in puddles, pools and streams.

You can choose to think of the characteristics these doomed young people have bequeathed us and our language as common human traits or as problematic afflictions. Narcissistic personality disorder and echolalia (the apparently mindless repetition of what is said) are both classified in the *Diagnostic and Statistical Manual of Mental Disorders*, which medically and legally defines mental illnesses. Narcissistic personality disorder, much talked about these days, is marked by vanity, self-importance, a grandiose hunger for admiration, acclaim and applause, and above all an obsession with self-image. The feelings of others are railroaded and stampeded, while such considerations as honesty, truthfulness or integrity are blithely disregarded. Bragging, boasting and delusional exaggeration are common signs. Criticism or belittlement is intolerable and can provoke aggressive and explosively strange behaviours.*

Perhaps narcissism is best defined as a need to look on other people as mirrored surfaces who satisfy us only when they reflect back a loving or admiring image of ourselves. When we look into another's eyes, in other words, we are not looking to see who *they* are, but how we are reflected *in their eyes*. By this definition, which of us can honestly disown our share of narcissism?

---

* No one we know, of course . . .

LOVERS

Tristan and Isolde, Romeo and Juliet, Heathcliff and Catherine, Sue Ellen and J.R. – the doomed lovers we know all owe a great debt to the tragic Greek tradition that preceded them.

Pyramus and Thisbe

When we hear the name 'Babylon' we think of a Middle Eastern civilization famed for ribaldry and excess. Its Hanging Gardens were one of the original Seven Wonders of the World and for a time Babylon was the largest city in the world.* The Babylonian Empire took in much of Asia Minor, indeed some believe that this story really took place in Cilicia, the kingdom that Cilix founded before he joined Cadmus and the other sons of Agenor in their quest for Europa. Ovid, however, in his version of the tale, is happy to locate the action plum in the centre of Babylon and so that is where I have placed it too.

In Babylon, then, lived two families who had been feuding, no one quite remembers why, for generations. Their great palaces stood next to each other on the main street of the city, but the children of each household were raised as enemies, forbidden so much as to speak, write or sign to one another.

---

* The remains of Babylon lie under, or poke through, the sands of Iraq, about fifty miles south of Baghdad.

345

One of the families had a son called PYRAMUS and the other a daughter called THISBE who somehow fell in love with each other despite the obstacles in their way. They had discovered a small hole in a shared wall between their adjoining homes. Through this aperture they whispered, swapping views of life, poetry and music until they found themselves falling very deeply in love. The hole in the wall was too small to allow them to touch, but the heat of their young and ardent passion could be breathed from one mouth to another through that benevolent chink, intensified by the forbidden nature of their feelings and their thrillingly unbridgeable proximity.

This exchange of hot, youthful breath enflamed them so much that one night, maddened beyond endurance, they arranged each to escape their respective palaces and meet at night in the grounds of the tomb of Pyramus's ancestor, the Assyrian King NINUS, founder of the great city of Nineveh.

And so, the following evening, the nimble and quick-witted Thisbe slips past the guardians of her room and the sentries on duty outside her father's palace and is soon beyond the city walls, built all those years ago by her ancestor, Queen SEMIRAMIS. When she reaches the trysting-place, Thisbe encounters not her lover Pyramus, but a savage lion whose jaws drip with the blood of its recent prey, an ox. Frightened by its roars, Thisbe runs from the cemetery. In the hurry and panic of her flight she drops her veil. The lion approaches the veil, snuffles it, takes it between its jaws and shakes it from side to side, staining it with some of the ox-blood on its muzzle before letting it fall back to the ground, giving one last roar and padding off into the night.

A little later Pyramus arrives on the scene and sets himself to wait for his beloved under a tall mulberry tree loaded with its heavy summer burden of snow-white fruit. A shaft of moonlight shoots between the tree's branches and illuminates Thisbe's veil, which is lying on the ground all smeared and dabbled with gore. Pyramus snatches it up. Horror-struck, he can make out the embroidered crest of Thisbe's family in the bloodstained linen, and more than that, he recognizes the scent of the girl with whom he has exchanged the fierce fever of love's breath so many times. Paw prints on the ground bear witness to the presence of a lion.

Blood, paw prints, the family crest, the unmistakable scent of Thisbe herself: the clear and tragic meaning of it all bursts in on Pyramus. With a cry of despair he draws his sword and stabs himself deep in the stomach, ripping the wound wider from side to side in his hurry to join his dead beloved. Blood spurts up from him like a fountain, dyeing the white mulberries purple.

'You took my beloved Thisbe away before we could be united for the short span of our lives,' Pyramus cries to the heavens, 'so let us be one in the endless night of eternal death!' With these noble words he expires upon the ground.*

Enter Thisbe. In the dead hands of Pyramus she sees her own veil, smeared and spattered with blood. She sees the lion's paw prints and reads all too clearly the story written there.

'Oh gods, can you have been so jealous of our love that

---

* In the farcical production in *A Midsummer Night's Dream*, Pyramus (played by Bottom) cries out as he stabs himself:

Thus die I, thus, thus, thus.
   Now am I dead,
   Now am I fled;
My soul is in the sky.
   Tongue, lose thy light;
   Moon, take thy flight;
Now die, die, die, die, die.

you could not grant us even one short moment of happiness?' she cries.

She sees Pyramus's sword. It is still hot and wet with his blood. She throws herself upon it, plunging it deep into her belly with a cry of triumph and ecstasy in one of the most Freudian suicides ever.

When the two families are taken to the site of the tragedy they fall weeping on each other's necks and beg forgiveness. The feud is over. The lovers' bodies are cremated and their ashes mixed together in a single urn.

As for their spirits – well, Pyramus was turned into the river that bore his name for millennia and Thisbe into a spring whose waters run into it. The flow of the Pyramus (now called the Ceyhan) has been dammed for hydroelectric energy, so the power of the two lovers now goes to light Turkish homes.

Moreover, in honour of the couple's love and sacrifice, the gods decreed that the mulberry fruit would from that moment on be always a deep crimson purple: the colour of their passion and their blood.

GALATEAS

Acis and Galatea

Amongst the many daughters of the Oceanid Doris and the sea god Nereus, was one Nereid called GALATEA. Named for her milk-white complexion she was adored by POLYPHE-MUS, a Cyclops. Not one of the original Cyclopes – Polyphemus was the savage and ugly offspring of Poseidon and the Ocea-nid THOOSA.

Galatea herself loved ACIS, a Sicilian shepherd boy of simple charm and beauty. Though the son of the river nymph SYMA-ETHIS and the god Pan, Acis was only mortal. One day the jealous Polyphemus caught sight of Acis and Galatea in each other's arms and hurled a boulder down onto the boy, crushing and killing him. The grieving Galatea was able to call upon sufficient power and resources, or perhaps had enough friends on Olympus, to be able to turn Acis into an immortal river spirit with whom she consorts for eternity. Their story is the subject of Handel's pastoral opera *Acis and Galatea*.

Galatea II

While on the subject of girls called Galatea there are two more worth meeting.

PANDION of Phaestos in Crete had a son, LAMPROS, who married a Galatea. Lampros had no interest in fathering girl-children and told his wife that if she gave birth to a daughter she was to kill it and they would keep trying until she bore the son he craved. Their first child was a beautiful baby girl. Galatea did not have the heart to kill her – what mother would? – and told her husband that the baby had been born a healthy boy, and that she wanted to call him LEUCIPPOS (white horse).

Lampros took his wife at her word without bothering with any anatomical inspections and thus, raised male, Leucippos grew up to be a fine, intelligent, universally liked and accepted boy. Teenage years approached, however, and Galatea became more and more afraid that her beloved child's lush natural curves and striking lack of any downy growth on the chin must eventually give the game away to Lampros, who was not the kind of man to overlook such a deception.

For safety's sake Galatea took Leucippos and sought refuge in a temple of Leto (the Titaness mother of Apollo and Artemis), where she prayed that her daughter might change her sex. Leto answered the prayer and on the instant Leucippos was transformed into a masculine youth. Hairs pushed through where they should on a male, the correct bulges appeared, the incorrect bulges disappeared. Lampros was none the wiser and they all lived happily ever after.

For generations after this, the city of Phaestos celebrated a festival they called the Ekdusia.* In this ritual all young Phaestian boys lived amongst women and girls, wore female clothes and had to swear an oath of citizenship before they could graduate from their *agela*, or youth corps, and acquire full male dress and status.†

---

* A word that covers moulting, shedding, casting off and re-evaluating. Slipping out of one thing and popping on another.

† For more on this fascinating subject, see David D. Leitao, 'The Perils of Leukippos: Initiatory Transvestism and Male Gender Ideology in the Ekdusia at Phaistos', in *Classical Antiquity*, vol. 14, no. 1 (1995).

Leucippos II, Daphne and Apollo

Interestingly, another myth tells of a different sex-changing LEUCIPPOS – this one a son of OENOMAUS – who fell in love with the naiad DAPHNE, whom Apollo also loved but had not so far wooed or seduced.

In order to be near Daphne, this Leucippos disguised himself as a girl and joined her company of nymphs. The jealous Apollo saw this and caused the reeds to whisper to Daphne that she and her attendants should bathe in the river. Accordingly they slipped out of their clothes and splashed about naked. When Leucippos, for obvious reasons, refused to remove his maidenly garb the girls teasingly stripped him bare, discovered his embarrassing and unmistakable secret, and angrily speared him to death.

By this time Apollo's own lustful blood was up. He materialized and began a pursuit of Daphne. The terrified girl leapt out of the river and ran away as fast as she could, but he quickly gained on her. He had almost reached her when she sent up a prayer to her mother, Gaia and her father, the river god LADON. Just as Apollo closed in and touched her he felt her flesh change under his fingers. A thin bark formed over her breasts, her hair began to slither out into shining yellow and green leaves, her limbs wreathed themselves into branches and her feet slowly drove down roots into her mother Gaia's receiving earth. A stupefied Apollo found that he was clutching not a naiad but a laurel tree.

For once in his life the god was chastened. The laurel became sacred to him and its wreath thenceforward crowned the brow, as I have said, of the winners of his Pythian Games at Delphi. To this day the winner of a great prize is still called a laureate.*

Galatea III and Pygmalion Too

The island of Cyprus, being the landing ground of spume-born Aphrodite, had long worshipped the goddess of love and beauty with a special fervour, earning Cypriots a reputation for libertine licentiousness and libidinous loose-living. Cyprus was thought of by the mainland as a degenerate place, an Island of Free Love.

In the southern port town of Amathus, a group of women known as the PROPOETIDES, or 'daughters of Propoetus', were so indignant at the amount of sexual licence that pervaded there, they even had the temerity to suggest that Aphrodite should no longer stand as the island's patroness. To punish such blasphemous impertinence the wrathful Aphrodite visited upon these sanctimonious sisters feelings of insatiable carnal lust, at the same time ridding them of any sense of modesty or shame. So cursed, the women lost the ability to blush and began eagerly and indiscriminately to prostitute their bodies about the island.

A sensitive and wildly attractive young sculptor called PYGMALION saw the flagrant and shameless behaviour of the

---

* Daphne should not be confused with DAPHNIS, a Sicilian youth of great beauty who was found as a baby under the laurel bush that gave him his name. Both Hermes and Pan fell in love with him, the latter teaching him to play the pipes. He became so proficient that later generations credited him with the invention of pastoral poetry. In the second century AD Longus, an author from Lesbos, wrote a romance (like *The Golden Ass* a contender for the title First Ever Novel) called *Daphnis and Chloë* which tells of two bucolic lovers who undergo all kinds of ordeals and adventures to test their love. Offenbach composed an operetta based on this tale. Even better known is the revolutionary 1912 ballet with music by Maurice Ravel, choreographed by Fokine and danced by Nijinsky.

Propoetides and grew so disgusted that he decided to fore-
swear all love and sex in perpetuity.

'Women!' he muttered to himself as he set to work one
morning on a commission to render in marble the face and figure of a general from Amanthus. 'You won't find me wasting
my time on women. Oh no. Art is enough. Art is all. Love is
nothing. Art is everything. Art is . . . well now, that's strange . . .'

Pygmalion stepped back to look at his work and wrinkled
his brow in surprise. His general was taking shape in the
oddest way. He could have sworn the man had a beard. Furthermore, the old warrior may have been a little on the tubby
side, but Pygmalion was sure he didn't sport a pair of swelling breasts. Nor were his neck and throat so slender, smooth
and irresistibly . . .

Pygmalion went out into the yard and dipped his head in
the fountain of cold water that played there. Returning
refreshed to the studio he looked again at his work in pro-
gress and could only shake his head in bewilderment. The
general, when Pygmalion had been permitted to go round to
his villa to study the great man's features, had struck him as
being constructed more on the lines of a warthog than anything human, and yet here he was emerging from the marble
as nothing short of a refined and miraculous beauty. A distinctly *feminine* beauty at that.

Picking up a chisel, Pygmalion ran his artist's eye over the
work and knew that with some merciless and well-aimed
blows he could easily enough get back on course and not
waste the valuable block of marble for which he had paid a
month's income.

Crack, crack, crack!

This was more like it.

Tap, tap, tap!

Must have been some weird subconscious urge.

Chip, chip, chip!

Or indigestion perhaps.

Now, let's step back again and see . . .

No!!!

Far from rescuing the work and bringing the general's masculine and martial glare back to the face of his sculpture he had somehow managed only to amplify its soft femininity, grace, sensuality and – goddammit – sexiness.

He was in a fever now. Deep inside he knew he was no longer rescuing the general. He was on a mission to see through to the end the madness that had seized him.

The madness was of course the work of Aphrodite. She had not been pleased when one of the handsomest and most eligible young men of her island had chosen to turn his back on love. A young man moreover, whose seaside dwelling happened to be exactly where Aphrodite had made landfall after her birth in the waves and, she reasoned, ought therefore to vibrate with a special intensity of amorousness. Love and beauty, as most of us find out in the course of our lives, are remorseless, relentless and ruthless.

For days and nights Pygmalion laboured on in a frenzy of creativity, of literal *enthusiasm*. Generations of artists in all media since might have recognized the agonized, breathless ecstasy of inspiration that had seized him. No thought of food or drink – no conscious thought at all – came into his mind, as he tapped, hammered and hummed.

At last, as the pink flush of Eos and a nacreous flash of light from the east betokened the beginning of his fifth continuous day of work, he stepped back with the miraculous knowledge that only true artists understand: somehow, yes certainly, at last – it was finished.

He hardly dared raise his eyes. All his work thus far had been up close, detailed – the lineaments of the complete figure existed only in some dark inaccessible corner of his mind. For the first time he could take it all in. He took a deep breath and looked.

He cried out in shock and dropped his chisel.

From its exquisitely rendered toes to the perfectly worked flowers that wreathed the hair on its head the sculpture was far and away the best thing he had ever done. More than that, it was surely the most absolutely beautiful work of art that had ever been seen in the world. To a true artist like Pygmalion this meant it was more beautiful than any *person* that had ever been seen on earth, for he knew that art always exceeds the best that nature can manage.

Yet he saw that the figure he had rendered in marble from his enraptured imagination was even more than the most absolutely beautiful thing now in the world. She was *real*. To Pygmalion she was more real than the ceiling above his head and the floor beneath his feet.

His heart was beating fast, his pupils had dilated, his breath was short and the very core of his being stirred in the most powerful and disturbing manner. It was joy and pain all at once. It was love.

The expression and posture of the girl – whose name he knew should be Galatea, for her marble loveliness was white as milk – were caught in a moment of sublime hesitation, between awakening and wonder. She seemed a little surprised, as if on the verge of gasping. At what? At the beauty of the world? At the handsomeness of the young artist who was feasting his eyes so hungrily upon her? Her features were regular and perfect, but so were the features of many girls. There was more to her than conventional appeal. An inner loveliness of soul sang from her very core. Her lines were sweepingly, swoopingly, swooningly smooth, supple and sensuous. Her breasts seemed softly to be pushing out, her nakedness made so much more alluring by the way her hand touched her throat in a gesture of sweetly modest alarm.

Pygmalion walked around her to take in the thrilling generosity of the curve of her buttocks and the glorious fullness of her thighs. Dared he put a hand to that flesh? He reached out – gently, so as not to bruise her. But his fingers met cold marble. Hard, unyielding marble. To the eye and through to the depths of her Galatea seemed quick, warm and alive, but to Pygmalion's stroking hands and to the loving cheek he rested on her side she was as cold as death.

He felt both sick and supercharged with life at one and the same time. He jumped up and down. He shouted out loud. He groaned. He laughed. He sang. He swore. He exhibited all the wild, deranged, furious, euphoric and despairing behaviours of a young man tempestuously and frighteningly in love.

At last he threw himself at his Galatea, encircled her with his arms and with his legs, nuzzled himself against her, kissing and pawing and rubbing until everything inside him exploded.

The madness that consumed his soul did not abate after that first frenzy. He now devoted himself to Galatea with all the ardour and attentive tenderness of a true lover. He called her affectionate names. He went out to the market and bought her gowns, garlands and trinkets. He adorned her wrists with bangles and bracelets and her throat with necklaces and pendants of jasper and pearl. He bought a couch that he adorned with silks of Tyrian purple. He lay her upon it and sang ballads to her. Like most great visual artists he was an incompetent musician and a deplorable poet.

His love was passionate and generous but – except to his

fevered imagination in its most optimistic moods – wholly
unreciprocated. This was a one-way wooing and in the
depths of his bursting heart he knew it.

The day came for the festival of Aphrodite. Pygmalion
kissed the cold but lovely Galatea goodbye and left the house.
All of Cyprus and thousands of visitors from the mainland
had gathered in Amanthus for this annual holiday. The great
square in front of the temple was crowded with pilgrims who
came to pray to the goddess of love and beauty for success in
matters of the heart. Garlanded heifers were sacrificed, the
air was thick with frankincense and every column of the
temple had been entwined with flowers. The prayers came
thick, fast and loud.

'Send me a wife.'

'Send me a husband.'

'Improve my performance.'

'Slow me down.'

'Take these feelings away from me.'

'Make Menander fall for me.'

'Stop Xanthippe from cheating on me.'

Beseeching cries and wails filled the air.

Pygmalion shouldered blindly through the press of ped-
lars and petitioners. He reached the temple steps, bribed the
guards, coaxed the priestesses and at last was led into the
inner sanctum where only the richest and most influential
citizens were allowed to pray directly in front of a great statue
of Aphrodite. He fell to his knees before it.

'Great goddess of love,' he whispered. 'It is said that you
grant wishes to ardent lovers on this your festal day. Grant
the wish of a poor artist who begs that you might . . .'

At the altar rail important men and women were babbling their imprecations to Aphrodite, and although the

chances of Pygmalion being overheard were slim, some kind of modesty or shame stopped him from uttering his real desire.

'. . . poor artist who begs that you might provide him with a real living girl just like the one he fashioned from marble. Grant this, dread goddess, and you will have won a devoted slave whose life and art will be devoted always to the service and praise of love.'

An amused Aphrodite saw through the prayer. She knew perfectly well what Pygmalion really wanted. The candles on the altar in front of him flared up and leapt in the air nine times.

Pygmalion flew home. To his dying day he could not tell you the way he went or how long he took. He may have knocked over one person or forty as he charged through the crowds.

The lifeless statue is lying on its gorgeous couch just as he left it. Never has the carved figure seemed less accessible or more icily remote. Yet, with the faith and demented fury of the lovestruck, Pygmalion kneels down and kisses the cold brow. He kisses it once, twice . . . twenty times. Then he kisses its neck, its cheeks . . . and, *wait*! Is it just that the fire of his kisses has warmed the marble, or can he feel a growing heat beneath his hungry lips? *He can!* Beneath the touch of his mouth the unyielding stone is easing into flesh, into quick, warm delicious flesh!

Again and again he kisses, and as the wax from the honeycomb softens and melts in the sun, so the cold ivory of his beloved softens from each gentle caress of mouth and hand.

He is amazed. He cannot believe it. He puts a finger to the veins of her arm and feels the surge and pulse of hot human blood! He stands. Can it be true? Can it be true? He cradles

Galatea in his arms and feels her frame expanding as she takes in her first breaths of air. It *is* true! She lives!

'Aphrodite I bless you! Aphrodite greatest of all the gods, I thank you and pledge myself to serve you always!'

He bends down to meet warm lips that eagerly return his kisses. Soon the pair are in each other's arms laughing, weeping, sighing and loving.

Nine times the moon changes before the union of this happy pair is blessed with the birth of a child, a boy they call PAPHOS, and whose name will be given to the town in which Pygmalion and Galatea live out the remainder of their loving and contented lives.

Just once or twice in Greek myth mortal lovers are granted a felicitous ending. It is that hope, perhaps, that spurs us on to believe that our quest for happiness will not be futile.*

Hero and Leander

The Greek Sea, or 'Hellespont', is called the Dardanelles in our age and is best known as the scene of some of the most furious fighting around Gallipoli during the Great War. As part of the natural boundary that separates Europe and Asia, these straits have always been strategically important for war and trade. Despite the size of the symbolic gap between them, they are in reality narrow enough to be crossed by a strong swimmer.

LEANDER's† home was in Abydos, on the Asian side of

---

* Paphian became a word to describe Aphrodite and the arts of love. George Bernard Shaw chose *Pygmalion* as the title for his play about a man who tries to turn a cockney girl into a Mayfair lady.

† Little is known about Leander. Christopher Marlowe's poem tells us nothing much more than that he was a youth who met Hero and fell in love. Leigh Hunt wrote another, which is no more informative.

the Hellespont, but he was in love with a priestess of Aphrodite called HERO, who lived in a tower in Sestos on the European side. They had met during the yearly festival of Aphrodite. Many youths had been smitten by 'the meadow of roses in her limbs'* and her face as pure as Selene, but it was only the handsome Leander who awoke a like passion in her. In the brief time they had together at the festival they hatched a plan that would allow them to see each other once they were back home and separated by the straits. Each night Hero was to set a lamp in the window of her tower and Leander, eyes fixed on this point of light in the darkness, would breast the currents of the Hellespont, climb up and be with her.

As a priestess, Hero was sworn to celibacy, but Leander persuaded her that the physical consummation of their love would be a holy thing, a consecration of which Aphrodite would approve. In fact, he said, it was surely an insult to devote herself to the goddess of love and yet remain a virgin. It would be like worshipping Ares but refusing to fight. This excellent argument won Hero over and each night the lamp was lit, the straits swum and love made. They were the happiest couple in all the world.

All summer long this blissful state of affairs prevailed, but summer all too soon turned to autumn and before long the equinoctial gales blew. One night the three winds Boreas, Zephyrus and Notus – the North, West and South Winds – howled together, sending blusters and gusts all around, one of which blew out the lamp in Hero's window. With nothing to guide him across the Hellespont and with the winds

---

* In Marlowe's poem she wears a veil of flowers so realistically embroidered that she has to swat bees away . . .

stirring up the waves into heaving walls of water, Leander lost his way, got into trouble and drowned.

Hero waited up all night for her lover. The next morning, as soon as Eos had cast open the gates of dawn and there was light enough to see, she looked down to see Leander's broken body spread out over the rocks beneath her tower. In an agony of despair she leapt from her window and dashed herself on those same rocks.*

Since Leander many others have swum the Hellespont. None more notably than the poet Byron, who managed it on 3 May 1810 – at the second attempt. In his journal he proudly recorded a time of one hour and ten minutes. 'Did it with little difficulty,' he noted. 'I plume myself on this achievement more than I could possibly do on any kind of glory, political, poetical, or rhetorical.'

Lord Byron swam in the company of one Lieutenant William Ekenhead of the Royal Marines who obtained his own share of immortality with his inclusion in this stanza from Byron's mock epic masterpiece, *Don Juan*. Praising his hero's prowess in swimming across the Guadalquivir in Seville, Byron writes of Juan:

> He could, perhaps, have passed the Hellespont,
> As once (a feat on which ourselves we prided)
> Leander, Mr. Ekenhead, and I did.†

---

* Leander's name lives on in England's venerable and exclusive rowing club, whose candy pink socks, tie and oar-blades are such an alarming feature of the Henley Regatta.

† The achievement clearly meant a lot to the club-footed but superbly athletic poet. He wrote this to his friend Henry Drury: 'This morning I *swam* from *Sestos* to *Abydos*. The immediate distance is not above a mile, but the current renders it hazardous; – so much so, that I doubt whether Leander's conjugal affection must not have been a little chilled in his passage to Paradise.'

Six days after his feat Byron even wrote a mock heroic poem on the subject, 'Written after Swimming from Sestos to Abydos' (overleaf):

Shakespeare seems to have been especially fond of the ancient lovers' story, giving a character in *Much Ado About Nothing* the name Hero and putting these wonderfully cynical anti-romantic words into the mouth of Rosalind in *As You Like It*:

> Leander, he would have lived many a fair year though Hero had turned nun if it had not been for a hot midsummer night, for, good youth, he went but forth to wash him in the Hellespont, and, being taken with the cramp, was drowned; and the foolish chroniclers of that age found it was Hero of Sestos. But these are all lies. Men have died from time to time, and worms have eaten them, but not for love.

If, in the month of dark December,
  Leander, who was nightly wont
(What maid will not the tale remember?)
   To cross thy stream, broad Hellespont!

If, when the wintry tempest roared,
  He sped to Hero, nothing loth,
And thus of old thy current poured,
  Fair Venus! how I pity both!

For me, degenerate modern wretch,
  Though in the genial month of May,
My dripping limbs I faintly stretch,
  And think I've done a feat to-day.

But since he crossed the rapid tide,
  According to the doubtful story,
To woo, – and – Lord knows what beside,
  And swam for Love, as I for Glory;

'Twere hard to say who fared the best:
  Sad mortals! thus the gods still plague you!
He lost his labour, I my jest:
  For he was drowned, and I've the ague.

A later work of Byron which refers to Leander's home, although unrelated to the myth, is *The Bride of Abydos* (1813).

ARION AND THE DOLPHIN

The Greeks, like all great civilizations, set a great price on music – placing it so high in the arts that it took its name from all nine of the daughters of Memory. Music festivals and music prizes, so ubiquitous a feature of our cultural life today, were quite as important in the Greek world.

Few earned a finer reputation in their lifetime as singer, minstrel, bard, poet and musician than ARION, from Methymna on the island of Lesbos.* He was the son of Poseidon and the nymph ONCAEA, but despite this parentage he chose to devote his musical talent to the celebration and praise of the god Dionysus. His instrument of choice was the *kithara*, a variation of the lyre.† He is accepted everywhere as the inventor of the poetic form known as the dithyramb, a wild choral hymn dedicated to wine, carnival, ecstasy and delight.

With his dreamy brown eyes, sweet voice and bewitching ability to cause the toes to tap and hips to rotate, Arion soon became something of an idol around the Mediterranean world. His patron and most enthusiastic supporter was the tyrant of Corinth, PERIANDER‡ and it was he who found out about a big music festival being held in Tarentum, a

---

* Only Orpheus, whose story belongs to the later Age of Heroes, exceeded Arion in skill and fame.

† The word 'guitar' derives from the word *kithara*.

‡ 'Tyrant' is just the Greek word for 'autocratic ruler', sometimes a self-appointed king. Periander was a real historical figure, cited as one of the so-called 'Seven Sages of Greece', who were mentioned by Socrates as exhibiting all the qualities of gnomic wisdom to which mankind should aspire.

prosperous port city set in the instep of Italy's heel. Periander gave Arion the money to get himself across the sea and take part in the competitive elements of the festival on the condition that he agreed to split the prize money on his return.

The outward journey was uneventful. Arion arrived in Tarentum, entered the competitions and easily won first prize in every category. The judges and members of the public had never heard such thrilling and original music. A treasure chest of silver, gold, ivory, precious stones and exquisitely wrought musical instruments was his reward. In gratitude for so generous a prize Arion gave a free concert for the townspeople the following day.

The Tarentum region was famous for the great wolf-spiders commonly found in the countryside all around. The locals called them, after their town, 'tarantulas'. Arion had heard that tarantula venom could provoke hysterical frenzy and so he improvised for the crowd a variation on his wild dithyrambs that he called a *tarantella*. The delirious rhythms of this folk dance* maddened the excitable Tarentines, but towards the end he tamed them with a medley of his softest, most romantic airs. By the early hours he could have had his pick of any girl, boy, man or woman in southern Italy and it is reported that, like the successful musician he was, he did.

A large crowd was there to see Arion off the next morning, many of the people blowing kisses and a good few sobbing their hearts out. He and his luggage, including the box of treasure, were rowed out to sea in a tender, where a small but serviceable brig crewed by a sea-captain and nine civilian sailors was standing off. Arion was soon comfortably settled aboard. The crew hoisted sail and the captain set a course for Corinth.

---

* The tarantella is still popular throughout Europe.

Overboard

As soon as land was out of sight and they were in the open sea, Arion sensed that something was wrong. He was used to being stared at – he was after all as outrageously beautiful as he was talented – but the looks that were being directed at him by the crew were of a different order. Days passed in this sullen and threatening atmosphere and he grew more and more uncomfortable. There was something in the sailors' eyes that resembled lust, but suggested a darker purpose. What could be wrong? Then one hot afternoon, the ugliest and meanest looking of the sailors approached him.

'What you got in that chest you're sitting on, boy?'

Of course. Arion's heart sank. That would account for it. The sailors had heard tell of his treasure. He supposed they wanted some of it, but he was damned if he was going to share his hard-won prize with anyone but Periander. He had earlier planned in his mind to tip the crew generously at the end of the voyage, but now his heart hardened.

'My musical instruments,' he replied. 'I am a kitharode.'

'You're a *what*?'

Arion shook his head sorrowfully and repeated slowly, as if to a child. 'I – play – the – kith – ara.'

Such a mistake.

'Oh – do – you? Well – play – us – a – tune – then.'

'I'd rather not, if you don't mind.'

'What's going on here?' The captain of the brig approached.

'Snotty kid says he's a musician but won't play. Says he's got a *kithara* in that box of his.'

'Well now, I'm sure you won't mind showing it to us, will you, young man?'

The full ship's complement had circled round him now.

'I – I'm not feeling well enough to play. Perhaps tonight I'll be in better shape.'

'Why don't you go below and rest in the shade?'

'N-no, I prefer the fresh air.'

'Seize him, lads!'

Rough hands lifted Arion up as easily as if he were a new-born puppy. 'Let me go! Leave it alone. That's not your property!'

'Where's the key?'

'I've . . . I've lost it.'

'Find it, boys.'

'No, no! Please I beg you . . .'

The key was easily found and wrenched from round Arion's neck. Low whistles and murmurs arose as the captain loosened the latch and raised the lid. Light from the glitter of gold and flash of gemstones danced on the sailors' greedy faces. Arion knew he was lost.

'I am quite p-prepared to sh-share my treasure with you . . .'

The sailors seemed to find the offer highly amusing and laughed heartily.

'Kill him,' said the captain, taking out a long rope of pearls and holding it up to the light.

The ugliest sailor took out a knife and approached Arion with an evil smile.

'Please, please . . . may I – may I at least sing one last song? My threnody, my own funeral dirge. You owe me that, surely? The gods would punish you if you dared send me to my death without a cathartic obsequy of some kind . . .'

'I'll stop you spouting those bloody words,' snarled the ugly sailor, drawing closer.

'No, no,' said the captain. 'He does have a point. We'll let our Cygnus sing his swan song. I suppose you'll need this lyre.' He fished the *kithara* from the chest and gave it to Arion who tuned it, closed his eyes and began to improvise. He dedicated the song to his father Poseidon.

'Lord of the Oceans,' he sang, 'King of Tides, Earth Shaker, beloved father. Often have I neglected you in my prayers and sacrifices, but you, O great one, will not neglect your son. Lord of the Oceans, King of Tides, Earth Shaker, beloved –'

Without warning, clutching his *kithara* tightly to him, Arion leapt overboard and dropped into the waves. The last thing he heard was the laughter of the crew and the captain's dry voice: 'That was easy! Now for the spoils.'

If any of them had bothered to look down, a remarkable sight would have met their eyes. Arion had plunged below the surface and was fully intending to open his mouth and let the seawater in without a struggle. Someone had told him that drowning is a sweet and pleasant death, a slow passing into sleep, as long as you don't fight it. *Choking* is a terrible panicky nightmare, but true *drowning* is a serene and painless release. So he had been told. Despite this comforting knowledge, Arion kept his mouth firmly clamped, and with bulging cheeks he kicked at the water, hugging his *kithara*.

And then, just as his lungs were ready to burst, something amazing happened. He felt himself being pushed upwards. Pushed hard and fast. He was surging through the water. He had broken the surface! He could breathe! What was going on? It must be a dream. The rush of the water, the bubbles and spray, the tilting, rocking horizon, the booming in his ears, the soaking, the roar and the dazzle – it all prevented him from understanding what was happening until he dared look down and through stinging eyes saw that . . . that . . . he was on the back of a dolphin! *A dolphin*! He was riding it over the waves! But its skin was slippery and he began to slide off. The dolphin barrelled and twisted and Arion was somehow righted again. The animal had deliberately manoeuvred to keep him safe! Would it mind if he stretched out one hand and held onto the dorsal fin, much as a horseman might grip the horn of a saddle? The dolphin did not mind, indeed it bucked a little, as if in approval, and increased its speed through the water. Arion slowly reached for the strap of his *kithara* and swung the instrument behind him so that he could enjoy the ride with two hands on the fin.

The brig was out of sight now. The sun shone down, dolphin and man ploughed furrows through the sea, sending up plumes of iridescent spray. Where were they going? Did the dolphin know?

'Hey, dolphin. Set your course for the Gulf of Corinth. I'll direct you when we get there.'

The dolphin gave a series of squeaks and clicks that seemed to indicate understanding and Arion laughed. On and on they went, chasing the never-nearing horizon. Arion, confident of his balance now, pulled his *kithara* back round and sang the song of Arion and the Dolphin. It is lost to us, but they say it was the most beautiful song ever composed.

At length they reached the gulf. The dolphin negotiated this busy shipping lane with graceful, zipping ease. Sailors on the busy barques, barges and small boats turned to stare at the remarkable sight of a young man riding a dolphin. Arion steered on the fins with gentle tugs this way and that and they did not stop until they had reached the royal docks.

'Send word to King Periander,' he said, stepping from the dolphin onto the quay. 'His minstrel is returned. And feed my dolphin.'

The Monument

Periander was overjoyed by the homecoming of the musician he loved. The story of his rescue filled the court with wonder and amazement. They feasted all night and into the morning. It was evening by the time they set out to see, praise and pet the heroic dolphin. But a sad sight met their eyes. Ignorant dock workers had brought the animal ashore to be fed. It had languished overnight without any water to keep its skin moist and then lay all morning and afternoon on the quayside, surrounded by inquisitive children, the hot sun burning down and drying it up. Arion knelt on the ground and whispered into its ear. The dolphin rippled an affectionate reply, heaved a shuddering sigh and died.

Arion recriminated himself bitterly and even Periander's instructions that a high tower be constructed to commemorate the dolphin and glorify its memory failed to raise his spirits. For the next month all his songs were sad ones and the palace mourned along with him.

Then came news that the brig crewed by the nine sailors and its villainous captain had been blown by a storm into Corinth. Periander sent messengers to command the crew to come before him, bidding Arion to stay away while he questioned them.

'You were supposed to be conveying my bard Arion back from Tarentum,' he said. 'Where is he?'

'Alas, dread majesty,' said the captain. 'So very sad. The poor boy was swept overboard in the storm. We recovered the body and gave him a most respectful burial at sea. Great pity. Charming lad, popular with all the crew.'

'Aye. Indeed. Pleasant fellow. Terrible loss . . .' muttered the sailors.

'Be that as it may,' said Periander, 'news reaches me that he won his singing competition and came to you with a treasure chest, half of which is my property.'

'As to that . . .' the captain spread his hands. 'The chest was lost during the violent pitching of the storm. It opened as it slid down the deck and into the sea and we managed to recover *some* small bits and pieces. A silver lyre of some kind, an *aulos* – one or two trinkets. I wish it had been more, sire, really I do.'

'I see . . .' Periander frowned. 'Assemble tomorrow morning by the new monument at the royal docks. You can't miss it. There's a carved dolphin on top. Bring what treasure remains and perhaps I will allow you to keep Arion's share, now that the poor boy is dead. You are free to go.'

'Have no fear,' said Periander to Arion as he related to him all that had been said. 'Justice will be done.'

Next morning, the sea-captain and his nine men arrived early at the monument. They were laughing and relaxed, amused that they had to return only a small amount of Arion's treasure and might even expect to be given a share of that by the gullible tyrant.

Periander arrived with his palace guards at precisely the appointed hour. 'Good morning, captain. Ah, the treasure. That's all you managed to save? Yes, I see what you mean, not much at all, is it? Now, remind me what befell Arion?'

The captain repeated his story fluently and easily, every word exactly the same as it had been the day before.

'So he really is dead? You really did recover the body, prepare it for burial and then return it to the waves?'

'Absolutely.'

'And these trinkets are all that remain of the prize treasure?'

'It grieves me to say so, majesty, but yes.'

'How then,' Periander asked, 'do you account for the discovery of all *this* hidden in the hollow of your ship's timbers?'

At a sign, some guards came forward bearing a litter on which was disposed the bulk of the treasure.

'Ah. Yes. Well . . .' the captain gave a winning smile. 'Foolish of us to attempt to deceive you, dread lord. The poor boy died, as I said, and there was his treasure. We are but poor working sailors, sire. Your cunning and wisdom has found us out.'

'That is handsome of you,' said Periander. 'But I am still puzzled. I had a *kithara* made for Arion in silver, gold and ivory. He never went anywhere without it. Why is it not here amongst the other things?'

'Well now,' said the captain. 'I told you how fond we were of young Arion. Like a younger brother to us, isn't that right, lads?'

'Aye, aye . . .' muttered the sailors.

'We knew what his *kithara* meant to him. We included it with him in his shroud before committing his body to the waves. How could we have done otherwise?'

Periander smiled. The captain smiled. But suddenly his smile disappeared. From the mouth of the golden dolphin at the top of the column emerged the sound of a *kithara*. The captain and his men stared in amazement. Arion's voice joined the notes of the *kithara* and these were the words that came from out of the carved dolphin's mouth:

> 'Kill him, men,' the captain said.
> 'Kill him now and seize his gold.'
> 'We'll kill him now,' the sailors cried,
> 'And throw him to the sharks.'
> 'But stop,' the minstrel said. 'Only let me sing
> One final farewell song.'

One of the sailors let out a scream of fear. The others fell quaking to their knees. Only the captain, white-faced, stayed upright.

A door opened in the plinth and Arion himself stepped from the monument, strumming his *kithara* and singing:

> But the dolphin came and saved him.
> He rode it on the rolling waves.
> They crossed the sea to Corinth,
> The dolphin and the bard.

The sailors began to weep and blubber, begging forgiveness. They blamed each other and most especially they blamed the captain.

'Too late,' said Periander, turning on his heel. 'Kill them all. Now, come with me, Arion and sing me a song of love and wine.'

At the end of the musician's long and successful life, Apollo, to whom dolphins and music were sacred, set Arion and his rescuer amongst the stars between Sagittarius and Aquarius as the constellation Delphinus, the Dolphin.

From their position in the heavens, Arion and his rescuer could aid navigators below and remind all of us of the strange and marvellous kinship that exists between mankind and dolphins.

PHILEMON AND BAUCIS, OR
HOSPITALITY REWARDED

In the hills of eastern Phrygia, in Asia Minor, an oak and a linden grow side by side, their branches touching. It is a simple, rural setting, far from any glittering palaces or soaring citadels. Peasant farmers scratch out their livings here, wholly dependent on the clemency of Demeter for the ripening of their crops and the fattening of their pigs. The soil is not rich and it is always a struggle for the people to fill their barns with enough provender to last them through the winter months, when Demeter languishes and mourns the absence from the upper world of her bright daughter Persephone. That oak tree and the lime tree, unimpressive as they seem when compared to the grand poplar groves and elegant cypress avenues that line the highways connecting Athens and Thebes, are nonetheless the holiest trees in the Mediterranean world. The wise and the virtuous make pilgrimage to them and hang votive gifts in their branches.

Many years ago a settlement had grown up in the valley below. It was somewhere between a town and village in size. It called itself, with that hopeful desperation that always marks out the naming of failed settlements, Eumeneia which means 'the place of the good months' – in the forlorn expectation perhaps that Demeter would bless the barren soil of the place and provide bountiful harvests. She rarely did.

At the centre of the agora, the main square, there stood a large temple of Demeter, opposite to one of almost equal size dedicated to Hephaestus (for the people needed their forges and workshops blessed). Around the town could be seen many votive shrines to Hestia and Dionysus. The sparse vineyards that straggled up the hillsides were as carefully tended as any of the olive trees or fields of corn. Life was hard, but the men and women here found much solace in the sour wine of their region.

At the top of a winding lane leading out of the town, in a small stone cottage, lived an old couple called PHILEMON and BAUCIS. They had been married since they were very young and now in their old age they loved each other as deeply as ever, with a quiet unwavering intensity that amused their neighbours. They were poorer than most, their fields were the meanest and most barren in all of Eumeneia, but they had never been heard to complain. Every day Baucis milked their one goat, hoed, stitched, washed and mended, while Philemon sowed, planted, dug and scratched at the earth behind their cottage. In the late afternoons they gathered wild mushrooms, collected firewood or simply walked the hills, hand in hand, talking of this and that or content to be silent companions. If there was enough food to make a supper they would eat, otherwise they would go to bed hungry and fall asleep in each other's arms. Their three children had long since moved out and were bringing up their own families far away. They never visited and no one else was likely to knock on their door. Until one fateful afternoon.

Philemon had just returned from the fields and was sitting down in preparation for his monthly haircut. There was very little these days to crown his bald old head, but this was a monthly ritual that gave them both pleasure. The loud rat-a-tat-tat on their door almost caused Baucis to drop the razor she had been sharpening. They looked at one another in great surprise, each unable to remember the last time anyone had come calling.

Two strangers stood on the threshold, a bearded man and his younger, smooth-faced companion. His son perhaps.

'Hello,' said Philemon. 'How may we help you?'

The younger man smiled and removed his hat, a strange round cap with a shallow brim. 'Good afternoon sir,' he said. 'We are a pair of hungry travellers, new to this part of the world. I wonder if we might trespass upon your good nature . . .'

'Come in, come in!' said Baucis, bustling up behind her husband. 'It's chilly to be out at this time of year. We are higher up than the rest of the town you know and feel the cold a little more. Philemon, why don't you scare up the fire so that our guests might warm themselves?'

'Of course, my love, of course. Where are my manners?' Philemon stooped down and blew into the hearth, awakening the embers.

'Let me take your cloaks,' said Baucis. 'Have a seat, sir, by the fire. And you, sir, I beg.'

'That is most kind,' said the older of the two. 'My name is Astrapos, and this is my son Arguros.'

The younger man bowed at the mention of his name with something of a flourish and seated himself beside the fire. 'We are very thirsty,' he said, with a loud yawn.

'You must have something to drink,' said Baucis. 'Husband, you fetch the wine jug and I shall bring dried figs and pine nuts. I hope you gentlemen will consent to dine with us. We can't offer rich fare, but you would be most welcome.'

'Don't mind if we do,' said Arguros.

'Let me take your hat and staff . . .'

'No, no. They stay with me.' The young man pulled the staff close to him. It was of a most curious design. Was it a vine that was carved all around it, Baucis wondered? He was twisting it so deftly that the whole thing seemed alive.

'I'm afraid,' said Philemon coming forward with a jug of wine, 'that you may find our local wine a little thin and perhaps a little ... *sharp*. People from neighbouring regions mock us for it, but I assure you that once you are used to the taste it can be really quite drinkable. We think so at least.'

'Not bad,' said Arguros after a sip. 'How did you get the cat to sit on the jug?'

'Ignore him,' said Astrapos. 'He thinks he's amusing.'

'Well, I have to admit that *was* rather funny,' said Baucis, approaching with fruit and nuts on a wooden plate. 'I hate to think, young sir, what you're going to say about the appearance of my dried figs.'

'You're wearing a blouse so I can't see them. But the preserved fruit on this plate looks pleasant enough.'

'*Sir!*' Baucis slapped him playfully and went very pink. What a strange young man.

The slight awkwardness that usually attends the drink and nibbles phase of an evening was quickly mellowed by the cheek and cheerfulness of Arguros and the ready laughter of their hosts. Astrapos seemed to be of a gloomier disposition, and as they went to the table Philemon put a hand on his shoulder.

'I hope you will forgive the inquisitiveness of a foolish old man, sir,' he said, 'but you seem a little distracted. Is there anything we can help you with?'

'Oh, ignore him. He's always down in the dumps,' said Arguros. 'That's where he gets his clothes from, haha! But, in truth, there's nothing wrong with him that a good meal won't put right.'

Baucis met Philemon's eyes for a brief instant. There was so little in the larder. A side of salted bacon that they had been saving for the midwinter feast, some preserved fruit

376

and black bread, half a cabbage. They knew they would go hungry for a week if they fed so much as half the appetites of two such hearty men. But hospitality was a sacred thing and the needs of guests must always come first.

'Another glass of that wine wouldn't hurt,' said Arguros.

'Oh dear,' said Philemon, looking at the jug, 'I fear that there isn't any more . . .'

'Nonsense,' said Arguros snatching it away, 'plenty left.' He filled his cup and then Astrapos's too.

'How strange,' said Philemon. 'I could have sworn the pitcher was only a quarter full.'

'Where are your cups?' asked Arguros.

'Oh please, we don't need any . . .'

'Nonsense,' Arguros leaned back in his chair and reached for two wooden beakers on the side-table behind him. 'Now then . . . Let's have a toast.'

Philemon and Baucis were amazed, not only that there was enough wine in the pitcher to fill their beakers to the brim, but that its quality was so much better than either of them remembered. In fact, unless they were dreaming, it was the most delicious wine they had ever tasted.

In something of a daze, Baucis wiped the table down with mint leaves.

'Darling,' Philemon whispered in her ear, 'that goose that we were going to sacrifice to Hestia next month. It's surely more important to feed our guests. Hestia will understand.'

Baucis agreed. 'I'll go out and wring its neck. See if you can get the fire hot enough to give it a fine roasting.'

The goose, however, would not be caught. No matter how carefully Baucis waited and pounced, it leapt honking from her grasp every time. She returned to the cottage in a state of agitated disappointment.

'Gentlemen I am so very sorry,' she said, and there were tears in her eyes. 'I'm afraid your meal will be crude and disagreeable.'

'Tush, lady,' said Arguros, pouring more wine for everyone. 'I've never partaken of a finer feast.'

'Sir!'

'It's true. Tell them, father.'

Astrapos gave a grim smile. 'We have been turned away from every house in Eumeneia. Some of the townspeople swore at us. Some spat at us. Some threw stones at us. Some set dogs on us. Yours was the last house we tried and you have shown us nothing but kindness and a spirit of *xenia* that I was beginning to fear was vanished from the world.'

'Sir,' said Baucis, feeling for Philemon's hand under the table and squeezing it. 'We can only apologize for the behaviour of our neighbours. Life is hard and they have not always been brought up to venerate the laws of hospitality as they should.'

'There is no need to make excuses for them. I am angry,' said Astrapos, and as he spoke a rumble of thunder could be heard.

Baucis looked across into the eyes of Astrapos and saw something that frightened her.

Arguros laughed. 'Don't be alarmed,' he said. 'My father is not angry with you. He is pleased with you.'

'Leave the cottage and climb the hill,' said Astrapos, rising. 'Do not look back. Whatever happens do not look back. You have earned your reward and your neighbours have earned their punishment.'

Philemon and Baucis stood, holding hands. They knew now that their visitors were something more than ordinary travellers.

'There is no need to bow,' said Arguros.

His father pointed to the door. 'To the top of the hill.'

'Remember,' Arguros called after them, 'no looking back.'

Hand in hand Philemon and Baucis walked up the hill.

'You know who that young man was?' said Philemon.

'Hermes,' said Baucis. 'When he opened the door to let us go, I saw the snakes twined around his staff. They were *alive*!'

'Then the man he called his father was . . . must have been . . .'

'Zeus!'

'Oh my goodness!' Philemon paused on the hillside to catch his breath. 'It's getting so dark, my love. The sound of the thunder is getting closer. I wonder if . . .'

'No darling, we mustn't look back. We mustn't.'

Disgusted by the hostility and shameless violations of the laws of hospitality shown to him by the townspeople of Eumeneia, Zeus had decided to do for this community what he had done back in the time of Deucalion and the Great Flood. The clouds gathered into a dense mass at his command, lightning flashed, thunder boomed and the rain began to fall.

By the time the elderly couple struggled to the top of the hill, torrents of water were gushing past them.

'We can't just stand here in the rain with our backs to the town,' said Baucis.

'I'll look if you will.'

'I love you Philemon, my husband.'

'I love you Baucis, my wife.'

They turned and looked down. They were just in time to see the great flood inundating Eumeneia before Philemon was turned into an oak tree and Baucis into a linden.

For hundreds of years the two trees stood side by side, symbols of eternal love and humble kindness, their intertwining branches hung with the tokens left by admiring pilgrims.*

---

* This *theoxenia*, this divine testing of human hospitality, is notably similar to that told in the nineteenth chapter of Genesis. Angels visit Sodom and Gomorrah and only Lot and his wife show them decency and kindness. The debauched citizens of Sodom of course, rather than setting the dogs on the angels wanted to 'know them' – in as literally biblical a sense as could be, giving us the word 'sodomy'. Lot and his wife, like Philemon and Baucis, were told to make their getaway and not look back while divine retribution was visited on the Cities of the Plain. Lot's wife did look back and she was turned, not into a linden, but into a pillar of salt.

PHRYGIA AND THE GORDIAN KNOT

The Greeks loved to mythologize the founders of towns and cities. Athena's gift of the olive to the people of Athens and her raising of Erechtheus (the issue of Hephaestus and the semen-soaked fillet, you will recall) to be the founder of the city seems to have helped foster the Athenian sense of self. The story of Cadmus and the dragon's teeth did the same for Thebans. Sometimes, as is the case with the founding of the city of Gordium, elements of the story can move from myth to legend to actual, identifiable history.

In Macedonia there lived a poor but ambitious peasant called GORDIAS. One day, as he laboured in his barren stony fields, an eagle landed on the pole of his oxcart and fixed him with a fierce glare.

'I knew it!' Gordias said to himself, 'I have always felt that I was marked for greatness. This eagle proves it. I have a destiny.'

He raised his plough and drove the ox and cart many hundreds of miles towards the oracle of Zeus Sabazios.* As Gordias lumbered along, the eagle gripped the pole fast with its talons, never flinching no matter how violently the cart bumped and swayed over the potholes and boulders.

On the way, Gordias encountered a young Telmissian girl endowed in equal measure with great prophetic powers and

---

* Sabazios was a horse-riding incarnation of Zeus worshipped by the Thracians and Phrygians

an alluring beauty that stirred his heart. She seemed to have been expecting him and urged that they make haste at once to Telmissus, where he should sacrifice his ox to Zeus Sabazios. Gordias, fired by the coming together of all his hopes, undertook to follow her advice so long as she agreed to marry him. She bowed her head in assent and they set off for the city.

It so happened that, at this very moment, the King of Phrygia had just died in his bed. Since he left no heir or obvious successor, the people of his capital hurried to the shrine of Zeus Sabazios to find out what should be done. The oracle told them to anoint and crown the first man to enter the city in a cart. So it was that the townspeople were clustering excitedly round the gates at the very moment that Gordias and the prophetess arrived. The eagle flew from his perch with a great cry as they crossed the threshold. The populace threw their caps in the air and cheered until they were hoarse.

In a very short time Gordias had gone from scratching a lonely living in the Macedonian dirt to being wed to a beautiful Telmissian seer and crowned King of Phrygia. He drew up plans to rebuild the city (which he immodestly named Gordium in his own honour) and settled down to reign over Phrygia and live happily ever after. Which he did. Sometimes, even in the world of Greek mythology, things go well.

The oxcart became a holy relic, a symbol of Gordias's divine right to rule. A carved post of polished dogwood was placed in the agora and the yoke of the cart secured to it with a rope tied up in the most intricate knot the world had seen. Gordias was determined that the cart should never be stolen from the town square. The legend arose, in that mysterious and unattributable way that legends do arise, that whoever untied this fiendish knot would one day rule Asia. Many tried – master mariners, mathematicians, toymakers, artists, artisans, tricksters, philosophers and ambitious children, but none could even begin to unpick its elaborate interwoven hitches, loops and twists.

The great Gordian knot lay unsolved for more than a thousand years until a reckless and brilliant young Macedonian conqueror and king called Alexander rode with his army into town. When told of the legend he took one look at the great tangle of rope, raised his sword and swept it down, cutting the Gordian knot and earning the delighted praise of his own and future generations.*

Meanwhile, back in time, Gordias's son Prince MIDAS grew up to be a friendly, merry young man, loved and admired by all who knew him.

---

* When I first heard this story I thought not more of Alexander but less. 'He *cheated*!' I said. Suppose I 'solved' a randomized Rubik's cube by jemmying it open with a screwdriver until all the pieces fell out and then pressing them back again in the right order? Who would praise that? But Alexander is congratulated by history for 'thinking outside the box' and called 'the Great'. One rule for the genius warrior kings of the world and another for the rest of us.

MIDAS

The Ugly Stranger

In due time Gordias died and his son Midas succeeded him as king. His life was simple but elegant – who had grown up to be a friendly, merry young man, bred and admired by all – Phrygia was not an especially rich kingdom, but most of the time and money that Midas did possess were lavished on a magnificent rose garden in the palace grounds. It became known as one of the wonders of the age. Midas loved nothing more than to roam this paradise of colour and fragrance and tend to his plants – each one of which bore sixty glorious blooms.

One morning, as he wandered the garden, noting with habitual delight how exquisitely the beads of dew twinkled on the delicate petals of his darling roses, Midas tripped over the slumbering form of an ugly, pot-bellied old man, curled up on the ground and snoring like a pig.

'Oh,' said Midas, 'I'm so sorry. I didn't see you there.'

With a belch and a hiccup, the old man rose to his feet and bowed low. 'Beg pardon,' he said. 'Couldn't help but be drawn by the sweet scent of your roses last night. Fell asleep.'

'Not at all,' said Midas politely. He had been brought up always to show respect for his elders. 'But why don't you come into the palace and partake of some breakfast?'

'Don't mind if I do. Handsome of you.'

Midas had no way of knowing that this ugly, pot-bellied old man was Silenus, boon-companion of the wine god Dionysus.

'Perhaps you would like a bath?' he suggested as they made their way indoors.

'What for?'

'Oh, nothing. Just a thought.'

Silenus stayed for ten days and ten nights, making deep inroads into Midas's meagre cellar, but rewarding him with outrageous songs, dances and stories.

On the tenth night Silenus announced that he would be leaving the next morning.

'My master will be pining for me,' he said. 'Don't suppose your people could conduct me to him, could they?'

'With pleasure,' said Midas.

The next day Midas and his retinue led Silenus on the long journey to the southern vineyards that Dionysus liked to frequent at that time of year. After many hours of struggling through the heat and tangle of choked lanes, steep hills and narrow byways they came upon the wine god and his attendants picnicking in a field. Dionysus was overjoyed to see his old friend.

'Wine tastes sour without you,' he said. 'Dances go wrong and music falls flat on the ears. Where have you been?'

'I got lost,' said Silenus. 'This kind fellow –' he pushed the reluctant Midas forward to face the god, '– took me in to his palace and gave me the run of the place. I drank most of his wine, ate most of his food, pissed in his water jars and sicked up over his silk cushions. Never complained. Thoroughly good soul.' Silenus slapped Midas on the back. Midas smiled as best he could. He hadn't known about the water jars and the silk cushions.

Dionysus, like many deep drinkers, could easily become very emotional and affectionate. He pawed gratefully at Midas. 'You see?' he declared to the world in general. 'You *see?* Just when you lose faith in humanity, they show their worth like this. This is what my father means by *xenia*. Makes my heart burst. Name it.'

'Excuse me?' Midas was keen to leave. Ten days and nights of Silenus had been quite enough. He yearned now to be alone with his flowers. A drunken Dionysus with a full entourage of Maenads and satyrs might just be too much even for his patience.

'Name your reward. Anything. Whatever you – hic! – desire I will providely divine. Which is to say,' Dionysus amended with dignity, 'I will divinely provide. So there,' he added belligerently, turning suddenly round to face off no one in particular.

'You mean, my lord, that I can ask anything of you?'

Which of us has not entertained joyous fantasies of genies and fairies granting us wishes? I am sorry to say that, at this offer from Dionysus, Midas had rather a rush of blood to the head.

I have mentioned that Phrygia was one of the poorer kingdoms, and while Midas was not considered by his friends to be rapacious or avaricious, he did long, like any ruler, for more money to spend on his armies, his palace, his subjects and his municipal amenities. The expenses of a royal household mount up and Midas had always been too benevolent a king to burden his people with heavy taxes. And so he found a most extraordinary wish making its way from his fevered brain to his mouth.

'Then I ask this,' he said; 'that everything I touch be turned to gold.'

Dionysus smiled a rather diabolical smile. 'Really? That's what you want?'

'That is what I want.'

'Go home,' said the god. 'Bathe yourself in wine and go to bed. When you arise in the morning, your wish will be granted.'

It is probable that Midas did not believe that anything would come of this exchange. The gods were notorious for dodging, twisting and sliding out of their obligations.

Nevertheless, just in case – after all, what harm could it do? I mean, one never knows – that night, Midas poured a few hogsheads from his diminishing store of wine into the royal bath. The fumes from it ensured that when he went to bed he enjoyed a deep and untroubled sleep.

Midas awoke to a sparkling morning that cast all ideas of wild wishes and drunken gods from his mind. With thoughts only for his flowers, he sprang from bed and hurried to his beloved garden.

Never had the roses looked more beautiful. He leaned down and sniffed a pink young hybrid that was in that perfect state midway between bud and full bloom. The exquisite fragrance made him giddy with joy. He lovingly made to unfurl the petals. In an instant the stem and flower had been transformed into gold. Solid gold.

Midas stared in disbelief.

He touched another rose and then another. The moment his fingers touched them they turned to gold. He ran up and down around the garden in a whooping frenzy, brushing his hands along the bushes until every one had been frozen into hard shining precious, priceless, glorious, golden gold.

Skipping and shouting with joy Midas beheld what had once been a garden of rare roses and was now the most valuable treasure in all the world. He was rich! He was insanely, monumentally rich! No man on earth had ever been richer.

The sound of his exultant shouts attracted his wife,

who came out of the palace doors and stood looking down, their infant daughter in her arms.

'Darling, why are you shouting?'

Midas ran up to her and encircled mother and child in a tight hug of excited joy. 'You won't believe it!' he said. 'Everything I touch turns to gold! Look! All I have to do is – *oh!*'

He stepped back to see that his wife and infant girl were now one fused golden statue, glittering in the morning sun, a frozen mother and child group that any sculptor would have been proud of.

'I'll attend to that later,' Midas said to himself. 'There must be a way to recover them . . . Dionysus wouldn't be so . . . meanwhile – *Zim! Zam! Zoo!*'

A guard on sentry, the great side-door to the palace and his favourite throne were now entirely gold.

'*Vim! Vam! Voo!*'

The side-table, his goblet, his cutlery – solid gold!

But what was this? *Crack!* His teeth almost broke on a hard golden peach. *Tunk!* His lips met metallic wine. *Thwop!* A heavy gold nugget that had once been a linen napkin crushed and bruised his lips.

The unbounded delight began to fade as Midas realized the full import of his gift.

You may imagine the rest. All at once the thrill and pleasure of his ownership of gold were changed to dread and fear. All Midas touched turned to gold, but his heart turned to lead. No words of his, no shrieks of imprecation to the heavens could return his cold solidified wife and daughter to quick warm life. The sight of his beloved roses dropping their heavy heads caused his own to bow in misery. Everything around him glinted and glittered, gleamed and glimmered with a gorgeous gaudy golden glow but his heart was as grim and grey as granite.

And the hunger and thirst! After three days of food and drink turning to inedible gold the moment it touched him, Midas felt ready for death.

Atop his golden bed, whose hard heavy sheets offered no warmth or comfort, he fell into a fevered sleep. He dreamed of his flowers blooming back into soft, delicate life – his roses, yes, but most of all the flowers that he now understood mattered most, his wife and child. In the wild, contorted dream he saw the soft colours returning to their cheeks and the light shining once more in their eyes. As these beguiling images danced and flickered in his mind the voice of Dionysus boomed inside him.

'Foolish man! It is fortunate for you that Silenus is so fond of you. Only for his sake do I show you mercy. When you awaken in the morning, betake yourself to the River Pactolus. Plunge your hands in its waters and your enchantment will be dissolved. Whatever you wash in the fast-flowing stream will be restored to you.'

The next morning Midas did what the voice in his dream had instructed. As promised, contact with the waters of the river relieved him of his golden touch. Mad with joy, he spent a good week shuttling back and forth immersing his wife, his daughter, his guards, servants, roses and all of his possessions in the river and clapping his hands in delight as they returned to their valueless – but priceless – original state.

After this, the waters of the Pactolus, which wind around the foothills of Mount Tmolus, became the single greatest source of electrum, a natural alloy of gold and silver, in all the Aegean.

King Midas's Ears

You would think that Midas had learned his lesson by now. The lesson that repeats and repeats throughout the story of man. Don't mess with the gods. Don't trust the gods. Don't anger the gods. Don't barter with the gods. Don't compete with the gods. Leave the gods well alone. Treat all blessings as a curse and all promises as a trap. Above all, never insult a god. Ever.

In one respect Midas had certainly changed. He now spurned not just gold, but all riches and possessions. Shortly after Dionysus lifted the curse, Midas became a devoted follower of Pan, the goat-footed god of nature, fauns, meadows and all the wild things of the world.

With flowers in his hair, sandals on his feet and the merest suggestion of clothing covering his modesty, Midas left his wife and daughter in charge of Phrygia and devoted himself to a hippy-happy life of simple bucolic virtue.

All might have been well had not his master Pan taken it into his head to challenge Apollo to a competition to determine which was the superior, the lyre or the pipes.

One afternoon, in a meadow lying on the slopes of Mount Tmolus, Pan put the syrinx to his lips before an audience of fauns, satyrs, dryads, nymphs, assorted demigods and other lesser immortals. A coarse but likeable air in the Lydian mode emerged. It seemed to summon barking deer, rushing waters, gambolling rabbits, rutting stags and galloping horses. The rough, rustic tune delighted the audience, especially Midas, who really did worship Pan and all the frolicking mirth and madness that the goat-footed one represented.

When Apollo stood and sounded the first notes of his lyre, a hush fell. From his strings arose visions of universal love, harmony and happiness, a deep abiding joy in life and a sense of heaven itself.

When he had finished the audience rose as one to applaud. Tmolus, the deity of the mountain, called out, 'The lyre of the great lord Apollo wins. All agreed?'

'Aye, aye!' roared the satyrs and fauns.

'Apollo, Apollo!' cried the nymphs and dryads.

One lone voice demurred.

'No!'

'No?' Dozens of heads turned to see who could have dared dissent.

Midas rose to his feet. 'I disagree. I say the pipes of Pan produce the better sound.'

Even Pan was astonished. Apollo quietly put down his lyre and walked towards Midas.

'Say that again.'

It could at least be said of Midas that he had the courage of his convictions. He swallowed twice before repeating, 'I – I say the pipes make a better sound. Their music is more . . . exciting. More artistic.'

Apollo must have been in a soft mood that day, for he did not slaughter Midas on the spot. He did not peel the skin from him layer by layer as he had done to Marsyas when that unfortunate had had the temerity to challenge him. He did not cause Midas even the slightest amount of pain but just said softly, 'You honestly think Pan played better than me?'

'I do.'

'Well, in that case,' said Apollo, with a laugh, 'you must have the ears of an ass.'

No sooner were these words out of the god's mouth than Midas felt something strange and warm and rough going on in his scalp. As he put an enquiring hand to his head, howls and hoots and screams and screeches of mocking laughter started to come from the assembled throng. They could see what Midas could not. Two large grey donkey ears had pushed their way through his hair and were twitching and flicking back and forth for all the world to see.

'It seems I was right,' said Apollo. 'You do indeed have the ears of an ass.'

Crimsoning with shame and mortification, Midas turned and fled the meadow, the taunts and jeers of the crowd sounding all the more clearly in his great furry ears.

His life as a camp-follower of Pan was over. Tying his head in a kind of turban, he returned to his wife and family in the palace of Gordium and – his carefree experiment in country living decidedly done with – settled back down into the life of a king.

The only person who saw his ass's ears was, necessarily, the servant who cut his hair every month. No one else in Phrygia knew the terrible secret and Midas was determined it should stay that way.

'Here's the deal,' Midas told the barber. 'I give you a bigger salary and a more generous pension than any other member of the palace staff and you keep quiet about what you have seen. If, however, you breathe a word to *anyone* I will slaughter your family before your eyes, cut out your tongue and leave you to wander the world in mute poverty and exile. Understood?'

The frightened barber nodded.

For three years each side kept to the bargain. The barber's wife and family waxed fat and happy on the extra money that came in and no one found out about the king's asinine auditory appendages. Turbans in the Midas style caught on throughout Phrygia, Lydia, Thrace and beyond. All was well.

But secrets are terrible things to have to keep. Especially

such juicy ones as that to which the royal barber was privy. Every day he would wake up and feel that the knowledge was writhing and swelling inside him. The barber loved his wife and family and was in any case loyal enough to his monarch not to have any wish to humiliate or embarrass him. But that bulging, ballooning secret had to be released somehow before he burst. No unmilked cow with swollen udders, no mother of overdue twins, no gut-stuffed gastronome straining on the privy, could ever feel such a desperate need for relief from their agonies than this poor barber.

Finally he hit upon a scheme which he felt sure would rid him of his burden without endangering his family. Awaking from a tortured night in which he had dreamed that he revealed the secret to the gaping populace of Gordium from a balcony in the main square, he went out at first light deep into the remote countryside. In a lonely place by a stream he dug a deep trench in the ground. Looking about him in all directions to make sure that he was alone and that there was no possibility of being overheard, he knelt down, cupped his hands around his mouth and shouted these words into the hole:

'Midas has ass's ears!'

Scrabbling frantically to close up the hole before the words could escape, he failed to notice one tiny seed floating down and settling at the bottom . . .

When the backfilling was done, the barber stamped fiercely up and down on the earth to seal in the dreadful secret. He skipped all the way back to Gordium, headed straight for his favourite tavern and ordered a flagon of the house's best wine. He could drink now without fear that the wine might loosen his tongue. It was as if he were Atlas and the sky had finally been lifted from his shoulders.

Meanwhile, over the next few weeks, back in the remote

field by the stream that tiny seed, warmed by the soft breath of Gaia below, began to germinate. Soon, a delicate little reed was shouldering its way through the topsoil and pushing its delicate head into the air. As the breeze caught the reed it softly whispered 'Midas has ass's ears.'

The faint words reached the rushes and sedges that fringed the riverbank. 'Midas has ass's ears . . .'

The susurration of rushes and the hiss of sedges was swept on by the grasses and leaves of the trees and swiftly the soughing of cypresses and sallows sent the sound through the breeze.

'Midas has ass's ears,' sighed the branches.

'Midas has ass's ears,' sang the birds.

And at last the news reached the city.

'Midas has ass's ears!'

King Midas woke with a start. There was laughter and shouting in the street outside the palace. He crept to the window, crouched down and listened.

The humiliation was too much for him to bear. Without stopping to wreak his vengeance on the barber and the barber's family, he mixed a poisonous draught of ox-blood, raised his eyes heavenwards, gave a bitter laugh and a shrug, drained the drink and died.

Poor Midas. His name will always mean someone fortunate and rich, but truly he was unlucky and poor. If only he had kept to his roses. Green fingers are better than gold.

APPENDICES

The Brothers, a Sidebar

A final word about Epimetheus and Prometheus, the sons of Clymene (or Asia) the Oceanid and Iapetus the Titan, and younger brothers of sky-shouldering Atlas and thunderbolt-exploded Menoetius. It is generally held that Prometheus means 'forethought' and Epimetheus 'afterthought', from which it is usually inferred that Epimetheus blundered into things without considering consequences while his elder brother Prometheus deliberated with more perspicacity. It might be convincingly argued that there was nothing especially cautious, forward-thinking or prescient about Prometheus's actions in bringing fire to man. It was impulsive, generous . . . loving even, but not especially wise. Epimetheus was a kindly, well disposed individual also, and his failings were only . . . I was going to say only human, but that can hardly be right, for he was a Titan. His failings were certainly titanic in their consequences. The perceived difference between the brothers is used to this day by philosophers to express something fundamental about us all.

In Plato's dialogue *Protagoras* the title character suggests a creation myth somewhat different from the traditionally accepted one.

The gods (so Protagoras tells Socrates) decided to populate nature with new strains of mortal life, there being only immortals in the world at that time. Out of earth and water and with divine fire and divine breath they created animals and man. They charged Prometheus and Epimetheus with the task of allocating to these creatures all the attributes and characteristics that would enable them to live fulfilled and successful lives. Epimetheus said he would do the distributing and Prometheus could come and check up on his work. This the brothers agreed upon.

Epimetheus set to with a will. He gave armour to some animals – the rhinoceros, the pangolin and the armadillo, for instance. To others, almost at random it seemed, he handed out heavy weatherproof fur, camouflage, venom, feathers, tusks, talons, scales, claws, gills, wings, whiskers and goodness knows what else. He assigned speed and ferocity, he apportioned buoyancy and airworthiness – every animal was fitted out with its own cleverly designed and efficient speciality, from navigational skills to expertise in burrowing, nest-building, swimming, leaping and singing. He was just congratulating himself for providing the bats and dolphins with echolocation when he realized that this had been the very last of the available gifts. He had, with his characteristic lack of foresight, completely omitted to consider what he would bestow on man – poor, naked, vulnerable, smooth-skinned, two-legged man.

Epimetheus went guiltily to his brother and asked what they should do now that there was nothing left at the bottom of the gift basket. Man had no defences with which to arm himself against the cruelty, cunning and rapacity of these now superbly provisioned animals. The very powers that had been lavished on the beasts would surely finish off weaponless mankind.

Prometheus's solution was to steal the arts from Athena and flame from Hephaestus. With these, man could use wisdom, wit and industry to pit himself against the animals. He might not swim as well as a fish, but he could work out how to build boats; he might not run as swiftly as a horse, but he could learn to tame, shoe and ride one. One day he might even construct wings to rival those of the birds.

Somehow then, by accident and error, man alone of all mortal creatures was given qualities from Olympus – not so that he could rival the gods, but merely so that he could fend off the more perfectly equipped animals.

Prometheus's name means, as I have said, 'forethought'. Forethought has far-reaching implications. Bertrand Russell in his *History of Western Philosophy* (1945) has this to say:

> The civilized man is distinguished from the savage mainly by prudence, or, to use a slightly wider term, forethought. He is willing to endure present pains for the sake of future pleasures, even if the future pleasures are rather distant . . . True forethought only arises when a man does something towards which no impulse urges him, because his reason tells him that he will profit by it at some future date . . . the individual, having acquired the habit of viewing his life as a whole, increasingly sacrifices his present to his future.

This is perhaps a way of suggesting that Prometheus is father of our civilization in a way more subtle than as the provider of fire, whether real or symbolic. Prometheus also bequeathed us this quality of forethought, of being able to act beyond impulse. Was it Promethean forethought that raised us from being from hunter-gatherers to agriculturalists, town dwellers and traders? You do not toil and plant, plan and build, store and exchange unless you are capable of looking to the future.

Lest we take worship of the potentially Christlike and ideal Prometheus too far (a favourite Greek motto was, after all, *mēdén ágan* 'nothing too much'), Russell reminds us that the Greeks seemed to be aware of a need to counter his influence with darker, deeper, less stable passions:

It is evident that this process [acting on prudence and forethought] can be carried too far, as it is, for instance, by the miser. But without going to such extremes prudence may easily involve the loss of some of the best things in life. The worshipper of Dionysus reacts against prudence. In intoxication, physical or spiritual, he recovers an intensity of feeling which prudence had destroyed; he finds the world full of delight and beauty, and his imagination is suddenly liberated from the prison of every-day preoccupations. Without the Bacchic element, life would be uninteresting; with it, it is dangerous. Prudence versus passion is a conflict that runs through history. It is not a conflict in which we ought to side wholly with either party.

The complexity and ambiguity of Prometheus is remarkable. He gave us fire, the creative fire, but he also gave us civilizing forethought – which tamped down another, wilder, kind of fire. It is their refusal to see any divine beings as perfect, whole and complete of themselves, whether Zeus, Moros or Prometheus, that makes the Greeks so satisfying. To me at least . . .

Hope

What Elpis being left behind in Pandora's jar meant to the Greeks, and what it might mean for us today, have been matters of intriguing debate amongst scholars and thinkers since the invention of writing and perhaps even before that.

For some it reinforces the terrible nature of Zeus's curse on man. All the ills of the world were sent to plague us, they argue, and we were denied even the consolation of hope. The abandoning of hope, after all, is often used as a phrase that preludes the end to caring or striving. Dante's gates of hell commanded all who entered there entirely to abandon hope. How terrible then to believe that hope might abandon us.

Others have maintained that Elpis means more than 'hope', it suggests expectation and not only that but expectation of the *worst*. Foreboding, in other words, dread, an impending sense of doom. This interpretation of the Pandora myth submits that the final spirit locked in the jar was in fact the most evil of them all, and that without it man is at least denied a presentiment of the awfulness of his own fate and the meaningless cruelty of existence. With Elpis locked away, in other words, we are, like Epimetheus, capable of living from day to day, blithely ignorant of, or at least ignoring, the shadow of pain, death and ultimate failure that looms over us all. Such an interpretation of the myth is, in a dark manner, optimistic.

Nietzsche looked at it in yet another, slightly different way. For him hope was the most pernicious of all the creatures in the jar because hope prolongs the agony of man's existence. Zeus had included it in the jar because he wanted it to escape and torment mankind every day with the false promise of something good to come. Pandora's imprisonment of it was a triumphant act that saved us from Zeus's worst cruelty. With hope, Nietzsche argued, we are foolish enough to believe there is a point to existence, an end and a promise. Without it we can at least try to get on and live free of delusional aspiration.

Hopefully, or hopelessly, we can decide for ourselves.

Giant Leaps

There are some stories in Greek myth of a GIGANTOMACHY, or 'war with the giants'. A hundred of this warrior race (who, as I have mentioned, were not especially tall or gigantic in the modern sense) were born of Gaia and the blood of the gelded Ouranos. It may be that the war was Gaia's last attempt at wresting control of the cosmos. In some sources there seems to be an overlap or fusion with the Titanomachy. What seems certain is that a violent uprising of some sort did take place and that it was led by the King of the Giants, EURYMEDON, against the gods.

We do not have the names of all the participants, but the fates of a few of the mightiest were certainly recorded. The most powerful of all, ENCELADUS (the noisy one) was buried by Athena under Mount Etna, from which prison he continues to grumble volcanically.* POLYBOTES was crushed under Nisyrus, a section of the island of Cos that Poseidon broke off and thrust on top of him.† DAMYSUS (the conqueror) was killed early in the struggle, but came to fame later, when his body was exhumed by the centaur Chiron for spare parts. Hephaestus emptied a vat of molten iron all over the unfortunate MIMAS (the imitator); CLYTIUS (the renowned) was consumed in the flames of Hecate's torches; SYCEUS, with Zeus in hot pursuit, was saved from extinction when Gaia turned him into a fig tree.‡ Hippolytus (the stampeder of horses) was slain by Hermes, who cheated by wearing his invisibility cloak; and Dionysus killed TYPHOEUS (the smoulderer), with his sacred *thyrsus*.

I have read of one giant, called ARISTAEUS (the best),§ who was spared from the war by being hidden away in the shape of a dung beetle by his mother, Gaia. But how THOON (the swift), PHOITIOS (the reckless), MOLIOS, EMPHYTOS (the rooted one) and goodness knows how many others of the

---

* Scientists now tell us that the moon of Saturn named after Enceladus, a mere 800 million miles from earth, appears to offer the necessary conditions for life. So perhaps all along Gaia had laid plans for the expansion of her bloodline on other worlds.

† My Greek–English lexicon isn't of much help with Polybotes' name. It seems to mean 'much-nourishing' or 'many feeding'. *Fertile*, perhaps.

‡ The fig thereafter bore Syceus' name.

§ Not to be confused with a minor god of bee-keeping with the same name.

giant race all met their ends remains, as far as we know, unrecorded.

Oddly one account tells how the ferocious giant PORPHY-RION, (the purple one), in the act of trying to rape Hera was killed by Zeus and Hercules, which places his death much later in the timeline than the rest of the Gigantomachy. As if such a consistent and stable a device as a timeline could ever be used to delineate the complex, kaleidoscopic and disorderly unfolding of Greek myth.

Feet and Toes

Like us the Greeks used feet as a measurement. One *pous* (plural *podes*) was made up of about fifteen or sixteen toes (*daktyla*) and was approximately as long as a British or American foot. There were one hundred podes to a *plethron* (the width of a running track), six of those to a *stadion* (the length of a running track, from which we get our word 'stadium') and eight *stadia* to the mile, or *milion*. The foot business – podiatrists, octopuses (or octopodes), tripods and so on – shows the interesting journey of the letter 'P' as it strangely contorted to 'F' the further west it went: so *pous* became *Fuss* in German and *foot* in English. *Pfennig*, *Pfeife* and *Pfeffer* are still stuck in the middle in modern German but have become *penny*, *pipe* and *pepper* in English (though *fife* exists too). The early nineteenth-century philologist Friedrich von Schlegel first noticed this 'Great Fricative Shift', which subsequently became part of Grimms' Law – so named in honour of the Brothers Grimm, who were the ones who really put in the work and showed how most of the languages of Europe and the Middle East could be traced all the way back to India and their notional Proto-Indo-European ancestor.

AFTERWORD

I have assembled below a few thoughts on the nature of myth and a brief outline of some of the sources I have had recourse to in the writing of this book.

I cannot repeat too often that it has never been my aim to interpret or explain the myths, only to tell them. I have, of course, had to play about with timelines in order to attempt a coherent narrative. My version of the 'ages of man', for example, varies from the well-known one by the poet Hesiod in order more clearly to separate the eras of the rule of Kronos and the creation of humans. So energetic was the explosion of stories in Greece almost three thousand years ago that necessarily all sorts of events seemed to happen at once. If anyone tells me that I have got the stories 'wrong' I believe I am justified in replying that they are, after all, fictions. In tinkering with the details I am doing what people have always done with myths. In that sense I feel that I am doing my bit to keep them alive.

Myth v. Legend v. Religion

Much as a pearl is formed around grit, so a legend is taken to have been built up around a grain of truth. The legend of Robin Hood, for example, seems to have derived from a real historical figure.* The narrative substance that accretes as the

---

* Robin of Loxley/Locksley and Lord Fitzooth, the Earl of Huntingdon, are popular candidates.

story is handed down over the generations, embellished and exaggerated on the way, at some point takes on the properties of legend. It is likely to be written down, for the word derives from the gerundive of the Latin *legere*, meaning 'to be read'.*

Myths, however, are imaginative, symbolic constructs. No one believes that Hephaestus ever truly existed. He stands as a representation of the arts of metalwork, manufacture and craftsmanship. That such a figuration is portrayed as swarthy, ugly and hobbling tempts us to interpret and explain. Perhaps we noticed that real blacksmiths, while strong, are often dark, scarred and so muscle-bound as to be bunched and alarming to look upon. Perhaps cultures required that the fit, tall and whole always be taken into the ranks of fighting men and that, from the first, the halt, lame and shorter male children might be trained in the forges and workshops rather than drilled for battle. Any god of blacksmiths that the collective culture imagined, therefore, would be likely to reflect the human archetype they already knew. Gods of this kind are created in our image, not the other way round.

Symbolical rather than historical in origin as myths and mythical figures might be, they underwent the same fictional remodelling and embellishments as more factually rooted legends. They too were written down, and the Greek myths especially, thanks to Homer, Hesiod and those that followed, were chronicled and detailed in ways that have granted us the timelines, genealogies and character histories that allow for story-telling of the kind I have attempted with this book.

Myths, to put it simply and obviously, deal with gods and monsters that can't be observed or pointed at. It may be that

---

* Interestingly, the absolute origin of the verb *legere* and its supine form *lectum* bears the meaning of 'gather' – as in 'college' and 'collect'. So maybe legends are as much to do with stories that are collected as with those that are written down and read.

some members of the ancient Greek population *believed* in centaurs and water dragons, gods of the sea and goddesses of the hearth, but they would have had a hard time proving their existence and convincing others. Most of those who told and retold the myths would have been aware, I think, at some level of their consciousness, that they were telling fictional tales. They might have thought the world was once peopled with nymphs and monsters, but they could be fairly certain that such beings no longer existed.

Prayer, ritual and sacrifice, the taxation paid to the invisible forces of nature, those are different things. At some point myth becomes cult becomes religion. It moves from stories told around the fire to a systematized set of beliefs to which obedience is owed. Priestly castes arose who ordained how people should behave. How myths become codified into scriptures, liturgies and theologies is a subject for another book and quite beyond my scope. We can, however, say that the ancient Greeks had no written revealed texts akin to the Bible or the Qur'an. There were 'mysteries' and initiations of various kinds that involved ecstatic states, perhaps not unlike the shamanic ones seen today in other parts of the world, and there were plenty of temples and shrines. It is true, as well, that even in the great Athenian age of reason and philosophy a man like Socrates could be executed for religious reasons.*

The Greeks

It is always a mistake to think of the Greeks as superior human beings uniquely endowed with enlightened wisdom and rational benevolence. We would find much in ancient

---

* He was accused of an irreligious refusal to recognize the Athenian state's gods.

Greece alien and distasteful to us. Women could play no real part in affairs outside the home, slavery was endemic, punishments were harsh and life could be brutal. Dionysus and Ares were their gods quite as much as Apollo and Athena. Pan, Priapus and Poseidon too. What makes the Greeks so appealing to us is that they seemed to be so subtly, insightfully and animatedly aware of these different sides to their natures. 'Know thyself' was carved into the pronaos of the temple of Apollo at Delphi. As a people – if we read them through the myths as much as in their other writings – they did their best to attend to that ancient maxim.

So while they may have been far from perfect, the ancient Greeks seem to have developed the art of seeing life, the world and themselves with greater candour and unclouded clarity than is managed by most civilizations, including perhaps our own.

Location, Location

Greece. What and where is that? It was no kind of a nation at the time of the myths. There is a politically identifiable sovereign landmass and collection of islands we can now visit, but the Greek world of *Mythos* includes much of Asia Minor, incorporating Turkey, parts of Syria, Iraq and Lebanon as well as areas of North Africa, Egypt, the Balkans, Albania, Croatia and Macedonia. The story of 'Arion and the Dolphin' takes us to southern Italy and other myths deal with people who might at times have described themselves as Hellenic, Ionian, Argive, Attic, Thracian, Aeolian, Spartan, Doric, Athenian, Cypriot, Corinthian, Theban, Phrygian, Sicilian, Cretan, Trojan, Boeotian, Lydian . . . and much more besides. It is all, I am well aware, confusing and probably irritating to anyone but a scholar or a Greek citizen. There is the map to consult, but otherwise I really hope you don't bust a boiler trying to work it all out. Goodness knows I bust mine often enough and I wouldn't wish the same confusion and worry on you.

Sources Ancient

To retell Greek mythical stories is to tread in the footsteps of giants. In the Foreword to this book I shared Edith Hamilton's observation that Greek myth is 'the creation of great poets'. While its deepest origins lie in prehistory and unrecorded folklore, in preparing material for this book I have been able, as any one of us can, to consult the very first poets of the Western tradition, who just happened to be Greek and whose subject matter just happened to be myth.

There is a unique treasury of extant sources that chart the chronology of Greek myth from the creation of the universe and birth of the gods all the way to the end of their interaction and interference in human affairs. It begins with HOMER, who may or may not have been a single (blind) Ionian bard, but whose name is attached to the two great epic poems, the *Iliad* and the *Odyssey*, that were put together some time, it is thought, in the eighth century BC. Their setting is the siege of Troy and its aftermath, but Homer makes countless useful references back to earlier myths. His approximate contemporary, the poet HESIOD (undoubtedly an individual), did the most to create what might be called a timeline for Greek mythology. His *Theogony* (Birth of the Gods) narrates the creation, the rise of the Titans, the origin of the gods and the establishment of Olympus. His *Erga kai Hemerai* (Works and Days) tells the great human creation stories of Prometheus and Pandora as well as laying out mankind's Five Ages – Golden, Silver, Bronze, Heroic and Iron.

Other Greek and subsequent Roman poets, writers and travellers filled in gaps, elaborated, embroidered, fused, confused and just plain fabricated Greek mythical stories that mostly descended from Hesiod's genealogical plan. Of these the *Bibliotheca* (Library), a great dictionary of myth is perhaps the most valuable source. It was originally thought to have been the work of the scholar APOLLODORUS OF ATHENS, who worked in the second century BC, but this is now doubted; these days the work is attributed to an unknown who goes by the demeaning soubriquet of PSEUDO-APOLLODORUS and dated to the first or second century AD. Other compelling and/or reliable sources – all of them probably from the second century AD – include the Greek traveller and guide-book compiler PAUSANIAS, the 'novelists' LONGUS (who wrote in Greek) and APULEIUS (who wrote in Latin) and the Latin prose writer HYGINUS.

Towering above them all is the Roman poet OVID (43 BC–AD 17), whose *Metamorphoses* ('Transformations') tells of those mortals, nymphs and others who were changed by the gods into animals, plants, rivers or even stones as a punishment or out of pity. His other works, principally the *Ars Amatoria* (Art of Love) and *Heroides* (Heroines) also contain recastings of Greek myth, using always the Latin names for the gods – 'Jove' or 'Jupiter' for Zeus, 'Diana' for Artemis, 'Cupid' or 'Amor' for Eros. and so on. Ovid is prolific, profuse, irreverent, saucy and cinematic in his energy and restless switching of points of view. It is clear from the wealth of references in his plays and poems that Shakespeare, amongst many other writers and artists, was hugely influenced by him. Ovid was happy to add, subtract and invent, and this has influenced and emboldened me to be – shall we say *imaginative*? – in some of my retellings too.

Many children on both sides of the Atlantic grew up, as I did, on classic collections of the Greek myths by four enduringly popular Americans. Two were nineteenth-century writers: Nathaniel Hawthorne, who gave us *A Wonder-Book for Girls and Boys* (1851) and its sequel, *Tanglewood Tales* (1853); and Thomas Bulfinch, whose *The Age of Fable* (1855), later incorporated into the compendious *Bulfinch's Mythology* (1881), has run through dozens and dozens of editions in its 160 years of life. The twentieth century was dominated by the matchless Edith Hamilton's *Mythology: Timeless Tales of Gods and Heroes* (1942), which is still happily in print, and by Bernard Evslin's evergreen *Heroes, Gods and Monsters of the Greek Myths* (1967). British equivalents include Charles Lamb's *The Adventures of Ulysses* (1808) and L. S. Hyde's *Favourite Greek Myths* (1905), this last being a great favourite of mine when I was a boy.

Estimable as all of these were, and still are, they tend shyly to skirt round or bowdlerize the erotic and violent episodes that form such an essential part of the Greek mythic world. The poet and novelist Robert Graves had no such compunctions, but his two eccentrically structured and narrated volumes of *The Greek Myths* (1955), while meticulous, scholarly and inspiring, chart a more literary and mythographical course – often with a view to highlighting his obsession with cults of a 'white goddess'. The approaches of James Frazer and those who came after, including Joseph Campbell, valuable as they are, also have other, less specifically Greek and more academic, psychological, comparative and anthropological, fish to fry. Online these days there are plenty of sites devoted to helping the young 'find' Greek myth – though you may feel like a lie-down after reading those that describe Cadmus as 'a homie', Hermes as 'cool' and Hades as 'a dude with issues'.

The one website I would most heartily recommend is theoi.com – a simply magnificent resource entirely dedicated to Greek myth. It is a Dutch and New Zealand project that contains over 1,500 pages of text and a gallery of 1,200 pictures comprising vase paintings, sculpture, mosaics and frescoes on Greek mythological themes. It offers thorough indexing, genealogies and subject headings. The bibliography is superb, and can lead one on a labyrinthine chase, hopping from source to source like an excited butterfly-collector.

Spelling the Names

Because many Greek myths and the characters in them come down to us by way of Latin writers, and because our alphabet is more Roman than Greek, the spelling of personalities and places can be rather hit and miss. I could have chosen only to offer Greek spellings, so that Kerberos, Iason and Kadmos are used instead of Cerberus, Jason and Cadmus. Should I have given 'Cronus' instead of Kronos? Maybe I ought to have favoured 'Aktaion' over Actaeon? 'Narkissos' seems bloody-minded when we all know Narcissus so well. In the end I've been inconsistent, but consistently so.

Saying the Names

My advice is to pronounce them in your head the way that seems most comfortable to you. The Greek letter *kappa* covers hard 'k' sounds, and the letter *chi* covers the more aspirated and guttural fricatives found in the 'ch' of 'loch' and 'Bach', though you are quite safe pronouncing all 'ch' instances as if they are standard 'k' sounds. The *eta*, or long Greek 'e', was sounded as 'ee' when I was taught ancient Greek at school – so the letter itself was pronounced 'eater'. Nowadays it's taught to rhyme with 'waiter'. I get the sense that this modern pronunciation has entered American English more readily than British. Americans will tend to say 'baiter' for *beta* where we say 'beater', for example.

So is Thetis 'Theetis', 'Thettis' or 'Thaytis'? Is it 'Maytis', 'Mettis' or 'Meetis' for Metis, and 'Hearer' or 'Hairer' for Hera? 'Ahr-ease' or 'Air-ease' for Ares? Modern Greeks pronounce it one way, English and American academics their ways and common usage, inasmuch as there is common usage, goes its way. Anyone who tells you that there is a definitive right or wrong can be doubted, in my opinion.

ACKNOWLEDGEMENTS

Firstly to my beloved husband Elliott for being patient enough to endure my long periods spent away in the mythic landscape of ancient Greece. To my beloved persistent sister and assistant, Jo Crocker, for sculpting my life into a shape that allowed me the hours in which to write.

As ever thanks to my agent, Anthony Goff, and to Louise Moore and everyone at Michael Joseph, the friendly imprint of Penguin Random House that is obliging enough to publish me. Most especially to my diligent, maddening, charming, thoughtful and stubbornly insightful editor, Jillian Taylor.

Picture Credits

Section One

1. *Gaia, Mother Goddess* Greek relief. Ancient Art Architecture Collection Ltd / Alamy.

2. Attic Red-Figure Cup, bpk / Antikensammlung Berlin.

3. *Polyphemus*, Johann Heinrich Wilhelm Tischbein, 1802. Landesmuseum Oldenburg.

4. Bronze head of Hypnos, c.275 BC. British Museum / Alamy.

5. *The Mutilation of Uranus by Saturn* by Giorgio Vasari, c.1560. Palazzo Vecchio, Room of the Elements.

6. *The Birth of Venus*, Sandro Botticelli, c.1485. Uffizi Gallery. Florence / Bridgeman.

7. *Saturn Devouring One of His Sons*, Francisco de Goya, c.1823. Prado Museum, Madrid / Alamy.

8. Attic Red Figure attributed to the Nausicaa Painter, c.475 – 425 BC. Metropolitan Museum of Art, New York.

9. *The Feeding of the Child Jupiter*, Nicolas Poussin, c.1640. National Gallery of Art, Washington DC. / Bridgeman.

10. Marble Relief of the Battle of Giants, Gigantomachy. Getty Images / De Agostini Picture Library.

11. Attic Black-Figured Hydria, c.540–530 BC. Staatliche Antikensammlungen, Munich.

12. *The Dance of the Muses*, Joseph Paelinck, 1832. Private Collection / Alamy.

13. Relief of the Three Moirai. Alte Nationalgalerie, Berlin.

14. *The Battle Between the Gods and the Giants*, Joachim Antonisz Wtewael, c.1608. Art Institute of Chicago /Bridgeman.

15. *The Gods of Olympus*, Sala dei Giganti, c.1528. Palazzo del Te / Bridgeman.

Section Two

1. Hierogamy, unknown artist, 1st Century AD. Museo Archeologico Nazionale, Naples / Bridgeman.

2. *Vulcan Forging Jupiter's Lightening Bolts*, Peter Paul Rubens, 1636–38. Prado Museum, Madrid / Bridgeman.

3. Head of Ares, after Greek original by Alkamenes, 420 BC. State Hermitage Museum, St Petersburg, Russia / Alamy.

4. *Venus and Mars*, Sandro Boticelli, c.1485. National Gallery, London / Alamy.

5. Black-figure Amphora, 6th century BC. Louvre, Paris / Bridgeman.

6. *Minerva or Pallas Athena*, Gustav Klimt, 1898. Wien Museum Karlsplatz, Vienna / Bridgeman.

7. Red-Figure Cup, 5th century BC. Louvre, Paris / Bridgeman.

8. *Apollo*, Italian School, 17th century. Musee Massey, Tarbes, France / Bridgeman.

9. *Diana*, Paul Manship, 1925. National Gallery of Art, Washington, DC, USA / Alamy.

10. *Prometheus Bringing Fire to Mankind*, Friedrich Heinrich Fuger, 1817. Neue Galerie, Kassel, Germany / © Museumslandschaft Hessen Kassel / Ute Brunzel / Bridgeman.

11. *Prometheus Bound*, Jacob Jordaens, c.1640. Wallraf-Richartz-Museum, Köln, Germany / Alamy.

12. *Charon Crossing the River Styx*, Joachim Patenier or Patinir, 1515–24. Prado, Madrid, Spain / Bridgeman.

13. *Pandora*, John William Waterhouse, 1896. Private Collection / Alamy.

14. *The Return of Persephone*, Frederic Leighton, c.1891. Leeds Museums and Galleries (Leeds Art Gallery) UK / Bridgeman.

15. *Cupid and Psyche*, Francois Edouard Picot, 1817. Louvre, Paris / Bridgeman.

16. *The Fall of Phaeton*, Peter Paul Rubens, c.1604–8. National Gallery of Art, Washington DC / Bridgeman.

17. *Drunken Silenus Supported by Satyrs*, Peter Paul Rubens (studio of), c.1620, National Gallery, London / Bridgeman.

18. *Apollo and Marsyas*, Michelangelo Anselmi, c.1540. National Gallery of Art, Washington DC / Bridgeman.

19. *The Spinners, or The Fable of Arachne*, Diego Rodriguez de Silva y Velazquez, 1657. Prado, Madrid / Bridgeman.

INDEX

438